HAMPSTEAD AND HIGHGATE

The Story of Two Hilltop Villages

Books by the same author

TWO VILLAGES, *The Story of Chelsea and Kensington*
THE BRITISH HOTEL THROUGH THE AGES
COVENT GARDEN
A WEEK IN LONDON
BACKGROUND TO ARCHAEOLOGY
THE YEARS OF GRANDEUR, *The Story of Mayfair*
WILLINGLY TO SCHOOL, *A History of Women's Education*

HAMPSTEAD AND HIGHGATE

The Story of Two Hilltop Villages

MARY CATHCART BORER

W. H. ALLEN · LONDON
A Howard & Wyndham Company
1976

PRINTED AND BOUND IN GREAT BRITAIN BY T. & A. CONSTABLE LTD,
HOPETOUN STREET, EDINBURGH EH7 4NF
FOR THE PUBLISHERS, W. H. ALLEN & CO. LTD,
44 HILL STREET, LONDON WIX 8LB

ISBN 0 491 01827 4

Contents

Acknowledgements

For permission to reproduce photographs the publishers would like to thank the following for the use of copyright material. Illustrations nos. 1, 2, 3, 4, 5, 6, 9, 12, 13, 19, 21, 22, 23, 26, 29, and 30 are reproduced from the Local History Collection of the London Borough of Camden Public Libraries; no. 10 the Greater London Council, The Iveagh Bequest, Kenwood; nos. 7, 8, 11, 14, 24, 25, 27 and 32, the National Portrait Gallery, London; nos. 15, 16, 17, 18, 20, 28, 31, 33, 34, 35, 36, 37, and 38 Mike Humphrey.

I

The Medieval Villages

In 1965 Hampstead and Highgate became part of the large London Borough of Camden, one of the most densely populated areas of the capital. The borough, comprising the former boroughs of St Pancras and Holborn, is roughly crescent-shaped, the longer arm, a wide belt stretching from the City of London to Shaftesbury Avenue, running northwards to the borough boundary at Islington and Harringay, the short arm turning westwards at this point, enclosing Highgate, Hampstead Heath and Hampstead and running on to the boundary with Brent. Through the heart of the borough, stretching for five miles in a continuous line, from north-west to south-east, are North End, Haverstock Hill, Camden High Street, Eversholt Street, Southampton Row and Kingsway. The Finchley Road lies due west of North End and Haverstock Hill. The Kentish Town Road and Fortess Road branch off from Camden High Street to the north-east, the Hampstead Road and Tottenham Court Road to the south-west, while New Oxford Street and High Holborn link the southern ends of Tottenham Court Road, Southampton Road and the Gray's Inn Road.

Camden includes some of the oldest survivals of London – St Giles High Street, Drury Lane, Great Queen Street, Lincoln's Inn Fields, Chancery Lane, Gray's Inn, Hatton Garden and Ely Place, Red Lion Square, Bloomsbury with its Georgian squares, and, to the north, Chalk Farm, Primrose Hill, Belsize Park and the heart of old Hampstead, with the wide stretch of the beautiful heath separating it from Highgate to the east.

Although much of the material evidence of the borough's history has inevitably been swept away during the transformation of London over the last hundred years or more, there are still many intriguingly romantic survivals, and this is particularly true of Hampstead and Highgate. The imagination must be stretched to its limits to visualise the greater part of Camden covered with the dense forest which the Romans encountered when they landed in Britain, or even to see it as the gentle land of hills and streams, fields and farms and isolated hamlets of three hundred years ago, yet there are corners of Hampstead and Highgate where one can drift quite effortlessly back to the eighteenth century, for here, despite a full integration with London in most aspects, the individuality and spirit of the villages have survived, as well as many of the beautiful seventeenth- and eighteenth-century houses.

Both Hampstead and Highgate were relatively late in developing, for they stand on twin hills which were not easily accessible to the pioneers, and it is these geographical and geological factors which have helped to mould their history and give them their distinctive charm.

When the Romans arrived in Britain they found a primitive country, large areas of which were uninhabited and as yet unexplored by the thinly scattered population of Celts. The Romans built Londinium on the north bank of the Thames, on the first rising ground above the estuary, and at the point where the Walbrook flowed into the main river.

As they probed north of London they encountered the dense Middlesex forest, stretching north-westwards to the Chilterns, which was part of the thick oak and ash forest covering nearly all the midlands of Britain.

As they cut their way through the forest, to build the continuation of Watling Street from London to the north-west, they avoided the first high ground they encountered, only four miles from the city, and chose for their permanent road a route to the west, about where the Edgware Road now lies, while Ermin Street, their road to the north by way of Lincoln and York, ran just east of Highgate Hill. This high ground, their first obstacle, was a crescent-shaped ridge of hills. The southern arm rose steeply on its southern face and descended more gently to the north. The highest part, at its western end, rising to 440 ft, is today known as Hampstead Hill. The eastern end is Highgate Hill, with an even steeper face than Hampstead Hill, although its height is some sixteen feet less. Between these two hills, rising above the clay of the lower, forested slopes, stretched a waste of sandy heathland, beautiful with its conifers and heather and little sand hills, but infertile and useless as agricultural land: and the crest of this heath is today marked by the Spaniards Road.

Beyond Highgate the southern arm of the crescent of the northern heights of London reached to Muswell Hill, and the northern arm swung back at this point westwards to Finchley and Hendon, the two arms enclosing the valley of the Mutton Brook, which sank gradually westwards to join the valley of the river Brent.

Both the steep southern approach of the Hampstead and Highgate ridge and the gentler northern slope fell away in broken country of forested hills and valleys. From today's Hampstead High Street, Rosslyn Hill runs into Haverstock Hill, which in turn leads down to Primrose Hill, while Parliament Hill is an isolated spur between Hampstead and Highgate.

In the valleys were a number of little streams, most of which have long since been converted into lakes, reservoirs and culverts. The western arm of the Fleet river once flowed across the Heath from the southern end of the Spaniards Road, through the Vale of Health and southwards to London and the Thames, but all that remains above ground today has been channelled into the Hampstead ponds, while the eastern arm of the river can be seen in the Highgate and Ken Wood ponds. The Leg of Mutton pond by Sandy Road and the lower ponds in Golders Hill Park are where tributaries of the Brent once flowed. The West Bourne river which was to become the Serpentine flowed from the south-west face of the Hampstead ridge. The Tyburn started at the old Shepherd's Conduit spring, about where the Lyndhurst Road runs into Fitzjohn's Avenue, and once ran southwards through the heart of Mayfair, across Piccadilly and the Green Park, to reach the Thames above Westminster. The eastward flowing streams from the Highgate and Muswell Hill ridge flowed into the river Lea.

There were a number of fresh water springs round the edge of the Heath, emerging at points where the porous and permeable sand joined the absorbent and relatively impermeable clay, and also one or two which were impregnated with iron – the chalybeate springs. These chalybeate springs were believed, from earliest times, to have curative properties for an unspecified number of ills, and two which were to become famous were where Well Walk and Kilburn were to arise.

Two thousand years ago, this supremely beautiful stretch of hill forest, topped by its wild heath, was the haunt of wolves and wild boar, stags and wild oxen, and a cover for partridge, pheasant and heron. It was uninhabited and isolated from the civilising influences of Rome.

The Legions passed close by, along Watling Street, in their advance to the north-west, and Boadicea, who no doubt correctly though less attractively, is now called Boudicca, may well have led the Iceni this way during her march on London, after sacking St Albans. Paulinus, the Governor of Britain, saved the situation for Rome only just in time, and the fleeing Boadicea drank poison rather than be taken prisoner.

The final battle must have taken place somewhere in this region north-west of London and for many years there was a legend that she lay buried in a tumulus between Ken Wood and Parliament Hill, but when, towards the end of the last century, it was excavated, no human remains had survived to prove or disprove the story.

The Romans rebuilt St Albans and it became an important residential and commercial centre and one of their most beautiful cities. They began to clear some of the lowland forests for agricultural land, but the Hampstead and Highgate forests remained untouched and little evidence has as yet come to light that the Romans visited them. One or two unimportant pottery lamps and vases and a large pottery funerary urn containing some fragments of human bones were discovered near the Hampstead Wells in 1733, and during modern building excavations at Shepherd's Hill, Highgate, a pottery vase full of third- and fourth-century coins was unearthed, while a few years ago a Romano-British pottery kiln was discovered in Highgate Woods, but none of these finds suggests any major settlement.

As the Roman empire disintegrated, during the fifth century, the Romans departed from Britain, leaving the undefended island open to the incursions and conquests of the Anglo-Saxons, the sea wolves that lived on 'the pillage of the world'.

The newcomers were solitaries, disliking towns and town life. 'None of the Germanic people,' said Tacitus, 'dwell in cities, and they do not even tolerate houses which are built in rows. They dwell apart, and at a distance from one another, according to the preference which they may have for the stream, the plain or the grove. They do not make use of stone cut from the quarry, or of tiles; for every kind of building they make use of unshapely wood, which falls short of beauty or attractiveness.'

Thus the first Englishmen built their lonely homesteads, sometimes widely scattered throughout the countryside, sometimes less than two miles apart. Most of these settlements developed into the characteristic English village, many of which still survive, but where the soil was poor and the reclamation particularly difficult, isolated hamlets or even solitary farmhouses remained unchanged for centuries.

The village of Hamstede or Hampstead may have derived its name from just such a lonely homestead, where some Saxon had made a forest clearing, not for the suitability of the soil for farming, for even the clay below the sandy summit of the hill was by no means good agricultural land, though it produced good grassland for grazing and oak wood for pigs, but because of the plentiful supply of game. But there are no records and all is conjecture. As for Highgate, its origins are even more obscure and its name is derived from later events. There are very few villages in England which were not founded in Saxon times, but it seems very doubtful if there were any dwellings at all yet on this lonely hilltop.

The first historical record of Hampstead is a tenth-century charter by which King Edgar of Wessex granted Hampstead land to a nobleman called Mangoda, but on Mangoda's death it reverted to the Crown and was granted by King Edgar's son, King Ethelred the Unready who ruled Wessex from AD 987 to AD 1016, to St Peter's Church at Westminster.

This land was a roughly diamond-shaped stretch of some six hundred acres, its apex about where the Spaniards Inn now stands. The boundary ran from here in a south-westerly direction to reach Watling Street at the Cucking★ Pool. This was one of the many pools formed by tributaries of the Brent and was used in medieval times for the ducking of scolds and suchlike troublesome women, who were strapped into a ducking-stool and immersed, to cool their tempers. The boundary turned south-eastwards from the Cucking Pool along the line of Watling Street to Kilburn. From here the boundary ran in a curving line through St John's Wood and Primrose Hill until it met Haverstock Hill. The fourth line of the diamond followed Haverstock Hill for a few yards, turned almost due north for a short stretch and then north-west through the Vale of Health and back to the site of the Spaniards.

It was a plot which enclosed the heart of the future village, where today Heath Street and the High Street meet, with the Church and Frognal a little to the west.

A few months before his death Edward the Confessor, son of Ethelred the Unready, confirmed the gift of Hampstead to Westminster, when he consecrated the newly-restored Abbey building. Later that year the Normans landed and by the time that the Domesday Book was compiled, some twenty years after the Conquest, the major part of

★ 'Cucking' was originally a lesser punishment than Ducking, where the offender had to sit on a chair in some public place. Ducking was reserved for scolds, but as the world grew harder, cucking came to involve ducking.

Hampstead was still in the possession of Westminster Abbey and they were using it as one of their home farms. One-fifth of the land had been bestowed on one of King William's Norman knights, Ranulf Peverel, who had married Ingelrica, the King's discarded mistress. However, Peverel seems to have been an absentee landlord and these changes in ownership had little effect on the lives of the Hampstead peasantry, which by this time numbered probably some fifteen or twenty families.

Hampstead was now called a manor, the word having been introduced by the compilers of the Domesday Book to record the fact that the district contained a house or 'manoir' in which a person of some consequence lived. This meant that in large villages there could be more than one manor, but in time the term 'manor' came to mean the whole of the estate over which its owner had manorial rights, the tenants being bound to him and his home farm.

Ranulf Peverel had no dwelling at Hampstead and since the rest of the land belonged to Westminster Abbey there was no secular manor house, the important dwelling being the Grange, where a few monks from Westminster lived, to superintend the cultivation of the farm for the Abbey and administer the small court of justice: and attached to it there would have been a small chapel. The site of this little settlement is uncertain, but it was most probably in the Frognal area.

The Normans built the first windmills in England, the overlords securing an additional income for themselves by charging for the services of the miller, and the site of the first windmill in Hampstead may well have been on Windmill Hill.

Although Verulamium declined with the departure of the Romans the fortunes of the city of St Albans, which arose on the site, revived during the tenth century, and by the time of the Norman conquest the Abbey was immensely powerful and rich, owning much of Hertford-shire, its lands south of the city extending through the forest of Middlesex to the hamlets of Barnet, Finchley and Hornsey – and the parish of Hornsey included the land where the village of Highgate was to arise.

The pilgrim way to St Albans from London lay along the route of Watling Street and the shrine of the saint was increasingly visited by travellers and merchants who were about to undertake the hazards of a journey overseas. But the pilgrimage to St Albans had its full share of danger too, for the forest through which the road passed was infested not only with wild animals but with thieves and outlaws. So in order to protect the pilgrims and at the same time ensure the steady flow of funds to the Abbey coffers, which they bestowed in thankfulness for spiritual blessing, the Abbot Leofstan not only improved the road but engaged a knight named Thurnothe who, with his band of followers, promised to defend it and make the journey of the pilgrims safe. For this service the knight, said Matthew Paris, received a 'goodly manor for his reward' and in gratitude 'gave privately to the Abbot about five ounces of gold, a beautiful palfrey for his own riding, and a very choice greyhound'.

Soon after his accession, King William began a triumphal tour throughout the country, and as he approached Berkhamsted, which was part of the St Albans Abbey land, Fritheric, the Saxon abbot of the Cathedral, was one of the few to show active resentment towards the Norman conquerors. He ordered trees to be felled and piled across the roadway to obstruct the royal progress. It was a futile gesture for the Normans merely made a détour, but King William did not overlook the insult. Shortly afterwards he sequestered all the southern parts of the Abbey lands – a tract of forest stretching from the boundary of Westminster's Hampstead lands in the west to Hornsey and Crouch End in the east, and from St Albans in the north as far south as the Heath. The power of St Albans was disastrously weakened and at the same time the King acquired a stretch of magnificent hunting country. Fritheric fled into exile to the lonely marshes of the Isle of Ely and the privilege of safeguarding the pilgrims to St Albans now came into the hands of the Bishop of London.

Hunting was the 'supreme felicity of royal life', the principal pastime of the King and also of his bishops, who lived in as princely a style as their royal master. They spent days on end indulging in their favourite sport and it was conducted with a fine display of pomp and ritual, involving a legion of retainers, all with their appointed tasks – the men of the bow, the grooms of the greyhounds and hart hounds and the master of the game, who blew the horn.

In order to preserve good hunting grounds, the King declared large tracts of the countryside including much of the Middlesex forest as royal forests, reserved for the King's hunts and subject to the especially created forest laws.

The stretch of the Middlesex forest which William took from St Albans Abbey he seems to have bestowed on his half-brother Odo, who was Bishop of Bayeux and Dean of Caen, as well as Earl of Kent. This is by no means certain, but the survival of the name of Caen or Ken Wood gives support to the suggestion. However, Odo was a scheming and avaricious man. 'Greediness he loved withal.' He very soon fell out with the King and when he attempted to seize power among the Barons opposing William he was arrested and kept in prison until the King's death in 1087.

In the meantime, his hunting ground had been sequestered and presented to the Bishopric of London, and as it was situated in the parish of Hornsey it was known as Hornsey Park. It was enclosed and the Bishop built a hunting lodge for himself at the highest point, Lodge Hill, where the Highgate golf club now lies. The lodge was a small, square, stone castle, moated and approached by a drawbridge. The main gate of the chase was at the top of the hill, and in that lonely spot, about where Highgate School now stands, a hermit established himself, to act as gate-keeper to the Bishop.

This was a not unusual practice. In medieval times hermits, both men and women, were to be found in many parts of the country, living in caves or the simplest of wooden huts, leading solitary lives of religious contemplation; but sometimes they undertook useful work, to serve the community, as well. The women occasionally taught a few girl pupils, until the Church frowned on the practice, reminding them that they should give their time entirely to their devotions. The attitude to the men hermits was rather different and they were sometimes allowed to act as gate-keepers or toll collectors to some ecclesiastical establishment or to undertake the maintenance of roads leading to the sacred shrines.

In time one of the Bishops of London built a private road through his chase, from the High Gate westwards, with a second gate about where the Spaniards Inn was eventually to be built, but there is no record of a hermit ever establishing himself at the Spaniards' end of the road.

For the next century or more the great chases were preserved. John of Salisbury, writing in the twelfth century, said bitterly that 'husbandmen with their harmless herds and flocks are driven from their cultivated fields, their meadows, and their pastures, that wild beasts may range in them without interruption', and urges the peasants and farmers that 'if one of these great and merciless hunters pass by your habitation, bring forth hastily all the refreshment you have in your house or that you can readily buy or borrow from your neighbours, that you may not be involved in ruin or even accused of treason'; and Fuller in his *Church History* declared that 'the bishops were the most powerful nobles in the land, each one having a cathedral for his devotion, many manors for his profit, parks for his pleasure, and castles for his protection'.

Yet despite these injustices, the prospect of Highgate and Hampstead from London was idyllic. Fitz-Stephen, writing his survey of London at the end of the twelfth century, said: 'On the North, are corn-fields, pastures, and delightful meadows, intermixed with pleasant streams, on which stand many a mill whose clack is grateful to the ear. Beyond them an immense forest extends itself, beautified with woods and groves, and full of the lairs and coverts of beasts and game, stags, buck, boars and wild bulls.'

There are no records describing any hunt of the Bishop of London in Hornsey Park, nor of any dwellings near the hermit's hut, for he dwelt in utter loneliness. In 1277, when Llewellyn, Prince of Wales, and the Barons of Snowdon came to London to pay homage to Edward I, their retinues were quartered nearby, but lower down the hill in Islington and the neighbouring villages, and they cannot be said to have enjoyed themselves.

> They liked neither the wine nor the ale of London, and though plentifully entertained were much displeased at a new manner of living, which did not suit their tastes, or perhaps their constitutions; they were still more offended at the crowds of people that flocked about them when they stirred abroad, staring at them as if they had been monsters, and laughing at their uncouth garb and appearance. They were so enraged upon this occasion that they engaged privately to rebel on the first opportunity, and resolved to die in their own country, rather than ever to come again to London, as subjects to be held in such derision,

recorded Carte in his *History of England*.

By the fourteenth century the sporting tastes of the Bishops of London were changing, influenced perhaps by the increasing criticism of contemporary writers such as Chaucer, who in his *Ploughman's Tale* accused many of the clergy of thinking 'more upon hunting with their dogs and blowing the horn than of the service they owed to God,' and the anonymous commentator of the time who said that 'Abbots and priors ride with horses and hounds as if they were knights, while poor men cower at the abbey-gate all day in hunger and cold'. But even before Chaucer's time the forest laws were being relaxed and work was under way of clearing some of the hitherto protected forests to provide more agricultural land to support the increasing population. During the reign of Henry III (1216-72) parts of the forest of Middlesex, on the lower slopes nearest to London, were cleared, but the Highgate and Hampstead woods were not yet touched and remained royal hunting grounds for another three or four hundred years, a succession of hermits guarding the eastern gate of the Bishop's wood at Highgate.

Away to the west, another hermit was making history. Early in the twelfth century a man of whom virtually nothing is known but his name, which was Godwin, built himself a little hermitage and chapel in the heart of the woodlands on the western edge of Hampstead, on the banks of the Kule-Bourne. How he came by the land no one knows, but he had probably inherited it from some member of his family who had bought it from the Abbey of Westminster. Here, for some years, Godwin lived a life of solitary contemplation, but then, perhaps growing weary of the loneliness, he consulted the Abbey and handed over his hermitage to three virgins, Emma, Gunilda and Cristina, who had been maids of honour to Queen Matilda, that most sternly devout queen of Henry I, who, every day during Lent, was said to have worshipped at Westminster Abbey barefooted and wearing a rough hair shirt.

These three women, on entering Godwin's hermitage, founded the Kilburn Priory, and Godwin remained as their warden and chaplain, it being decided that, after his death, this office should be in the appointment of the Abbey.

More nuns joined the convent, bringing with them many gifts, so that they were able to enlarge the building and the chapel, which was dedicated to St John the Baptist.

As the Kilburn Priory prospered, there were bitter arguments between the Bishop of London and the Abbot of Westminster about who should have ecclesiastical authority over the nuns, and eventually the increasingly powerful Bishop of London won the day and was given the privilege of consecrating the nuns and appointing their chaplain and prioress.

Throughout the thirteenth and fourteenth centuries, England's wealth lay in her wool, which was exported in large quantities to the weavers of Flanders, much of it through the Port of London, where it was brought from the sheep farms of the countryside by pack-horse train.

The steadily increasing export trade meant that there were many more travellers throughout the country, but the roads were appalling. Travellers and merchants between London and the North, by way of Lincoln and York, were still using the overgrown and ruined Ermin Street, which wound round the eastern slopes of Highgate Hill by way of Crouch End and Muswell Hill, a road which was becoming increasingly wearisome and difficult.

During the middle years of the fourteenth century a proposal was made to the Bishop of London that a new road should be built through his park, straight up Highgate Hill.

The old road was refused by way-faring men and carriers, by reason of the deepness and dirtie passage in the winter season; in regard whereof it was agreed between the Bishop of London and the countrie, that a new road should be layde forth through the said Bishop's park, beginning at Highgate, to lead to, as it now is accustomed, directly to Whetstone, for which new waie all cartes, carriers, packmen, and such like travellers yielde a certain tole unto the Bishop of London, which is farmed (as it is said at this daie) at £40 per annum, and for that purpose was the gate erected on the hill, that through the same all travellers should passe, and be the more aptlie staide for the same tole,

wrote Norden in his *Speculum Britanniaea*.

He suggested that the name of Highgate was derived from the High Gate or Gate on the Hill.

It is a hill over which is a passage, and at the top of the said hill is a gate through which all manner of passages have their way: so the place taketh the name of High Gate on the Hill, which gate was erected at the alteration of the way which is on the east of Highgate. When the way was turned over the said hill, to lead through the park of the Bishop of London as it now doth, there was in regard therof a tole raised upon such as passed that way – this gate was raised, through which, of necessity, all travellers pass.

The gate was spanned by an arch, which at first was wide enough for only one loaded pack-horse to pass through at a time, the hermitage being on the east side, where the new road joined the eastern end of the Bishop's private road.

The making of the road must have entailed a great deal of labour, and while there are no records of its actual construction, in 1364 Edward III gave permission for the hermit who at that time was established at Highgate, William Phelippe, to collect tolls from travellers, to reimburse him for the work and expense of its maintenance, since

we highly commend the pious motive which for the advantage of our people passing through the highway of Highgate and Smethefield, in many places notoriously miry and deep, you unremittingly and continually exert in the emendation and support of that way in wood and sand, and other things of that nature necessary thereto at your own cost; and since you assert that your own means are not sufficient for that purpose, we are willing upon due consideration to assent, and considering that those who from the performance of the said work obtain benefit and advantage to contribute to the same as is just. . . .

William Phelippe did a double service, for to maintain the steep road he dug gravel from the top of the hill, which produced a pond, in what is now Pond Square, which remained for years.

He caused gravel to be digged on the top of Highgate Hill, where is now a fair pool of water, and therewith made a causeway from Highgate to Islington; a two-handed charity, providing water on the hill, where it was wanted, and cleanness in the vale, which before, especially in the winter, was passed with much tribulation.

By this time a little chapel dedicated to St Michael was attached to the hermitage and here pilgrims paused to worship, on their way through the thick, dark woods, cut by the narrow, winding track of what is now Southwood Lane, to the shrine of Our Lady of Muswell, some two miles to the east. In 1386, Bishop Braybrooke of London gave to William Lichfield, a poor, infirm hermit, this office of 'keeping our chapel at Highgate, and the house annexed to the said chapel, hitherto accustomed to be kept by other poor hermits'.

The legend of Dick Whittington and Highgate Hill comes into the story now. About 1360, when he was still a young boy, the story goes that he ran away from his master's house in the City of London because of the cruelty of the cook. His only friend was his beloved cat, which he took with him, making his lonely way across the fields of Holloway and Islington. At the foot of Highgate Hill he paused to rest, and as he was about to continue his journey up the hill he heard the distant sound of the bells of Bow Church, echoing across the meadows. He paused to listen and they seemed to be singing to him: 'Turn again, Whittington, Lord Mayor of London Town'. The message was so clear and insistent that he obeyed them. With renewed courage, and marking the spot where he had first heard them, he retraced his footsteps, and from that time onwards his fortunes never flagged. He married his master's daughter, Alice Fitzwarren, and became Lord Mayor of London. The boyhood of the distinguished Lord Mayor of London, Sir Richard Whittington, bears little relation to this story, for his parents were wealthy; but he married an Alice Fitzwarren and held office for three separate terms, in 1397, 1406 and 1420. He founded Whittington College, built part of St Bartholomew's Hospital, the library of the Grey Friars Hospital, where Christ's Hospital was later to be established, and a chapel and library at the Guildhall, but there is no evidence to connect him with the legendary Dick, sad as it is to be unable to support such a well-loved nursery story, which was first circulated in the pedlars' chap-books of the sixteenth century.

The old Whittington stone at the foot of Highgate Hill seems to have been part of a wayside cross set up in front of the Lazar House and Chapel of St Anthony, which was established there in the second half of the fifteenth century, during the reign of Edward IV. It has even been suggested that it is nothing but the fragment of an old mounting block.

In medieval Hampstead life changed very little, but the land itself changed hands on several occasions. The manor of Chalcots in the south-east and the small manor of Wyldes in the north-west were granted to the hospital of St James, the leper hospital which once stood where the palace of St James was later to be built. In the thirteenth century the Knights Templar were given land to the north of the Kilburn Priory, around Shoot-Up Hill, and when the Templars were disbanded, in 1312, and their property appropriated by the King, their Hampstead land, on which sixty-six acres of wheat and twelve acres of winter wheat had already been sown, was granted to the hospital of St John.

As well as these main changes in ownership, succeeding Abbots of Westminster parcelled out smaller areas of their Hampstead land to numerous knights and wealthy merchants on long leases, and with heavy premiums, as a means of raising money: and these newcomers built their small manor houses, from which they managed their new estates.

One of the most important of these residents was Sir Roger de Brabazon, Lord Chief Justice to Edward II, who early in the fourteenth century came into possession of the manor of Belsize, which consisted of a house and fifty-seven acres of land; but on his death, in 1317, he bequeathed it back to the Abbey.

By the beginning of the fourteenth century there were five free tenants of the Hampstead manor, Roger de Brabazon and Robert de Kyngeswell being resident and the other three non-resident. There were forty-five householders, who between them rented 289 acres and also gave specified hours of labour to their manorial lords, as well as certain payments in kind, mainly of game, and the rest of the population were feudal peasants.

But changes were on the way. In 1349, while Edward III and the Black Prince were campaigning in France, Europe was ravaged by the terrible bubonic plague of the Black Death. Twenty-five million people – a quarter of the population of Europe – died, and in England the proportion was even higher. At least a third of the people perished, including half the labourers, and by the end of the King's reign the population of the country was reduced to only two million. The decimation was as bad in the country districts as in the medieval towns, for in places entire villages died. 'The sheep and cattle strayed through the fields and corn and there were none left who could drive them.'

By the time the plague had spent itself, the country was faced with a desperate shortage of labour, and with the price of food rising, the surviving landless peasants began demanding higher wages. For a few years they were repressed by the Statute of Labourers, hastily devised to tie them more firmly than ever to the land and oblige them to work for the same wages that they had received before the plague, on pain of imprisonment or outlawry. The Statute was the last stand of feudalism before its slow and painful end during the years following the Peasants' Revolt of 1381, which was a violent and bitter protest against the rich landlords, both lay and ecclesiastic, who held them in bondage. From Norfolk, Suffolk and Cambridgeshire, Hertfordshire, Essex and the counties of the south, the peasant army, a hundred thousand strong, rallied by their leader Wat Tyler, marched on London, pillaging manor houses and abbeys on the way.

Jack Straw was a generic name for a farm labourer, as Jack Tar still is for a sailor, and Jack Straw's Castle, the tavern on the Heath near the Vale of Health may well have been the site of the rallying ground for the people of Hampstead and the neighbouring villages to join the march on London.

Despite the initial success of Wat Tyler and the promise he obtained from the young Richard II that the serfs of England should be freed, Parliament, after recovering from the initial shock of the revolt, reversed the King's decision. Wat Tyler met his end at Smithfield and the charters of liberation were repealed.

Nevertheless, it was from this time that the old feudal powers began to decline. Even before the revolt, Westminster Abbey was no longer using Hampstead as its home farm, to be cultivated by feudal labour, but had resorted to letting out the Abbey land in a number of small holdings. By 1372 there were sixty of these little farms on their rent roll, occupied mainly by peasant subsistence farmers, but the whole population of Hampstead was less than two hundred souls.

During the fifteenth century the four mile stretch of country between London and the wooded hills of Hampstead and Highgate was gently rolling farmland, from which much of the timber had been cleared, and scattered through this countryside were little hamlets such as Kentish

Town and Gospel Oak, all with their sacred shrines. In Hampstead a legend was preserved which, some two hundred years later, seemed for a time as though it were to prove itself, for the story was told that when King Ethelred had granted the manor of Hampstead to the church at Westminster a miraculous well had sprung up, through the misadventure of an English saint. He had brought from Tours a precious phial containing four tears of the Virgin Mary, and one day, while praying in the fields, he dropped it and the tears fell into the ground. That night he had a consoling vision that he would find a healing spring at the spot where he had lost the tears, and when he returned to it the following morning he discovered the chalybeate spring which was destined in later years to bring fame to the village.

The last important record of medieval Hampstead is the granting by Henry VI to Eton College, which he founded in 1440, of the Hampstead lands which had formerly belonged to the St James's leper hospital. Presumably he reimbursed the hospital in some way, for it was still in existence nearly a century later, when Henry VIII arranged for the inmates to be moved and the hospital demolished for the building of St James's palace. At this time there seem to have been a number of obscure negotiations over land deals, but Henry VIII confirmed to Eton the manor of Chalcot, south of Belsize, which extended to some 226 acres, and also the manor of Wyldes in the north-west corner of the Hampstead manor.

In Highgate one of the last medieval records was an account of the strange attempt at murder by necromancy, which was made when Eleanor, the Duchess of Gloucester, devised a plan for destroying Henry VI by the age-old method of destroying his image. So strong was the belief that this method of murder was possible that victims had been known to die of sheer fright when they learnt that such magic was being used against them.

Medieval thinking was tortuous, and instead of making the wax model herself and burning it, which would seem to have been the most straightforward way of despatching the King, Eleanor had to call upon the services of a witch, Margery Jourdain, to fashion the model. Roger Bolingbroke, an astrologer, was engaged to destroy it with all due ceremony and ritual, and Thomas Southwell, a canon of St Stephen's Chapel at Westminster, promised to say masses for the departing spirit of the King.

And romantic, even in planning murder, the conspirators chose the loneliest spot they knew, the deserted Bishop's hunting lodge, deep in the thickets of Hornsey Park, which was by now falling into ruin, its moat dry and choked with scrub and trees already a hundred years old.

The ceremony was planned to take place at dead of night, for as Shakespeare said, in describing the scene:

> . . . wizards know their times:
> Deep night, dark night, the silent of the night,
> The time of night when Troy was set on fire;
> The time when screech owls cry, and ban-dogs howl,
> That time best fits the work we have in hand.

Henry VI, Part 2, Act I,
Scene IV

It was all to no avail. They lost their nerve, and when the Duchess fled to the sanctuary of Westminster suspicion was aroused that some sinister deed was afoot. Roger Bolingbroke was arrested and confessed, putting the blame squarely on the Duchess.

All four were eventually tried and sentenced to death, the charge being that 'they at the request of Eleanor, Duchess of Gloucester had devised an image of wax representing the King (Henry VI), which by their sorcery gradually consumed; intending thereby finally to waste and destroy the king's person'.

Henry was to live for another thirty years, but not as King of England, for a few years later the Plantaganets were fighting grimly for the succession, in the bitter and vicious Wars of the Roses. In 1485, after the battle of Bosworth and the defeat of Richard III, which secured the succession of Henry, Earl of Richmond as Henry VII the first sovereign of the Tudor dynasty, he rode back to London. And it was at Highgate that he was received by the magistrates of London and conducted, in solemn procession, to St Paul's cathedral.

II

Highgate during the Sixteenth and Seventeenth Centuries

The last hermit gatekeeper on Highgate Hill was William Forte, and the office was granted to him in 1531 by Bishop Stokeley, who adjured him to pray for the Bishop's soul, and the souls of his predecessors, as well as those of all the faithful deceased.

By this time the hermitage was a considerable gift, for it included the chapel, known as the Chapel of St Michael in the Parish of Hornsey, a small house, a garden and an orchard, as well as the tithes and offerings, but despite the beautiful surroundings, it was a solitary place.

Little is known of the people of Highgate during the sixteenth century, for the records have not survived, but, like Hampstead, the district was a wooded countryside of farmlands and small manors, with one or two Tudor mansions, for it was at this time that the nobles and merchant princes began to leave their London homes in the crowded, walled city and build houses for themselves in the adjoining country. They settled along the Strand, towards Westminster, and by the time Sir Thomas More had reached as far as Chelsea the heights of Hampstead and Highgate were also being explored. Yet although the road up Highgate Hill was a vast improvement on the old road to the east, it was very steep, and particularly difficult for the coach traffic which was soon to develop, so that Highgate village, at the top of the hill, was even slower in developing, during Tudor and Stuart times, than Hampstead.

John Norden said of Highgate: 'Upon this hill is most pleasant dwelling, yet not so pleasant as healthful; for the expert inhabitants there report that divers who have long been visited by sickness not curable by the "physicke" have in a short time repaired their Health by that sweet, salutary air'.

The village grew slowly round the hermit's pond and the green just to the west of it. The road to be known as West Hill had not yet been cut, but a few yards farther west Millfield Lane ran down from Hampstead Lane. This is the lane which runs due west from the village to join the Spaniards Road. Millfield Lane ran south-eastwards, past Fitzroy Park, which was still virgin woodland, towards the end of Swain's Lane, sometimes called at this time Swine's Lane. This narrow, steep track wound downhill, roughly parallel with Millfield Lane, in a south-westerly curve from the eastern end of the village.

Southwood Lane, winding eastwards from the hermitage, was the old pilgrim road to Our Lady of Muswell Hill, while Jackson's Lane, branching off about two-thirds of the way down, was the way to Hornsey and the parish church.

Apart from the chapel of the hermitage, the nearest place of worship was this little church at Hornsey, which was rebuilt in 1500 with stones taken from the ruins of the Bishop's Lodge in Hornsey Park.

With the Reformation, the ancient hermitage was abandoned, condemned for having been put to 'superstitious uses', but the archway over the road remained. It was a solid brick gateway, with rooms built over it which were approached from the western end by stairs, the eastern arm reaching across to the burying ground of the hermitage chapel.

At the western end, the first Gateway tavern soon came into existence, for the refreshment of travellers to and from London, particularly the cattle drovers, bringing their herds of cattle down to the medieval market at Smithfield. And it was here that the first ceremony of 'Swearing on the Horns' was probably inaugurated, a light-hearted penance which in time was to be inflicted by every landlord of the Highgate taverns on visitors passing through the village for the first time.

Each traveller was invited to submit himself to the ceremony. Having agreed, a pair of stag's horns fixed to a long pole was brought in by the clerk of the ceremony, while the landlord donned a black cloak, mask and wig. Then, with all due ceremony, the assembled company bared their heads, as the landlord recited the oath.

Upstanding and uncovered: silence. Take notice what I now say to you, for *that* is the first word of the oath; mind *that*! You must acknowledge me to be your adopted father, I must acknowledge you to be my adopted son. If you do not call me father, you forfeit a bottle of wine; if I do not call you son I forfeit the same. And now, my good sir, if you are travelling through the village of Highgate, and you have no money in your pocket, go call for a bottle of wine at any house you may think proper to enter, and book it to your father's score. If you have any friends with you, you may treat them as well; but if you have money of your own, you must pay for it yourself; for you must not say you have no money when you have; neither must you convey your own money out of your own pocket into your friend's pocket, for I shall search them as well as you, and if I find that you or they have any money, you forfeit a bottle of wine for trying to cheat and cozen your old father. You must not eat brown bread while you can get white, unless you like brown bread the best; nor must you drink small beer when you can get strong, unless you like small beer the best; you must not kiss the maid while you can kiss the mistress, unless you like the maid the best; but sooner than lose a good chance you may kiss them both. And now, my good son, for a word or two of advice: keep from all houses of ill-repute, and every place of public resort for bad company; beware of false friends, for they will turn to be our foes, and inviegle you into houses where you may lose your money and get no redress; keep from thieves of every denomination. And now, my good son, I wish you a safe journey through Highgate and this life. I charge you, my good son, that if you know any in this company who have not taken this oath, you must cause them to take it, for if you fail to do so, you will forfeit a bottle of wine yourself. So now, my son, God bless you! Kiss the horns, or a pretty girl, if you see one here, which you like best, and so be free to Highgate.

In this way the bewildered traveller was given the freedom of Highgate, which gave him the following privilege, solemnly recited by the landlord: 'If at any time you are going through Highgate, and want to rest yourself, and you see a pig lying in a ditch, you have liberty to kick her out and take her place; but if you see three lying together, you must only kick out the middle one and lie between the other two. God save the King!'

At the Gatehouse, the drovers who were putting up for the night would gather round the victim and watch him carefully. If he submitted cheerfully to the last detail of the ceremony, which was the kissing of the horns – or a pretty girl, if she happened to be on hand –

they considered him fit company for the rest of the evening and welcomed him to join them.

The joke went on all through the seventeenth and eighteenth centuries and even into the more sophisticated days of the early nineteenth. As coaches came to a halt at the posting inns, travellers were invited to alight and take the oath: and by Regency times there were no less than nineteen inns in Highgate, all of them equipped with their horns, either stag's, bullock's or ram's, in preparation for the ceremony.

Lord Byron was one who submitted, and later wrote:

> Many to the steep of Highgate hie;
> Ask, ye Boeotian shades! the reason why?
> 'Tis to the worship of the solemn Horn
> Grasped in the holy hand of Mystery
> In whose dread name both men and maids
>   are sworn
> And consecrate the oath with draught and
>   dance till morn.

Samuel Palmer, the friend of William Blake, put it more simply:

> It's a custom at Highgate, that all who
>   go through,
> Must be sworn on the horns, sir; and so
>   sir must you;
> Bring the horns, shut the door; now, sir
>   take off your hat.
> When you come here again, don't forget
>   to mind *that*.

This was a reminder that the first word of the oath was 'that'. Most initiates, struggling to repeat the oath, forgot it and had to start all over again.

The old gateway had been built for drovers and pack-horse men, and as carriers' carts became more usual for the transport of goods, and the first cumbersome, springless coaches came into use, the arch was found to be too low. It still stood, so the traffic had to be diverted through the inn yard, which if inconvenient for the travellers, was splendid for the custom of the inn.

One of the oldest mansions in Highgate of which there is any record was Arundel House, a Tudor mansion in South Grove, on the site of which the Old Hall, built late in the seventeenth century, is still standing.

Before Arundel House became the Highgate home of the Earls of Arundel, it belonged to the Cornwallis family. Sir Thomas Cornwallis was Treasurer of Calais and Comptroller of the Household to Mary Tudor: and it was here that the unhappy Princess Elizabeth came as a prisoner, when Queen Mary ordered her to be brought from Ashridge to the Tower of London, accused of complicity in the Wyatt rebellion.

The Princess was only twenty-one and had already known a life-time of trouble. The day after Wyatt's arrest, Sir Thomas Cornwallis, Sir Richard Southwell and Sir Edward Hastings, with an imposing array of two hundred and fifty attendants and troopers, arrived at Ashridge House in Hertfordshire at ten o'clock at night.

The Princess was ill and in bed, and sent a message that the envoys should discuss their business with her in the morning, but they 'came rushyng into her grace's chamber unbydden', telling her that the Queen wished to see her immediately. In vain the Princess protested that she was not well enough to travel. They told her they must bring her to London, 'quick or dead', and that she must be ready to travel by nine o'clock the next morning, assuring her, with cold comfort, that they had brought the Queen's litter, in which to carry her.

'Faynt and feeble', she was carried in the litter from Ashridge to Redbourn. The next day they reached St Albans. The third day they travelled as far as Mimms, and on the fourth they reached Sir Thomas's house at Highgate.

By this time the Princess was so ill that they were obliged to stay there all night and the whole of the following day, but when they eventually reached London the bitter and angry Queen Mary consigned her to the Tower immediately.

For a time it seemed that the Princess would follow Sir Thomas Wyatt to the scaffold, but she was eventually released: and only four years later Highgate saw a very different Elizabeth. Mary was dead and the new Queen Elizabeth rode in her chariot from Hatfield House to London, to prepare for her coronation, being met at Highgate by the Lord Mayor, Aldermen and Sheriffs, 'who conducted her Majesty in great pomp to the City; where she was received with equal acclamations both from Protestants and Papists, who seemed to vie with each other in their demonstrations of joy'.

During the Reformation and the dissolution of the monasteries and abbeys, many of the medieval grammar schools which had been attached to the ecclesiastical foundations had disappeared. Some were re-established and a few new ones were founded, with funds from the old endowments. During Edward VI's short reign another fifteen grammar schools were founded, although some were very small and poorly endowed; and during the reign of Queen Elizabeth many more were established, mainly by prosperous merchants or noblemen, who now gave to the cause of education the money which in pre-Reformation days would have been bequeathed to chantries or expended on pilgrimages.

With England's growing foreign commerce and widening horizons, far more people with an adequate education were needed to conduct her affairs, and by now it was generally considered fitting that wealthy citizens and the State should bear some of the responsibility for this education, which hitherto had been vested in the Church.

Amongst the London schools founded at this time were John Colet's new foundation at St Paul's, the Mercers', the Merchant Taylors', Charterhouse and Highgate. Mostly they were day schools and for the most part they were free, serving the needs of local boys: and the pupils were drawn from all levels of society except the lowest, who were thought, like girls of most ranks, to have no need for education.

By the middle of Queen Elizabeth's reign there were some three hundred and fifty of these small grammar schools throughout the country and there were few towns of any consideration which did not possess one. They were still under ecclesiastical supervision, however, and masters had to be licensed by the Church. Some disappeared during the educational changes of the eighteenth and nineteenth centuries, but others, like Highgate, were destined to weather the storms of controversy and become distinguished public schools.

It was Sir Roger Cholmeley who founded the little grammar school at Highgate. He reached high office during the reign of Henry VIII, being made Chief Baron of the Exchequer, and it was during these years that he acquired the Shoot-Up Hill manor of Hampstead, as well as property in Highgate. In Edward VI's time he became Lord Chief Justice of the King's Bench, but Queen Mary sent him to the Tower for a time, the charge being that he had taken part in a scheme to disinherit both her and her sister. After his release, he retired to Highgate, his home probably being the house which later was known as Dorchester House, standing on the west side of the Green, in the Grove at the southern end, close to the spot where West Hill was to reach the Green.

In 1565 Bishop Grindal, the Bishop of London, granted him the abandoned hermitage, together with its garden and orchard and two acres of pasture: and here Sir Roger planned to build a grammar school for Highgate. He died the same year, and his bequest was left in the hands of six governors, who set to work on his plans.

The hermitage was pulled down and a small brick and stone school built on the site. It allowed for the accommodation of a maximum of forty boys, who were to be accepted from Highgate, Holloway, Hornsey, Finchley or Kentish Town, 'if there be so many'. If there were not, then boys could be taken from 'other towns nearby'.

Nothing could show more clearly than this how small the population was in these northern suburbs of farms and fields and wooded glades. The boys were to be taught reading, writing and their grammar, as well as their ABC. The ABC was a standard text book containing the Lord's Prayer, the Ave Maria, the Creed, the Ten Commandments and the Catechism, as well as various maxims for good conduct, which are said to have been compiled by Henry VII. It does not specify in the rules whether 'their grammar' meant Latin or English grammar, but as the grammar schools were primarily established for the teaching of Latin, which was the international language of commerce, and as essential for anyone planning a career as a merchant as for entry into one of the learned professions, it seems probable that Latin was intended.

School hours, as in all these little day schools throughout the country, were from seven until eleven o'clock in the morning, from one till five in the afternoon in winter and one till six in summer.

Most grammar schools of this size – and many were much smaller – had an usher or assistant, as well as the master, but there was no provision for one at Highgate. The master did the job unaided and received for it fifty shillings a quarter and a free house, which was attached to the school. He also had the use of the two acres of ground, which had been enclosed from Highgate common, as well as the garden and orchard of the old hermitage. He was allowed eight loads of wood each year, from the Bishop of London's Hornsey Park, provided he used it for himself or the school, and did not try to make a little cash on the side by selling it. Each scholar had to pay fourpence on admission, which was to be spent on books for the school library, and another fourpence as a gift to the master.

A few years later, in 1578, the hermit's chapel adjoining the new school building was rebuilt. It became a very odd looking structure, with three pairs of small round windows above the three pairs of main chapel windows, to light three rooms of the master's house, which had been built over the nave; and a square, battlemented tower was added at the west end, which was oddly at variance with the pointed gables of the school-house windows.

Besides being the school chapel, this was used as a chapel of ease for the people of Highgate, the parish church for the majority being still at

Hornsey, although a few residents came into the parish of St Pancras.

It added considerably to the duties of the school master, for in addition to opening and closing school each day, with prayers prescribed by the Bishop, he had to read morning and evening prayers at the chapel every Sunday, except the first Sunday morning in the month, when people attended their parish church to receive Holy Communion. He also had to read morning prayers, with the litany, every Wednesday and Friday, and evening prayers on Saturdays.

The first master at the school seems to have been Johnson Charle. He agreed to obey all the rules, which included not cutting down any trees surrounding the school building, and he was allowed ten days holiday a year, provided he found a substitute to take over his duties. If he failed to do this he had to pay a fine of two shillings a day; and if, after three warnings, he still broke any rule, he was liable to instant dismissal.

Sir Roger Cholmeley left several bequests to Highgate, in addition to the money for the school, including forty shillings to the Lazar House at the foot of the hill outside which the legendary Dick Whittington was thought to have rested. It had been founded by William Pole during the reign of Edward IV. Pole, who held office as Yeomen of the Crown to the King, was stricken with leprosy himself, and when he expressed a wish to build a hospital for future sufferers, Edward IV granted him a piece of land on the highway leading from Holloway to Highgate, which was sixty feet long and thirty-four feet wide. Here William Pole built his hospital and chapel, 'to the honour of God and St Anthony, for the relief and harbour of such leprous persons as were destitute in the kingdom, to the end they should not be offensive to others in their passing to and fro'.

The Lazar House survived the Reformation and seems to have lasted as a hospital or poor house until the last years of the Commonwealth when, being officially Crown property, it was sold, with the land on which it stood, to Ralph Harrison of London, for £130.10s, after which it was demolished.

Sir Roger Cholmeley also left five pounds to the poor people of Highgate and another five pounds to Simon of Highgate, who, it has been suggested, may have been Johnson Charle's predecessor as master of the school for a year or two.

Lauderdale House, on the west side of Highgate Hill, was built on the site of an Elizabethan mansion, the first owner of which was Sir Richard Martyn. It then came into the possession of John Povey, styled 'citizen and embroiderer of London', who died there in 1599, leaving the property to his only child Katharine, wife of Alderman Sir William Bond: and while the Bonds were living here the unfortunate Arabella Stuart was lodged with them, from March 1611, as a state prisoner.

Arabella, born in 1575, was the daughter of Charles Stuart, Earl of Lennox, the younger brother of Lord Darnley. Through his mother, the Earl was grandson of Margaret, the eldest sister of Henry VIII, by her second husband, Archibald Douglas, Earl of Angus. Arabella was therefore next in line of succession to the throne, after her cousin James I, and there was a strong body of opinion which maintained that not only would England fare better under an English monarch than a Scottish one, who was likely to grant offices of profit to his own countrymen, but that her claim to the throne was even stronger than that of James, since she had been born in England, while James was an alien, and thereby disqualified from owning land in England.

Just before Queen Elizabeth died, she heard that Arabella was planning to marry William Seymour, who came from the Suffolk line to which Lady Jane Grey had belonged. Scenting danger to the succession, she ordered Arabella to be arrested and kept out of harm's way. However, when James succeeded peacefully to the throne, without incident, Arabella was released; and since she was perenially short of cash, depending entirely on the Crown for her subsistence, he awarded her a pension of £1,600 a year.

Only two years later came the Gunpowder plot of the Papists, but all the conspirators were brought to justice and neither Arabella nor Seymour was in anyway implicated.

In later years a story was circulated that the gunpowder plot conspirators waited in the fields just west of Millfield Lane on that fateful 5 November 1605 to watch the Palace of Westminster, where Parliament was assembling, go up in flames, and that afterwards the spot, today known as Parliament Hill Fields, was called Traitors' Field. Yet this is not a very likely story, for there were only six men concerned in the plot, besides Guy Fawkes, all of them well-known Catholics, and from the records they were mainly scattered throughout the Midlands, preparing to organise a rebellion if Guy had been successful.

The place may have had some concern with Jack Cade's rebellion and it probably was at some time the site of a gallows, but it seems to have been called Parliament Hill after the Middlesex elections were held here, during the seventeenth and eighteenth centuries.

Arabella Stuart and William Seymour were deeply in love, but they bided their time. Not until 1610 did they formally announce their intention of marrying, whereupon King James, still nervous and jealous of the Suffolk family, summoned them to appear before the Privy Council. The King reprimanded Seymour for presuming to marry royal blood, although there was as much of it in Seymour's veins as James's; and he forbade him to marry without his permission.

Six months later the couple made what they fondly hoped was a secret marriage, but within forty-eight hours the news had reached the King's ears. Seymour was arrested and imprisoned in the Tower and Arabella was taken in custody to the house of Sir Thomas Parry in Lambeth. James, angry and suspicious of her, decided that she should be sent north, as far away as possible from her husband and put in the charge of the Bishop of London.

When Arabella heard her intended fate, she stormed and screamed and refused to move, whereupon she was taken forcibly from her bed and carried down to the Thames. She was then rowed up-river to a landing stage, where a litter had been prepared for her journey to Durham.

The first stop that day was to have been Barnet, but as they approached Highgate Arabella became so ill that the physician accompanying the procession grew anxious, reporting 'that she was assuredly very weak, her pulse dull, melancholy, and very irregular and her countenance very heavy, pale and wan'. A message was hurriedly sent to Sir William Bond, whose house was presumably the most important near at hand, asking him to give the Lady Arabella two rooms for the night, 'because wee doubt the Innes there are full of Inconvenience'.

As the Gate House was probably the only inn in Highgate at the time and was usually full of cattle drovers and carters, the request was reasonable enough. So Arabella was taken to the Bonds' house and made welcome and it was reported to the Privy Council that Sir William had treated her and her entourage with especial care.

How long she stayed in Highgate is not clear, for accounts differ, but it seems to have been for about two months, until the following June. What is certain is that it was long enough for her to write heart-rending letters to her cousin, Lady Jane Drummond, begging her to plead with the King for a change of heart.

> Good Cousin, I pray you to do me the kindness to present this letter of mine in all humility to hir Matie and wh all my most humble and dutifull thanckes for the gratuitous commiseration it pleased hir Maty to have of me, as I hear to my great comfort. [This suggests

that even Queen Henrietta had pleaded Arabella's cause with the King, though in vain.]

And I do earnestly intreate you to moue hir Mate to vouchsafe the continuance of hir so gratious a beginning on my behalfe, and to perswade hir Majty to weigh my cause aright, and then I shall not doubt to receive that Royall Justice and fauour that my owne soule witnessethe I have ever deserued at his Masty handes, and will euer endeavour to deserue of him and his whilest I have breath, and so wh many thanckes to your selfe for your kind offices I take leave and rest,

Your very loving Cousin,
Arabella Seymour

The King was adamant, but by some means, never disclosed, she managed to get in touch with her husband in the Tower. Between them and some trustworthy friends, they hatched a plot for escape. The time had come for Arabella to continue her journey to Durham, under the escort of Sir James Croft. She adopted an air of docile resignation, to allay all suspicion, and they prepared to leave Sir William Bond's house at Highgate for Mr Conyer's at East Barnet, the next stopping place on the way north. In the confusion of the move and the arrival at East Barnet, Arabella managed to escape, disguising herself in men's clothing by

drawing a great paire of French-fashioned hose over her petticoats, and putting on a man's doublet, a man-like peruke, with long locks, over her hair, a black hat, black cloake, russet boots with red tops, with a rapier by her side, and walked forth, between three and four of the clock, with Mr Markham. After they had gone on foot a mile and a half, they reached a sorry inn, where one Crompton attended to their horses.

He had been warned of their coming and the horses were ready for them. At this point, Arabella became faint, and the ostler remarked that the young gentleman would hardly hold out to London, but they pressed on at a gallop and the ride revived her. They reached the river at Blackwall about nine in the evening, to find two boats waiting for them, one packed with the possessions of Arabella and her husband, the other prepared for herself and her small circle of attendants and servants who, when they were told of the plan, had agreed to accompany her and risk the hazards of discovery.

They sailed all night, making their way down river to Woolwich and then to Gravesend and Tilbury, and at last, as day was dawning, they reached Leigh. They saw the French barque which was waiting for them, lying at anchor about a mile out to sea. They made their way towards her. Everything went smoothly. A few minutes later, with no interruption or sign of danger, they had boarded her with all the luggage.

Nothing now remained but the safe arrival of William. Heavily disguised with a peruke and false, black beard, he had walked calmly from his lodging in the Tower the previous morning, following a cart which had been delivering wood. Unhurriedly and still undetected, he had reached the Tower wharf and stepped aboard the boat in which his friend Rodney was waiting for him: and quietly they made their way to Leigh.

Security at the Tower was lax, for William was a privileged prisoner. No one noticed his disappearance and the journey to Leigh was uneventful.

Unfortunately for Arabella, her attendants grew nervous, fully aware of the dangers they were running and the punishment that awaited them if they were discovered. They said it was too dangerous to linger near the English coast any longer. It would be far safer to cross the Channel at once and meet William in France. Arabella protested that they must keep to the arrangement to meet at Leigh. They refused to wait. Arabella pleaded in vain and the barque set sail without him.

Only a few minutes later, William and Rodney arrived. The sea was very rough but they saw what they thought was the French barque some distance away and hired a fisherman to take them out to it. When they drew alongside, they found it was a different boat, but then they spotted a collier, and with an offer of twenty pounds induced the skipper to take them to Calais.

By this time Lady Arabella's escape had been reported to the King and an urgent message was sent to the Tower to increase the guard on Seymour. Only then, when the Lieutenant visited his lodging, did they discover that he, too, had escaped.

This second calamity was duly reported to the irate King James, who at once gave orders that 'a pinnace that lay in the Downes put presently to sea, first to Calais Road, and then to saile up the road towards Dunkirke'.

The pinnace sighted the French barque, which was still on the look-out for William Seymour, and made towards her. She put on all speed for the French coast, but the pinnace fired thirteen shots at her and forced her to surrender. The Lady Arabella was arrested yet again and taken back to the Tower, with her retinue, and even in her distress she maintained that she was 'not so sorry for her own restraint as she would be glad if Mr Seymour might escape, whose welfare she protesteth to feel much more than her own'.

Arabella spent the next four years of her life imprisoned in the Tower. She was told nothing of the fate of her husband and no message from him ever reached her. Here she died in September 1615. Many believed she died of a broken heart, although by this time she was more than half-demented with grief and despair. At the last, she was given her royal due, for she was buried in the Royal Chapel at Westminster.

Though Arabella never knew it, William Seymour escaped safely to France and after Arabella's death he was forgiven and allowed to return to England. He inherited the title of Marquis of Hertford and fought for King Charles during the Civil War, although by this time he had taken as his second wife the sister of the Parliamentary general, the Earl of Essex. At the Restoration, King Charles II restored to him the title of Duke of Somerset, which his great-grandfather, Protector of Edward VI, had forfeited at his downfall, but in this same year, 1660, he died.

When Sir William Bond died, Mary Countess of Home bought his estate and mansion on Highgate Hill, and on her death in 1648 her daughter, wife of the Earl of Lauderdale, inherited the property, which henceforth became known as Lauderdale House. By this time the Civil War was raging, and only a few months later Charles I was beheaded. At the battle of Worcester, in 1651 – the last resistance of the Royalists to Cromwell – after which Charles II fled into exile until the Restoration, the Earl of Lauderdale was taken prisoner and sent to the Tower for the next nine years.

The Commonwealth sequestered Lauderdale House and bestowed it on John Ireton, brother of Cromwell's son-in-law General Ireton. It is this loose connexion with Cromwell that gave rise to the legend that the mansion on the opposite side of the hill, still known as Cromwell House, had been built by Oliver Cromwell for his daughter, when she married Henry Ireton, but the house was in existence long before this and there is no evidence that Henry Ireton or his wife ever lived there.

The original house and estate were bought from George Crowther in 1605 by Robert Sprigwell, son of Richard Sprigwell, a citizen and barber surgeon of London. Richard had grown wealthy in his profession and was a man of determination, though, to judge from his will, not of great gallantry, for in it he settled, once and for all, the question of whether or not he had loved his second wife.

'And now to satisfy the world concerning my last marriage,' he wrote,

> forasmuch as the said marriage between me and Frances my wife (with whom or any other I did never purpose to marrie nor had any entent to have married) was effected and compassed by her through her many and earnest solicitations and alurements, and by subtil devises and practices, used therein at sundry times, but then especially when I was with her at her lodgings, where uppon the sodaine (in some sort) she enforced me thereunto, not permitting me to send for or to use the advise of any friend being of any familiar or old acquaintance.

He left her an adequate income but bequeathed the bulk of his property to Robert, the only son of his first marriage, who bought the house and lived there for the next nineteen years. He died in 1624 and was buried in the school chapel at the top of the hill. His widow lived on in the house and was there when Lord Bacon, the former Lord Chancellor, was taken ill at Highgate and died there.

The brilliant and arrogant Francis Bacon had been dismissed from his high office for corruption and accepting bribes, misdemeanours which were almost universal at this time, and he was in dire financial straits, for his promised pension had never materialised. He had been forced to sell his country estate of Gorhambury, as well as York House, his mansion in the Strand, in order to settle his enormous debts of £22,000. He was obliged to move back to his old lodgings in Gray's Inn, where he had once practised as a lawyer, but he still lived in the grand manner and his misfortunes in no way dimmed the unflagging energy of his enquiring mind and his devotion to the cause of science. The story goes that one cold April day in 1626 he was driving in a coach towards Highgate Hill with Dr Witherborne, the King's Scottish physician.

The snow lay thick on the ground and it passed through Bacon's mind that snow, like salt, might preserve the human body after death. He and the doctor decided, there and then, to experiment. They stopped the coach at the bottom of the hill, called at a cottage and bought a hen. They induced the surprised cottager to draw it for them and then they stuffed it with snow to see what would happen to it. It was the first experiment in refrigeration, but it chilled Bacon so severely that, according to John Aubrey's account, he was taken suddenly ill. Not being able to make the journey back to Gray's Inn, he was carried to the Earl of Arundel's house in South Grove. The Earl was not in residence when Sir Francis arrived, but he was welcomed and a bed was made ready for him. Unfortunately the bed was damp, for it had not been slept in for the previous twelve months, and instead of recovering, Sir Francis grew steadily worse.

His friend and relative, Sir Julius Caesar, the Master of the Rolls, arrived to look after him, but he was so old that he was said to have been 'kept alive beyond Nature's course by the prayers of the many poor whom he daily relieved'. Through him, Bacon sent a letter to the Earl of Arundel, explaining what had happened and saying that

> when I came to your lordship's house, I was not able to go back, and therefore was forced to take up my lodging here, where your housekeeper is very careful and diligent about me, which I assure myself your lordship will not only pardon towards him, but think the better of him for it. For, indeed, your lordship's house was happy to me; and I kiss your noble hands for the welcome which I am sure you will give me to it.

Lord Bacon cannot have known that he was dying when he dictated that letter, but he lived only a few days longer. And the unfortunate hen? Bacon must have taken it with him to South Grove, for its ghost is said to haunt Pond Square to this very day, dismally flapping its wings in protest at its melancholy end.

The following year Robert Sprignell's widow died at Cromwell House and their only son Richard inherited the property. His name is listed as one of the governors of Highgate school in 1639, and it was about this time that he rebuilt the old house, and the new Cromwell House, of which parts still survive, arose on the site. It is a splendid, red brick Jacobean mansion, the shallow front courtyard protected from the road by a brick wall and gateway. Many of the rooms had carved oak panelling and beautifully moulded, plaster ceilings, with pedimented doorways, but the most striking feature was the magnificent staircase, built round a square well, with square oak newels at each corner and a heavily moulded handrail. Each newel was surmounted by a carved wooden figure, some eighteen inches high, of a soldier of the time of Charles I, including a targeteer, a drummer, a pikeman and a musketeer.

There were no doubt other mansions in Highgate in the early seventeenth century, but the records are scanty and the real development was not until after the Restoration and during the eighteenth century. Before this development, the old farmhouse of Sherrick's Hole farm stood where Fitzroy House was to be built and the Caen or Ken Wood estate had been deserted since the Reformation – the remains of some monastic buildings there having fallen into ruins. In 1658 Sir Harry Vane was writing to his friend John Bill that

> the estate of Ken Wood appeared to him to require handling well, the home domain being peculiarly good, and capable of much improvement, but that he felt the price asked too great by £100, and so persuaded his friend John Bill not to purchase, as that little castle of ruinous brick and stone could only be used for materials to build another house, near thirty acres in waste, as ponds and the moate, a deal of great trees to be cut down, and many serious expences he had not yet considered.

When the Civil War broke out, the Parliamentary generals are said to have placed cannon on the Traitors' Hill fields for the defence of London, and thereafter Traitors' Fields were known as Parliament Hill Fields, but there is no real proof of this and the theory that they took the name from the elections held there is just as possible.

John Ireton continued to live in Lauderdale House during the Commonwealth, while the Earl of Lauderdale was in the Tower, and the Earl was not the only man in Highgate to lose his home. Mr Carter, the master of Highgate school, was forcibly thrown out of his house by the Puritans, despite the fact that his wife was in labour when the soldiers came to evict him. The baby was born in the chapel porch and the family left to fare as best they could, while a new master, Humphrey Vernon, was installed at double the salary of the unfortunate Mr Carter.

The Sprigwell family still lived at Cromwell House and were close friends of John Ireton and his family across the road. Richard Sprigwell went mad and died about 1658, but his eldest son, Sir Robert, husband of Anne, daughter of Sir Richard Livesey, continued to live there until a few years after the Restoration, when the family sold out to George Hill.

Just above Lauderdale House and opposite Cromwell House was a delightful little half-timbered house, with a gabled roof and porch, and a little garden which adjoined the grounds of Lauderdale House. There were probably several such houses lining the hill and surrounding Highgate Green and the pond at this time, but the one next to Lauderdale House survived for many years, for it was the home of Andrew Marvell. Marvell was born in 1621 and left Cambridge in 1641, after which he spent four years travelling through Europe. By the time he returned to England the Civil War was raging. He was a Parliamentarian but took no part in the fighting and devoted himself to his poetry and writing, supporting himself mainly by tutoring. He tutored a ward of Cromwell's at Eton for a time and taught Latin to the daughter of General Fairfax. In 1657 he was appointed assistant to John Milton, in Milton's capacity of Foreign Secretary to the Council of State, the office being described as Latin Secretary, since all the correspondence was conducted in Latin; and in 1659 he took his seat in Richard Cromwell's parliament, as member for Kingston-upon-Hull, maintaining a close correspondence with his constituents, from his cottage on Highgate Hill.

With the Restoration, Marvell stayed on at his cottage, which he loved and of which he wrote:

> I have a garden of my own
> But so with roses overgrown
> And lilies that you would it take
> To be a little wilderness

He devoted much of his time to writing sharply critical tracts on the arbitrary methods of government during the Restoration years and the conduct of Church dignitaries such as Bishop Parker, whom he castigated for his persecution of the Nonconformists. Marvell was a rationalist and although he often dressed his criticism in a pungent wit, for he was essentially a lovable man, there were many who hated him, through fear of his pen, and would have been glad to see him destroyed.

'My foes are implacable, and I am frequently threatened with murder, and waylaid in my passing to and from Highgate, where I am fond of lodging,' he wrote.

Yet Charles II admired him and enjoyed his company. He even tried to buy his loyalty by offering him a place at Court: and knowing full well that he made only a poor living from his poetry, the King suggested the immediate gift of £1,000 as an added inducement, but Marvell, turning aside the offer with a graceful acknowledgment, was not to be bought and remained inflexibly loyal to his convictions.

One of his treatises, *An Account of the Growth of Popery and Arbitrary Government in England*, published anonymously in 1677, was considered to be so dangerous that a reward was offered for the discovery of the author and publisher. It was at this point that Marvell decided it would be prudent to retire to Hull, where a few months later he died, not without a suspicion that he had been poisoned, although the cause of death was officially said to have been a 'tertian ague'.

With the Restoration, John Ireton hastily moved from Lauderdale House and the Earl, freed from the Tower, returned to live there with his wife and family, and began his steady rise to power in the King's

Cabal, until he became one of the best-hated men in the country. He probably made many alterations to the old house at this time, but the Lauderdale House which stands today is the result of late Georgian rebuilding.

Although in the time of Charles I, Lauderdale had been one of the Covenanters responsible for selling the King to the English army, for his trial and execution, he now joined with Charles II in persecuting them. He was Lord-Deputy of Scotland and one of the first acts of the new Scottish Parliament, known as the Drunken Parliament, was the abolition of the legal sanction of the Presbyterian Church, which the Covenanters had won so hardly twenty-eight years earlier.

Lauderdale, the tyrant deputy of Scotland, with his big, red head, 'loud and coarse in mirth and anger', was, said Lord Macaulay, 'perhaps, under the outward show of boisterous frankness, the most dishonest man in the whole Cabal'.

Pepys paid a visit to Lauderdale House soon after the Restoration. On 28 July 1666 he recorded:

> Thence with my Lord (Bruncker) to his coach-house, and there put in his six horses into his coach, and he and I alone to Highgate . . . we went to my Lord Lauderdale's house to speake with him, about getting a man at Leith to joyne with one we employ to buy some prize goods for the King; we find (him) and his lady and some Scotch people at supper. Pretty odd company; though my Lord Bruncker tells me, my Lord Lauderdale is a man of mighty good reason and judgement. But at supper there played one of their servants upon the viallin some Scotch tunes only; several, and the best of their country, as they seemed to esteem them, by their praising and admiring them: but Lord! the strangest ayre that ever I heard in my life, and all of one cast. But strange to hear my Lord Lauderdale say himself that he had rather hear a cat mew, than the best musique in the world; and the better the musique, the more sicke it makes him; and that of all instruments, he hates the lute most, and next to that, the bagpipe.

The road to Highgate from London was still difficult. On 26 February 1664, when travelling to Barnet, Pepys rode with Mr Coventry 'through bad ways to Highgate'. On the following 4 August of that year, he and his cousin road out to Highgate, inspecting on the way the ditch where Walter Clun, a popular Drury Lane actor had been murdered two nights before by two thieves who attacked him as he was on the way home to his house in Kentish Town, after 'drinking with his whore'. He had received only one stab wound, recorded Pepys, but the robbers had bound him, tossed him into a ditch and left him to bleed to death.

On 11 July 1665 Pepys was again in Highgate, but in different and happier circumstances. It was a very hot night and he had slipped away from a solemn dinner at Trinity House, before it was half ended, in order to meet his friend Mary at the New Exchange.

And there, [said Pepys,] took coach and I with great pleasure took the ayre to Highgate, and thence to Hampstead, much pleased with her company, pretty and innocent, and had what pleasure almost I would with her, and so at night, weary and sweaty, it being very hot beyond bearing, we back again, and I set her down in St Martin's Lane, and so I to the evening 'Change' to hear the evening news.

Probably the most interesting reference to Highgate that Pepys made was his description of the Fifth Monarchy men who hid themselves in Ken Wood.

After Sir Harry Vane had advised John Bill, his future son-in-law, not to buy Ken Wood, it was acquired by Sir James Harrington, but with the Restoration Harrington hurriedly left the country, for he was listed with the Regicides and faced the probability of life imprisonment in the Tower. While on bail from the Sergeant-at-arms he fled to the Continent, leaving his wife and twelve children in dire distress. John Bill then bought Ken Wood, which at this time consisted of '200 acres of land well covered with large timber, and also is stated a capital messuage of brick, wood, and plaster, eight cottages, a farm house and windmill, fish-ponds, etc.'

Whether this capital messuage was a euphemistic agent's description of the ruinous old monastic buildings or a new house which Harrington had built in its place is not clear, but whichever it was, Bill pulled it down and 'formed a place that he could live in with comfort, and surrounded twenty-five acres with a brick wall'.

The Fifth Monarchy men were led by Thomas Venner, a wine-cooper, who was convinced that the second coming of Christ on earth was imminent and that he had been especially chosen to reform the world, in order to prepare the way. The imminent Fifth Monarchy was the reign of Christ and His Saints and was to last for a thousand years. The previous four monarchies were, declared Venner, the empires of Assyria, Persia, Greece and Rome, but no one seemed to have asked what the sixth monarchy was to be.

There seems to have been a good deal of muddled thinking about the entire movement, for if the second coming were so imminent, Venner's services would appear to have been superfluous, but he was obsessed with his mission and managed to acquire a following of perhaps only thirty but certainly no more than sixty men, all of whom were fully armed to conquer the world. They met in Coleman Street and their first venture was in St Paul's Churchyard. They accosted the first man they met and asked him 'who he was for?'. 'For God and King Charles!' replied the man, whereupon they murdered him. The Lord Mayor and a party of train-bands went in pursuit of them, but Venner's men, declaiming that 'King Jesus was their invisible leader', rampaged through the City like men possessed, committing several more murders before escaping to the refuge of Ken Wood for the night.

The next morning a few of them were captured, but the rest made their way back to the City, to do more damage. John Bill observed that he 'was glad to be rid of their company, he having in the meantime lost four sheep and two cows'.

For a day or two the City was in a ferment, waiting for the 'Fanatiques' to strike. Pepys, on 9 January 1661, found

> every body in arms at the doors. So I returned (though with no good courage at all, but that I might not seem to be afeared), and got my sword and pistol, which, however, I had not powder to charge . . . the streets full of Train-band, and great stories, what mischief these rogues have done; and I think near a dozen have been killed this morning on both sides.

The next day, when they had all been captured, Pepys discovered that this troublesome group of Fanatiques, who had

> routed all the Train-bands they met with, put the King's life-guards to the run, killed about twenty men, broke through the City gates twice; and all this in the day-time, when all the City was in arms, numbered only about thirty-one, whereas we did believe them (because they were seen up and down in every place almost in the City, and had been about Highgate two or three days, and in several other places) to be at least 500. A thing that was never heard of, that so few men should dare and do so much mischief. . . . Few of them would receive any quarter, but such as were taken by force and kept alive; expecting Jesus to come here and reign in the world presently, and will not believe yet but their work will be carried on though they die.

It was about this time, soon after the Restoration, that the well-intentioned though luckless William Blake made valiant efforts to establish a charity school at Highgate. He was a woollen draper with a business at the sign of the Golden Boy in Maiden Lane, Covent Garden, where all the fashionable mercers and drapers were establishing themselves, as society moved westwards from the City. He had a prosperous business and was a sincerely devout man, who wanted to establish his school for forty orphaned boys and girls. He spent almost his entire capital of £5,000 in buying Sir Roger Cholmeley's old house in the Grove, which after his death had been acquired by the Marquis of Dorchester and was known as Dorchester House. For its maintenance as a school Blake was confident that he would obtain voluntary subscriptions from the wealthy and titled women of London. The school was to be called the Ladies' Hospital or Charity School. The boys were to be taught painting, gardening, casting accounts and navigation and put to an apprenticeship when they left, and were to wear a uniform of blue lined with yellow, like the boys of Christ's Hospital. The girls were to be taught 'to read, write, sew, starch, raise paste, and dress, that they be fit for any service'.

He sent an appeal for funds to at least twenty-six noble-women, but, to his dismay, the response was negligible. About 1666 he published a little book called *Silver Drops; or Serious Things*, in which he outlined his plan in detail and included copies of the letters he had sent out appealing for support, though he did not give the names of the recipients, who had responded so meanly. Included in the book were odd scraps of spiritual advice, entitled *Short Hints but Sound Truths in Great Humility*.

Blake urged that the school should be available to the children of distressed French Protestant refugees, as well as the orphans of Highgate and the surrounding villages, observing very sensibly that it 'would be advantageous in matter of language'.

Against the advice of his family, and in a very shaky financial position, he opened the school, and by 1667 there appear to have been thirty-six boys, but there is no mention of any girls. Nor is it quite clear whether he first opened the school in some other building in Highgate and later moved to Dorchester House when it fell vacant.

The treasurer was Alderman Henry Cornish, the schoolmaster a minister in holy orders, for a time Henry Hurst, MA, a fellow of Merton College, Oxford.

But the money for maintaining the school did not come in quickly enough. Blake pleaded in vain, and complained that he was treated like a madman. It is true that his writings were mostly unintelligible, but one pamphlet, published in the 1680s, is clear enough, for in it he accuses his own brother of working against him, saying that 'he endeavours to hinder all others, setting your petitioner's wife and children to run it down, as an ill design full of pride, vainglory and hypocrisy'.

Poor Blake fell hopelessly into debt. He was imprisoned in the Fleet for more than two years, and after running for about twenty years, the school was closed. As he said sadly: 'the whole Design was Ravag'd, and my Family set against me to Obstruct all Charity, Keeping me in Prison to force the Sale of all for the Advantage of 2 or 3 Mortgages'.

William Blake, the mystic artist and poet, born in London in 1757, may well have been his great-grandson, although this is not certain, but the end of the school treasurer, Henry Cornish, is all too well authenticated. By 1680 he had become a sheriff of London, but five years later, during the reign of James II, he was tried and convicted of high treason by the Papists and was 'most barbarously hung, drawn and quartered, facing his own house, at the end of King Street, Cheapside'.

After Blake's school had been closed, Dorchester House was pulled down and the terrace of beautiful William and Mary houses which still stand in the Grove was built on the site. One of the first residents here was Sir Francis Pemberton, the eminent lawyer who had become Chief Justice of the Common Pleas and a member of Charles II's privy council. He died in 1697 and the new terrace of houses in the Grove was known for some time afterwards as Pemberton Row in his memory, and later, maintaining its air of expensive exclusiveness, as Quality Row.

The Earl of Lauderdale died in 1682 and during the next century Lauderdale House passed into the ownership of people who have no particular claim to fame. For a time it was a boys' school, and the story that Nell Gwynn once lived there is one of those popular myths for which no proof can be found.

One other interesting Highgate character during the second half of the seventeenth century was Dr Coysch, a Dutch physician who lived in an ancient, timber-framed house in the fields on the western side of Swain's Lane, not far down from the Green, but in the parish of St Pancras.

Dr Coysch arrived in England soon after the Restoration, coming from Amsterdam, where for many years he had made a particular study of antidotes for various kinds of poisons and infections. When the great plague broke out in Amsterdam, he not only gave valuable advice to people on how to avoid infection, but was successful in curing a number of people already stricken by it. The rich he charged for his services, but the poor he treated for nothing, and when the plague reached London, in 1665, hundreds came to love and honour him for the tireless and selfless work he did amongst the victims of one of the worst plague spots in all London, St Giles's, Holborn.

In some manuscript notes from an illustrated copy of Lysons' *Environs of London*, which once belonged to Lord Howard, there was an account of a further example of his humanity, at a time when people were living in mortal terror of the dreadful plague. The notes described

> his goodness to thirteen poor people who were flying for their lives from London and Clerkenwell and who intended to have gone north, away by Highgate, but were stopped in Holloway, as there the people would not let them pass, or not even suffer them to be in a barn for the night; so they crossed the fields towards Hampstead, when Dr Coysch, having heard of their distress, he had them brought to his barns, and there attended to and fed them for two days; he then saw them got safe to Finchley Common, where they intended to wait until they were in hopes the cold weather would check the infection.*

* Quoted in *The History of Highgate*, John Lloyd.

III

Hampstead during the Sixteenth and Seventeenth Centuries

Hampstead was an even lonelier rural hamlet than Highgate during Tudor times, for it was between the roads to the north and north-west and led to nowhere in particular. The Heath was still a royal hunting ground, for Henry VIII had a passion for the sport which was almost an obsession. He decreed that all the hare, partridge, pheasant and heron in the stretch of country from the palace of Westminster to St Giles-in-the-Fields, and from Islington to Our Lady of the Oke, to Highgate, Hornsey Park and Hampstead Heath should be preserved for his own 'disport and pastime' and that anyone hunting or hawking or in any way killing the game in this area would be imprisoned: and the decree added a royal hint of even sterner punishment, if the King felt so inclined.

At the time of the Reformation, the population of Hampstead was probably less than two hundred and fifty, most of the villagers occupied with farming their small plots, growing wheat and beans on their fields, grazing their cattle on the Heath and feeding their pigs in the woods, but it is at this time that we hear, for the first time, of another occupation. A colony of laundry women established themselves in the village, finding the slopes of the Heath, with their fresh, clean breezes, a splendid drying ground. It is said that the laundry of the Royal household was taken to Hampstead, and for centuries to come the laundry women of Hampstead find a vague mention in the records. As late as the days of the Regency, Beau Brummel, who was a connoisseur of such matters, commended their skill.

OLD CHAPEL.

1. The Old Chapel at Highgate.

2. Kilburn Priory.

3. The view from Moll King's house, Hampstead in 1760.

4. 'Swearing on the Horns' at Highgate c. 1784.

5. The Old Bull and Bush between 1783 and 1793.

6. Steele's Cottage, Haverstock Hill.

7. (*Above*) Sir Richard Steele.

8. (*Below*) Joseph Addison.

VIEW of CAEN WOOD, HAMPSTEAD, the SEAT of the EARL of MANSFIELD.

9. An early engraving of Ken Wood, the seat of the Earl of Mansfield.

10. The Adam Library at Ken Wood.

11. Mary-Anne Clarke.

12. (*Above*) Belsize House, Hampstead in 1760.

13. (*Below*) Belsize House in 1800.

At the time of the Dissolution, the manor of Hampstead, after being transferred to the Protestant Bishop of Westminster for a short time, returned to the Crown, but a few years later Edward VI bestowed the manor on an absentee landlord, Sir Thomas Wroth, a man from the West country who, said Strype, was 'one of those that received the largest share of benefits from the King, for he not only knighted him, but heaped great wealth, honours, offices and possessions on him'.

He was an enterprising character, and during the reign of Edward VI took part in a voyage to the Barbary coast, thereby becoming one of the earliest of the English merchant adventurers.

When Mary Tudor came to the throne Sir Thomas, as a devoted Protestant, retired to Strasbourg, although in consideration for his 'great learning, extraordinary worth and goodness', wrote Strype, he was allowed to keep his estates.

With the accession of Queen Elizabeth in 1558, he was back again in England, but whether or not he ever had time to visit Hampstead was never recorded, and when he died in 1573, he was living at his manor of Durants, in nearby Enfield.

No manor house seems to have been built to replace the medieval grange of the monks of Westminster in the Frognal area, nor is it clear how Frognal came to possess its strange name, unless it was because there was an abundance of frogs round the two or three ponds which stood there.

The road from London ran past Belsize and up Rosslyn Hill to the site of the present High Street, which was once known as Kingswell Street. It has been suggested that this name came about when King Henry passing through on his way to hunt, stopped to water his horse at a well in the heart of the village; but since one of the free tenants of Hampstead during the fourteenth century was Robert de Kyngeswell, it seems more likely that the street marked the site of his lands.

At the beginning of Queen Elizabeth's reign, sheep farming was still highly profitable and Lords of the Manor began to enclose lands which had hitherto been common, to pasture their own herds. At the same time, timber was becoming more valuable, and steps had to be taken to stop indiscriminate felling.

A few years before her accession, the Middlesex Commissioners had received a complaint that John Slannyng, a gentleman grazier of Hampstead, had cut down twenty acres of Ken Wood, to graze his 'horses, mares and cattle', fourteen acres of Wyldes Wood, leaving nothing but saplings on it, and six acres of Chalcotes Wood. Moreover, he was 'keeping 140 acres of Hampstead, and the farm of Chalcotes, containing 120 acres more, in pasture instead of tillage', which he was letting to 'butchers and inn-holders of London'.

There had been a similar complaint against Sir Thomas Wroth, while he was in exile at Strasbourg, for he was accused of selling some ninety acres of woods growing on the Heath, without the good will and consent of the tenants, thereby infringing their common rights.

Richard Reynes, John Jeymes and John Yerdley were also charged with cutting down many acres of woodland and Humfrey Crosse of Kilburn was 'presented' for cutting down 111 acres of wood and leaving no standards, 'in a wood called Florers Wood'.

Everyone had rights to the common, both owners and tenants of the adjacent land, but they were never clearly defined, a fact which was to lead to endless troubles during the litigation over the ownership of Hampstead Heath during the nineteenth century.

Generally speaking they had the right to a certain amount of wood for fuel and the use of the ground for pasturage. If anyone wanted to build a cottage on the common land, it could be done with the consent of the Lord of the Manor and the other tenants. A plot of land could be extended in the same way, but more often was achieved by surreptitiously altering the boundary fence a few yards. There was plenty of land and nobody minded very much if these incursions happened in a small way, but as soon as anyone was seen to be too greedy, there was inevitably a protest.

The chief trouble about these cases reported in the sixteenth century was the destruction of timber, which was needed for the navy, for ships were becoming bigger every year, both for overseas trading and for defence and war. Losses were heavy, replacements in constant demand and ship-building had become an important industry. Trees from the common lands produced the best timber for ship-building, for here the cattle had roamed for years, nibbling the young shoots of saplings so that, through the years, they had grown into mature trees of strangely twisted shapes which exactly suited the requirements of the shipwright, looking for curved timbers for ribs and beams.

These were the years of the great explorations and discoveries and the little village of Hampstead can claim a connection with one of the Elizabethan sea-dogs, Martin Frobisher, although it is by no means to the credit of himself. When he was about forty and had already made his voyage in search of a north-west passage to Cathay, and brought back stories of fabulous gold-mines in Labrador, he married a rich widow, many years older than himself and already a grandmother. He financed himself for his proposed Cathay Company with his wife's fortune, made preparations for his next voyage and departed, leaving her in Hampstead with her family.

He was away for months and in the meantime his wife was reduced to such straits that she at length wrote piteously to Sir Francis Walsingham for help, saying that she was 'the most miserable woman in the world, whose husband, Mr Captain Frobisher (whom God forgive) had not only spent that which her late husband left her but the portions also of her poor children.' He had 'put them all to the wide world to shift a most lamentable case', and 'to increase her misery, she having not to relieve herself, her children's children of her said first husband' had been sent to her, 'having a poor room within another at Hampstead near London, for her to keep at which place she and they are for want of food ready to starve, to your poor oratrix's intolerable grief and sorrow.'

No one knows the end of the story, but she cannot have survived for long, and perhaps she did starve to death, for soon after his share in the victory of the Armada, Frobisher married another widow.

Sir Thomas Wroth died in 1573 and his son succeeded to the property, but does not seem to have visited it. Sir Roger Cholmeley, as we have seen, acquired in 1546 the manor of Shoot-Up Hill, which had previously belonged to the Hospital of St John of Jerusalem. Eton College still owned Chalcot and Wyldes, although Henry VIII, during the course of his negotiations for acquiring the site of St James's Palace, seems to have filched some of the Chalcot land, as well as exchanging land in Westminster with certain estates in Kent and Suffolk.

The records of Tudor Hampstead list a few robberies and murders and summonses for not going to Church, and there were also determined efforts on the part of Londoners to arrange for some of the springs of Hampstead to be conveyed by pipe to London, to help the problem of their water supply. An Act was passed in 1546 allowing certain Hampstead streams to be diverted, but it was not until 1589 that anything was done about it, and then not with any great efficiency. They dug conduits and laid pipes to connect the Turnmill brook with the old Bourne, which joined the Fleet near Holborn bridge, but they failed lamentably in their efforts to clean and scour the Fleet, which remained in a deplorable condition for the next two hundred years.

While Sir Thomas Wroth was Lord of the Manor of Hampstead but with no manor house, the principal house in the parish was Belsize House, Belsize being the sub-manor which Sir Roger de Brabazon had willed back to Westminster Abbey on his death in 1317.

In 1496 the Abbey had made a contract for the production of 400,000 bricks at Belsize, a large proportion of which were probably used for the building of the Tudor mansion, standing where Belsize Park Gardens and Belsize Grove now meet. After the Dissolution this mansion and estate remained in the hands of the Dean and Chapter of Westminster Abbey, and during Queen Elizabeth's reign Armigall Waad, who had been Clerk to the Council to Henry VIII and Edward VI, leased it from the Abbey. Like Sir Thomas Wroth, he had ventured to sea in his younger days, in the van of the Merchant Adventurers, taking part in a private voyage to Newfoundland and North America, to report on the prospect of the land for King Henry.

The privations these men suffered in their frail vessels were terrible. They left Gravesend in April 1536 and when they reached Newfoundland they 'suffered famine in such a degree, that the ship's company began to devour one another, but were at length relieved by the arrival of a French ship well victualled, which they, contriving by some sleight to lay hold of, returned to England in, and arrived at St Ives in Cornwall about the end of October'.

Waad held high offices throughout his life, and amongst his multifarious activities was a keen interest in alchemy. Dr Dee had been the most famous wizard in England up till this time, and although during the reign of Mary Tudor he had been accused of using magic spells to bring about her death and had been forced to leave the country in a hurry, by the time Queen Elizabeth succeeded he was back in England. Lord Dudley had invited him to consult the stars and the spirit world in order to choose the most propitious time for the coronation. He had met the Queen and given her lessons in his mysteries, but she, in a friendly way, was by no means convinced.

When a new alchemist, Cornelius de Lannoy, appeared on the scene and offered, for a down payment of 2,000 crowns and a monthly allowance of 50 crowns, to produce 50,000 marks weight of pure gold each year, having presumably acquired the philosopher's stone by which the gold could be transmuted, the Queen and Cecil turned to Armigall Waad for advice.

Despite the suppression of the 'superstitious practices' of the Church of Rome, vestiges of paganism lingered on long after the sixteenth century, not only in the festivals of the countryside but in people's most private and personal way of thinking. Witches were still hunted, both in England and many countries of Europe, and the belief in sorcery and magic died hard.

The Queen and her advisers decided therefore to take a chance, and agreed that Cornelius should have a trial run, under Waad's super-vision, though with no pay until there were some tangible results.

All seemed to be going well until it came to the Queen's ears that Cornelius had promised to lend Princess Cecilia of Sweden, who had fled to England in distress, £10,000 by the following 1 May, from the proceeds of what the Queen regarded as her private mint. Cornelius was forbidden to have any further dealings with the Princess, but a few days later she wrote, asking for £3,000 immediately. Unwisely Cornelius replied, regretting that he had no such sum available as yet, but soon afterwards, from the kindness of his heart, he sent her twenty-five shillings, which did her and her household no good at all, for the following week her servants were arrested for debt.

Cornelius's activities were regarded with increasing suspicion, and Waad was soon convinced that he was a fraud and was making plans to escape to the Continent. He was arrested and sent to the Tower. Desperately he pleaded for his freedom, and begged the Queen to have pity on him and his wife and family; and Queen Elizabeth, who seemed to have a soft spot for necromancers, allowed him to leave the country in peace.

Waad died at Belsize in 1568 and by his wish was buried in the parish church at Hampstead, the first man of note to be interred there.

His son William, the eldest of his twenty children, by two wives, succeeded to Belsize House and his career followed the lines of that of his father, for he undertook various foreign missions for Queen Elizabeth, including a visit to Philip of Spain, just before the outbreak of the Spanish war with England. He was also the Queen's envoy to Mary Queen of Scots on one or two occasions and made her final arrest when she was charged with complicity in the Babington plot. Eventually he became Clerk to the Privy Council.

An interesting letter which he wrote from Hampstead to Lord Cecil in 1603, the year of the Queen's death, sheds light on the appalling conditions amongst the poor of London during the frequent epidemics which ravaged the City. He said that Londoners came from places of infection, bringing 'bedding and stuff with them, and presume noe man or officer will lay hands on them, because it is known the sickness is in their houses'. He suggests that they should be fined or arrested, except that no constable would come near them.

The Cages . . . are full of sick folkes and when they dye, the straw is thrown about the streets, fresh straw put in and new sicke persons. I have often seen three in one Cage together and people continually

about them. . . . Another lamentable thing very common: Divers
come out of the town and dye under Hedges in the fields and in divers
places further off, whereof we have experienced weekley here at
Hampsted and come in men's yardes, and outhouses if they be open
and dye there.

During the reign of James I, William Waad remained in high favour.
He was knighted and given among other appointments the position of
Lieutenant of the Tower, where he is said to have been unduly harsh,
though this may have been at the King's instigation.

He is known to have ordered the torture of three Jesuit priests who
were thought to have been implicated in the Gun Powder plot, in order
to wring a confession from them, yet nothing was ever proved against
them. He confined Raleigh more strictly and refused to allow his wife
and children to visit him. In 1613 he lost his Tower appointment during
the Overbury scandal. At thirteen, little Frances Howard had been
married to the fourteen-year-old Earl of Essex. As was usual, the
children were then parted for several years, but just before the Earl
returned to England to claim his bride, she fell madly in love with
Robert Carr, with whom King James was also in love.

When her husband presented himself, Frances refused to consum-
mate the marriage. There was talk of an annulment, but Carr's friend,
Thomas Overbury, a rising favourite at Court, did all he could to
prevent the dissolution, perhaps encouraged by the King, who did not
want to lose Carr, or perhaps by the Queen, who hated both Carr and
Frances. In 1613 Overbury was removed from the arena by his arrest
and committal to the Tower, on a nebulous charge devised by Frances,
who would brook no interference with her plans. Her marriage with
the Earl of Essex was annulled and she married Carr, who was
thereupon created the Duke of Somerset. At this point he arranged the
removal of William Waad from his appointment at the Tower,
asserting that though in some cases he had been too strict, in other
matters he was too lax. A friend of Somerset's was appointed in Waad's
place, and a few weeks later Thomas Overbury died in his cell in
mysterious circumstances which strongly suggested poison.

The scandal was so blatant that an enquiry had to be held. Ann
Turner, Frances's dressmaker and confidante, was arrested and
confessed that she had sent poisoned food to Overbury. She was
convicted of murder and hanged, after which both Frances and the
Duke of Somerset were arrested and committed to the Tower, for by
this time George Villiers had supplanted Somerset in the King's

affections and led the whispering campaign against him and Frances. At the trial at Westminster Hall, Frances confessed her guilt. Somerset denied all knowledge of the plot but was kept in the Tower with Frances for the next six years, and they ended up by hating each other.

After leaving the Tower William Waad retired altogether from public life and spent most of his remaining years at Belsize, until his death in 1623. His widow remarried, her second husband being Colonel Thomas Bushell, but with the outbreak of the Civil War Colonel Bushell fought for King Charles until the battle was lost and then went into hiding for a time. Belsize was occupied by one of Cromwell's men during the Commonwealth, but with the Restoration Bushell tried to return. However, the lease had nearly expired and by the time the litigation was ended, Belsize had been leased by Westminster to Colonel Daniel O'Neill and his third wife, the Countess of Chesterfield.

O'Neill had fought well during the Civil War and Charles II rewarded him handsomely, enabling him to build a new house at Belsize – a splendid Stuart mansion in place of the old Elizabethan house. It was a long, low house, built on two main floors, with dormer attic windows and short wings, and it was surmounted by a bell tower and weather cock. A balustrade ran from the front entrance, which was approached by a short flight of shallow steps, to the extremities of the wings.

O'Neill died in 1664. His widow stayed on, but survived him for only three years, leaving Belsize to her son by her second marriage, Lord Wotton.

On 17 August 1668, Samuel Pepys visited Belsize.

> Up, and by water to Whitehall, and so to St James's, and thence with Mr Wren by appointment in his coach to Hampstead, to speak with the Attorney-general, whom we met in the fields by his old route and house; and after a little talk about our business of Ackeworth, went and saw Lord Wotton's house and garden, which is wonderfull fine; too good for the house the gardens are, being, indeed, the most noble that ever I saw, and brave orange and lemon trees.

But when, eight years later, John Evelyn described his visit to Belsize, the gardens had apparently fallen into neglect.

> We returned in the evening by Hampstead to see Lord Wotton's house and garden – Belsize House – built with vast expense by Mr O'Neale, an Irish gentleman who married Lord Wotton's mother [he

recorded on 2 June 1676.] The furniture is very particular for Indian cabinets, porcelain and other solid and noble moveables. The gallery very fine, the gardens very large, but ill-kept, yet worthy and changeable. The soil a cold weeping clay yet not answering expense.

The Attorney-General whom Pepys had gone to visit was Sir Geoffrey Palmer, who also had a house in Hampstead at this time, an indication that the village was attracting more wealthy people from London as a place of residence.

It was in 1620, shortly before the death of William Waad, that the Manor of Hampstead changed hands, being bought from the Wroths by Sir Baptist Hicks, a wealthy City mercer who had already built himself a beautiful Jacobean mansion in Kensington, on land which he had acquired from Sir Walter Cope; and Sir Walter Cope at this time was ruining himself with the building of Cope Castle nearby, which was to become known as Holland House.

Sir Baptist, later to become Lord Campden, whose Kensington house was Campden House, had no snobbish attitude to shopkeeping and shocked the aldermen of the City of London by refusing to give up his business after James I had knighted him, in 1604. There is no record of his having ever lived in Hampstead, for his main seat was at Campden in Gloucestershire, but there was another interesting house in the village by this time, a small mansion which stood on the right-hand side of the road from London – now Rosslyn Hill. King James was as enthusiastic a hunter as Henry VIII had been, and this may have been his hunting lodge, or alternatively the country house of one of his courtiers, where the King sometimes stayed, for on two of the windows were painted portraits of King James and George Villiers, the Duke of Buckingham, and inscribed beneath them was the record that they had slept there on 25 August 1619.

The house, known as the Chicken House, survived into the nineteenth century, but long before this it seems to have been an inn of sorts, and then deteriorated into a disreputable thieves' kitchen.

Lord Campden died in 1629, leaving in his will an endowment for the little church at Hampstead, and the manor of Hampstead passed to his son-in-law Lord Noel, who became the second Lord Campden and died during the Civil War fighting for the King. His son Baptist, the third Lord Campden, raised his own troop of horse and a company of foot for King Charles, but was taken prisoner. He was released in 1646, but his estates and property were forfeited. With the Restoration, the tables were turned. The Royalists received back their possessions and retribution came to many of the Parliamentarians, including the brave Sir Harry Vane.

He was born in 1612, the son of the royalist Sir Henry Vane, of Raby Castle, Durham. He completed his education in Geneva and very early in his career became a radical and an advocate of freedom of conscience and religion, for he was a man of unassailable integrity, with a clear and logical mind. He believed that every man was entitled to his own beliefs and had the courage of his convictions.

The persecution of the Puritans during the reign of James I, as well as of the Roman Catholics, appalled him. In 1620 a little group of forty-one families of Puritans, calling themselves the Independents had sailed to American in their frail barque, the *Mayflower*, to establish a new home for themselves in Massachusetts. They suffered dire hardships in those early days, and by 1635 there were still less than four hundred of them. By this time King Charles was on the throne. He had a personal dislike of the Puritans and did nothing to help them. Harry Vane, already tending towards republicanism, joined the Pilgrim Fathers in Massachusetts and within a very short time they had elected him their governor. But Vane found their particular brand of Puritanism as intolerant and bigoted as any religious body in England, from which they had fled. He could not, in all conscience, call this religious freedom. After two years he was voted out of his governor-ship and returned to England.

He was elected member for Hull, was knighted and made one of the Treasurers of the Navy, which, after years of neglect, he helped to restore to its Elizabethan strength and efficiency. It was about this time that he chose Hampstead for his country home and built the beautiful Vane House, on Rosslyn Hill, just below the village, a large, three-storeyed Jacobean mansion set in large wooded grounds.

When the Civil War broke out, he declared for Parliament, and towards the end of the struggle Cromwell sent him to Edinburgh, to arrange terms whereby Scotland might join the Parliamentarians. Sir Harry handled the negotiations skilfully and the alliance with Scotland proved decisive in the defeat of the King. Yet he hated intolerance and refused to take any part in the trial of Charles.

During the early years of the Commonwealth, as Treasurer of the Navy, he refused the usual fees of office which went with such appointments, accepting only the nominal salary of £200. Gradually he grew sceptical of Cromwell's assumption of a military dictatorship, seeing it as yet another denial of true freedom, and shortly after the outbreak of the war with Holland, in 1652, their disagreements broke out into open quarrel. Cromwell settled the matter by dissolving Parliament and dismissing all the recalcitrant members. Angrily he raised the mace. 'What shall we do with this bauble?' he exclaimed. 'Take it away.'

It was the end of the Long Parliament. Sir Harry told him his action was against all right – all honour – and accused him of seizing supreme power illegally. When Cromwell later invited him to join his new Council of State, Sir Harry refused, and from henceforth Cromwell ruled England as Lord Protector.

Sir Harry retired to Raby Castle, where he wrote several pamphlets, the most forceful being *The Healing Question*, which was an attack on Cromwell for his tyrannical and illegal seizure of despotic power. He was summoned before the Council and when he refused to promise never again to criticise the Government, he was imprisoned at Carisbrooke for a time. However, Cromwell died in 1658 and Sir Harry was set free and returned to Hampstead. He took no part in Richard Cromwell's brief and inglorious Protectorate and by May 1660 King Charles II was back in England, restored to the throne.

Sir Harry remained at Vane House, but his name was included in the list of regicides to be brought to trial. Although Charles II had admired Andrew Marvell, he was afraid of Sir Harry Vane and his lucid thinking. 'He is too dangerous a man to let live,' he said, 'if we can safely put him out of the way.'

There is a story that at this stage Sir Harry took refuge with his daughter and son-in-law at Ken House, disguising himself as a labourer or servant, but this is so out of character, that the alternative description of his arrest as he was walking in his elm avenue at Vane House, watching a particularly beautiful sunset, seems far more likely.

His signature was not on the death warrant of Charles I and it was difficult to bring a precise charge against him, but Clarendon insisted on his imprisonment. He was taken first to the Tower and then to the Scilly Islands, where he was kept until June 1662. He was then brought to London for trial, the charge being that of 'compassing and imagining the death of the king, and conspiring to subvert the ancient frame of the kingly government of the realm', but he was not allowed a counsel to plead for him.

On 7 June 1662, Samuel Pepys recorded: 'Sir J. Robinson, Lieutenant of the Tower, said that yesterday Sir H. Vane had a full hearing at the King's Bench, and is found guilty; and that he did never hear any man argue more simply than he in all his life, and so others say'.

At his execution on Tower Hill, on 14 June, Pepys was one of the onlookers. There was 'a very great press of people,' he said. 'He made a long speech, many times interrupted by the sheriff and others, and they would take his paper out of his hand, but he would not let it go . . . the trumpets were brought under the scaffold that he might not be heard, at which he retorted: "It is a bad cause that cannot bear the words of a dying man".'

Many were shocked at the palpable injustice of Sir Harry's execution and those who witnessed it were loud in their praises of his gallant demeanour on the scaffold. 'At dinner at Lord Crewe's,' wrote Pepys, a few days later, 'the courage of Sir H. Vane at his death is talked on every where as a miracle.'

It was just about this time that the Fifth Monarchy men were scaring London, and a few people had the idea that Sir Harry had been in some way connected with the movement. Again Pepys had something to say on the matter. On 22 June 1662, a few days after the execution, he wrote:

> Coming home to-night, I met with Will Swan, who do talk as high for the Fanatiques as ever he did in his life; and do pity my Lord Sandwich and me that we should be given up to the wickedness of the world; and that a fall is coming upon us all; for he finds that he and his company are the true spirit of the nation, and the greater part of the nation too, who will have liberty of conscience in spite of this 'Act of Uniformity,' or they will die; and if they may not preach abroad, they will preach in their own houses. He told me that certainly Sir H. Vane must be gone to Heaven, for he died as much a martyr and saint as ever man did; and that the King hath lost more by that man's death, than he will get again a good while.

However, John Bill's account of the Fifth Monarchy men at Ken House, and his relief at their departure, makes any possible connection with Sir Harry highly improbable. The story was most likely spread by some scared and gullible villagers.

Hampstead was still essentially rural. The Hampstead woods reached as far as Kentish Town and down to Belsize and St John's Wood, but more people of wealth and standing were building houses up on the hill.

Close to Vane House was the house of Sir Isaac Wake, a courtier of Charles I. 'He had a fine seat at Hampstead in Middlesex, which lookes over London and Surrey, where he made those delicate walkes of pines and firres, also corme-trees etc.' wrote Aubrey in his *Brief Lives*. 'The Lord Chiefe Baron Wyld had it afterwards. His study was mighty pleasant.' And here Baron Wylde died in 1669.

As early as 1639 there is a mention of Pond Street in the parish register, a lane named after the pond which once lay on the Heath at its eastern end. In the following years one or two large mansions were built here and Pond Street remained a wealthy quarter for many years to come.

In 1646, out of a total of 1,289 acres held by the various owners of Hampstead land, the Lord of the Manor owned 356 acres, on which were seventeen tenants, the largest being John Maye, who paid a rental of £128.5s for 116 acres. John Withington paid £48 for 40 acres, William Crewes £38.15s for 34 acres and Humphrey Sumpster £36 for 29 acres. Sir William Robarts was another important landlord, with six tenants, the chief of whom was Widow Page, who had a house and 70 acres of land. Sir Thomas Alleyn, an absentee landlord, owned 177 acres, from which he drew £253.10s from his various tenants. John Hollgate, son-in-law of Lady Anne Waad, possessed 251 acres, which included 110 acres of wood and nine houses.

In this year there were 146 separate dwellings in the village, 68 of which were sizable houses, including, of course, the mansions of Belsize and Vane House, and 78 cottages, which shows that there was already an unusually high proportion of wealthy and comparatively wealthy inhabitants for a district where the main business was agriculture.

By 1649, the total holding of land was estimated at 1,408 acres, the extra 114 acres having presumably been filched from the Heath.

The tenants of these estates were farmers, engaged increasingly in specialised farming for London. Rents were high, compared with the national average for agricultural land, and they were tending to concentrate on dairying and stock-keeping, hay-farming for the London stables and cow houses, and the provision of pasturage for the cattle-drovers coming to London from the midlands. As arable land gave place to pasture, the plough gradually disappeared in Hampstead. There was little market gardening, for the ground was too hilly and the soil less suitable than the riverside stretches of Chelsea and Fulham and the fields of Kensington, where many acres of market gardens were established at this time, to supply Covent Garden and the London market.

The process of building houses and cottages beyond the original parish boundaries, on land enclosed from the Heath, increased towards the end of the seventeenth century. When anyone applied to the Lord of the Manor for ground for building a house, he would hesitate to part with agricultural land, which was yielding him a good income, but there was nothing to prevent him enclosing a few acres from the Heath. As Lord of the Manor he still had the right, with the consent of the holders of the ancient copyholds of the manor, to 'approve' or enclose pieces of the Heath and grant them to an applicant, who thereupon, after the payment of a small fee to the lord and his steward, became a copyhold tenant. This meant that the land was virtually his, to sell or bequeath to an heir, for copyhold land was land which a tenant held without any deed or transfer, in his own possession. It was a medieval form of land tenure in which a villein took an oath of fealty to his lord, in return for which he was granted his dwelling and land and allowed to bequeath them to his children, thus establishing the 'tenure of copyhold'.

The only legal limit to these piecemeal enclosures was that what remained of the Heath should be enough to meet the established rights of the copyholders to their pasture and turf, and as the enclosures were small and gradual, they appeared to have no effect on the Heath as a whole. Nevertheless, by the end of the seventeenth century the number of copyholders had risen to 146 and a 100 years later there were 300, while more than 100 acres of the Heath had been lost from the 540 acres it had once covered. Yet at the time, no one complained.

New building took place, therefore, not on the valuable agricultural land of the Lords of the Manor, but to the east, where the Heath reached close to the village, and particularly on the steep hill to the north and north-west, in many respects the most unlikely and awkward place on which to build, although it is the very steepness of the winding lanes and unexpected twists and turns which have given this part of Hampstead its unique charm. At the time the land was granted, the Lords of the Manor were able to keep their estates and the incomes from them intact, and in addition received fees from the new copyholders. They yielded nothing and made a clear profit.

One of these houses of the late seventeenth century, which has been beautifully preserved, is Fenton House built in 1693, perched crazily on the side of Hampstead Grove, which runs parallel to Heath Street and just to the west.

No one knows who built it nor for whom it was originally intended, but the date 1693 is scratched on one of the chimneys and also appears on a lead pump head in the garden. It is a typical William and Mary house, of brown brick, and is larger than it might appear at a first glance, for although it has only two storeys, in addition to a basement and attic floor, it is square in plan. The main entrance was originally to the south, giving on to Holly Hill, and approached by a pair of magnificent wrought iron gates set in the high brick wall enclosing the garden, but today, now that the house is a museum, it is entered by a doorway on the east front, looking on to Hampstead Grove.

The rooms are beautifully proportioned and for the most part panelled, while several have small, intriguing alcoves, large enough to have been used, perhaps, as powder closets.

Like nearly everything else in Old Hampstead, the garden is on a slope. It dips to the west, so that the gravel walk along the high wall separating it from Hampstead Grove is above the herbaceous border lining the upper lawn, and the lower lawn is reached by a flight of steps. The northern wall of the garden forms the south side of Admiral's Walk, and running down the hill along the west garden wall is still a narrow, rough track, shady and overgrown, which cannot have changed in the last two or three hundred years. Down towards the bottom, where the track runs into Windmill Hill, is a little gardener's gate, set in the wall, through which, one cannot help feeling, many a young thing must have slipped to a romantic tryst in the surrounding woods.

This was probably the home of a rich merchant, built at a time when the rising wealth of the upper middle classes of England enabled them to live in a style of dignified luxury which no other people in Europe could match. Such houses as these were filled with silver and porcelain, books, tapestries, pictures and beautiful furniture, and the high brick wall which invariably surrounded them was a protection against thieves and marauders.

Fenton House was first known as Ostend House, and in 1707 the owner, a man named Twysden, sold it to Joshua Gee. It remained in the Gee family for many years and then passed through several owners. By 1786 it was known as the Clock House, because of a clock built over the entrance, and in 1793 it was bought by Philip Fenton, a Riga merchant who had founded his fortune on the Baltic trade in tallow, oil and hemp, and he renamed it Fenton House.

It was while Fenton House was being built, at the end of the seventeenth century, that the curative properties of the chalybeate waters of Hampstead became widely known and the little village, with its scattered mansions, suddenly became a fashionable spa.

The legend of the healing waters must have persisted since medieval times amongst the villagers, but the earliest evidence of any attempt at commercialisation is a halfpenny token, made during the reign of Charles II, which was discovered many years ago. On one side it bears the inscription: *Dorothy Rippon at the Well in Hamsted,* and on the other is the representation of a well and bucket. So Dorothy Rippon must have been selling buckets of healing water, at a halfpenny a time, at a date before 1685.

Spas were becoming all the rage, and throughout the country there were many springs which were believed to have these healing properties. Some became famous and accommodation for visitors developed round them, while others remained of purely local interest. Tunbridge Wells was favoured by both Queen Henrietta, wife of Charles I, and Charles II's Queen, Catherine of Braganza, and thereupon became fashionable. The waters of Harrogate, Buxton, Astrop Wells in Northamptonshire, Barnet and Epsom were all visited for a time, those at Epsom being particularly popular, because of the added attraction of the race course, while the reputation of Bath, for such disorders as lameness and the palsy, was increasing steadily.

As early as 1634, when a young soldier from Norwich visited Bath, he found people of all descriptions and both sexes in the Cross Bath and said that 'their uncouth, naked postures' astonished him and made him think of the Resurrection. When Pepys visited it in 1668 he said it was 'only almost for the gentry' while the 'King and Queen's full of a mixed sort, of good and bad'. He sampled the Cross Bath and remarked that there were 'very fine ladies; and the manner pretty enough, only methinks it cannot be clean to go so many bodies together in the same water'.

By the time Celia Fiennes visited Bath, at the end of the seventeenth century, the baths were conducted with great discretion.

You generally sit up to the Neck in water – the gentlemen on seats in the middle the ladies round the side, [she recorded.] There is a serjeant belonging to ye baths that all the bathing tyme walked in gallerys and takes notice order is observed and punishes ye rude. . . . The Ladyes goes into the bath with Garments made of a fine yellow canvas, which is stuff and made large with great sleeves like a parsons gowne; the water fills it up so that its borne off that your shape is not seen, it does not cling. . . . The Gentlemen have drawers and wastecoates of the same sort of canvas. . . . As a lady leaves the bath a door shuts behind her while she is still partly in the water. In privacy you ascend more steps and let your Canvass drop off by degrees into the water . . . the women guides take it off and your maid flings a garment of flannell made like a Nightgown with great sleeves over your head.

The patient was then handed into a sedan chair and carried to her lodgings, where there was a large fire burning in her room to keep her warm. The chairmen 'sets you at your bedside where you go to bed, and lye and sweate some tyme you please'.

Celia also visited the spring at Barnet, where there were apparently no baths but merely arrangements for drinking the waters. They were dirty, she said, and the well was

> full of leaves and dirt, and every time they dip it troubles the water, not but what they take up and let stand looks clear but I could not taste it; its being very deep and not done at the bottom with a bason as Tunbridg, so that it appears not to be a quick spring as Tunbridg or the Spaw or Hamsted waters, which have all fine stone basons in which you see the springs bubble up as fast, and by a pipe runs off as clear and fast; it more resembles Epsom for which reason I dislike that. . . .

The Campden family had received back their estates, including the Hampstead lands, at the Restoration. The third Lord Campden died in 1682 and the manor of Hampstead passed to his son Edward Noel, who was created Lord Noel and later the Earl of Gainsborough. He died in 1689, and his son, the second Earl, the following year. The next heir was a cousin, who at this time was only a child.

In 1689 his mother and guardian, the Honourable Susanna Noel, widow of Baptist Noel, the third Lord Campden's second son, granted, in the name of the young third Earl of Gainsborough, 'six acres of waste land lying and being about certain medicinal waters called the Wells, for the sole use, benefit and advantage of the poor of the parish of Hampstead successively for ever'.

The land was on the east side of the village, reaching almost up to the High Street, and the spring ran from the hillside of the Heath into a small, natural pool, rusty looking from the iron in the water. Fourteen trustees were appointed to administer this Wells charity and develop the commercial possibilities of the waters.

From this time a great change came over Hampstead. From a rural village, it became, for a few years, a popular spa. Building proceeded apace and the population increased steadily.

IV

Hampstead Spa and Belsize

The first indication of the commercial development of the Hampstead waters was an announcement in *The Postman* on 18 April 1700.

> The Chalybeate Waters at Hampstead, being of the same nature, and equal in virtue with Tunbridge Wells, and highly approved of by most of the eminent physicians of the college, as likewise by many of the gentry, who formerly used to drink Tunbridge waters, are, by direction of the Trustees of the Wells aforesaid, for the conveniency of those who yearly drink them in London, carefully bottled up in flasks, and sent to Mr Phelps, Apothecary, at the Eagle and Child in Fleet street, every morning, at the rate of 3d per flask; and if any person desires to have them brought to their own houses, they will be conveyed to them upon their leaving a note at Mr Phelps's aforesaid at 1d per flask more. And to prevent any person being imposed upon, the true waters are nowhere else to be procured, unless they are sent for to the Wells at Hampstead. And the said Mr Phelps, to prevent Counterfeits, hath ordered his servants to deliver to each person who comes for any of the waters aforesaid, a sealed ticket, viz., a wolf rampant, with seven cross crosslets. Note. – The messengers that come for the waters must take care to return the flasks daily.

Phelps appears to have had the monopoly of selling the waters for a time, but the supplies were controlled by the Trustees and they were soon making arrangements for another spring to be brought into use, for in September 1700 there was an order in the Court Rolls of Hampstead that, 'the Spring by the purging Well be forthwith brought into the town of Hampstead, at the parish charge, and yt ye money and profit arising thereout be applied to the easing of the poors' rates hereafter to be made'.

There had been trouble with Widow Keys, one of the villagers who had been employed by the Trustees, to procure the water for bottling. Had she been helping herself and selling them on the side? No one will ever know, but she certainly brought down the wrath of the Trustees on her head, for they published a notice in *The Postman* that

> By order of the Trustees of Hampstead Mineral Waters. These are to certify, that the Widow Keys is discharged from the Wells, and carries to London no more of the said waters; the Trustees now only employing Mr Adams, a potter at Holborn Bars, to deliver out the said Mineral Waters. If any other person pretends to bring Hampstead waters, they are desired to try them, that so they be not cheated.

In the meantime the Trustees had made the waters available at several other London taverns and announcements stated that

> Hampstead Mineral water, for several distempers, is brought fresh from Hampstead Wells every day to Mr Adams, glass-seller, near Holborn Bars; to Mr Cresset's at the Sugar-loaf at Charing Cross; to Nando's coffee-house near Temple Bar; to Sam's coffee house near Ludgate; to the Salmon in Stock's market; and by Mr Pratt to the Greyhound in King Street, by Bloomsbury; to Howe's coffee house in Cheapside by the Half-moon tavern; and to the Black Post in King Street near Guildhall, and no where else in London.

At the Hampstead end of the business, the water was collected and brought to the old Flask Tavern, on the site of which the Victorian Flask now stands, and here it was bottled and taken by carrier's cart to London for distribution.

The waters had a good sale for a time and the Trustees decided on a more ambitious plan for promoting them. In *The Postman* advertisement which announced the downfall of Widow Keys they added a note that the trustees were prepared to 'let the said waters, with six acres of land, by lease or yearly rent,' and 'such as desire to treat about the same, may meet the Trustees at Craddock's coffee-house in Hampstead, every Saturday, from 10 to 12 in the morning, until the 29 September next'.

They soon found a speculator, John Duffield, who declared himself ready to embark on an ambitious programme of development. From 2 June 1701 he took a lease of the land and spring for twenty-one years at £50 a year, but this did not include the hillside spring, from which the flask water was obtained, the flask trade being kept as a separate venture, still in the hands of the Trustees. Moreover, in order to preserve the rights of the villagers, they were to be allowed to take away as much of the purging waters from the springs on his six acres as they liked, between the hours of five in the morning and midday, except for Widow Keys and her former assistant Michael Lydall, who were forbidden to go near Duffield's premises without his permission.

The widow had many sympathisers, for the people of Hampstead argued that the waters were theirs, to do with as they liked, and they were suspicious of what was happening, as the new buildings went up.

The large Assembly Room, ninety feet long and thirty-six feet wide, and more often called the Great Room, was built on the south side of the lane which came to be known as Well Walk, on the site of the present Gainsborough Gardens. It was planned to cater both for the genuine invalids seeking benefit from the waters and also for those who came to enjoy the diversions which were to be found at every eighteenth-century spa. Most of the space was therefore devoted to a concert and ball room, with smaller rooms for cards, but at the north end was the pump room, with a large basin filled from the chalybeate spring, for those who were taking the cure. It stood in large grounds, laid out with flower beds and lawns. There was a lake, with a small island, and at the back a bowling green, without which no establishment of this kind would have been considered complete.

By 1701 the venture was well under way and flourishing, for Dr Gibbons, who lived in Hampstead and attended many of the new seekers after health, did a great deal of valuable promotion work, declaring that the waters 'were full as efficacious in all cases where ferruginous waters are advised as any chalybeate waters in England, unless Scarborough Spa, which is purgative'.

Wealthy and fashionable people from London came to sample this new panacea for their ills, and some undoubtedly benefited, not from the waters, whose curative properties were later found to be negligible, but from the fresh, invigorating air of the Heath and the village. A certain amount of accommodation was available for those who came to stay for a spell. There were lodgings to be had at the Flask, which was known at this time as the Lower Flask, to distinguish it from the Upper Flask, built high up on the hill at the top of Heath Street, as well as at Jack Straw's Castle, the Bull and Bush and the Green Man, but these were not enough. Little cottages were hastily put up along the east side of the Heath and in Squire's Mount, while houses in secluded, tree-lined Pond Street were built for the wealthiest of the visitors.

Squire's Mount has survived almost intact, a row of charming white-washed cottages each with a tiny patch of garden in front, protected by white-painted wooden railings. Squire's Mount Croft, in the middle of the row, and a little larger than the others, bears the date 1704, and they must all have been built about the same time.

Larger houses were also built in Hampstead during these busy years of the early eighteenth century, as, for example, Numbers 92 and 94 Heath Street, which date from about 1700, when terraced houses like this were first being planned. The sashed windows with their delicate glazing bars are characteristic of the period, being relatively short on the ground floor, very tall on the first floor, which held the principal reception rooms, shorter on the floor above and square on the top floor.

Flask Walk was developed. It began as a narrow lane, leading from the High Street under an archway, over which extended part of a High Street building. It reached down to the Lower Flask and then opened out into a tree-lined avenue, ending in a small green. From the eastern end of the green Well Walk was laid out, leading to the Great Room and beyond to the Heath itself, and planted with a hundred lime trees to form a shady promenade for the fashionable visitors. It is true that the friends of Widow Keys, still smarting at the way she had been treated and still suspicious that strangers were profiting from the waters which were theirs by right, tore them all up again one night, but they were replanted and building continued. More houses went up and the development was known as New End. Some of them were small, weather-boarded cottages and lodging houses which did not have a very long life, but the terraced houses of New End were probably built as early as this and the handsome Burgh House, facing Well Walk, dates from 1703, when it was probably the home of Dr Gibbons.

As the villagers and tradesmen of Hampstead began to appreciate the new business that was coming to them, their resentment disappeared and they were quick to take advantage of all that was going. Lodging house keepers prospered. Tea shops, bun houses and souvenir shops opened, of the kind that were to be found in every spa and watering place at this time. The Whitestone tea-gardens, later to become the Green Man, were established where the present Wells Tavern stands, close to the Great Room.

From the outset, there was as much emphasis on the delights of the Great Room entertainments as on the health-giving properties of the waters, for Duffield had very little capital and needed to make as much money as he could, as quickly as possible.

He organised concerts in the Great Room which were advertised in *The Postman* and the *English Post.* In August 1701, *The Postman* announced:

At Hampstead Wells, on Monday next, being the 18th of this instant August, will be performed a Consort of both vocal and instrumental musick, with some particular performance of both kinds, by the best masters, to begin at 10 o'clock precisely. Tickets will be delivered at the said Wells for 1s per ticket; and Dancing in the afternoon for 6d per ticket, to be delivered as before.

A week later, on 25 August *The Postman* was advertising a more exclusive entertainment, beginning at 'four of the clock precisely', with tickets at 5 shillings each, 'to be had only at the Wells at Hamstead.' This had been arranged 'at the request of several people of Quality living at Hampstead', the star being Mr Abell, the 'celebrated lutenist and alto singer, formerly of his Majesty's Chapel extraordinary', who had been discharged for being a Papist and had had to live and work abroad for several years, but had retained his immense popularity.

The following month *The Postman* advertised:

In the Great Room at Hampstead Wells, on Monday next, being the 15th instant, exactly at 11 o'clock forenoon, will be performed a Consort of vocal and instrumental musick, by the best masters; and at the request of several gentlemen, Jemmy Bowen will perform several songs, and particular performances on the violin by 2 several masters. Tickets to be had at the Wells, and at Stephen's Coffee-house in King-street, Bloomsbury, at 1s each ticket. There will be Dancing in the afternoon, as usual.

By about late September or early October the entertainments at the Great Room ended for the season, beginning again about May, and at the opening of the 1702 season the *English Post* was announcing a concert to be given in the 'Great Room at Hampstead Wells on Monday the 11th May, with violin by Mr Dean, at 11 o'k rain or fair, and evening performances beginning at five o'clock, for the convenience of gentlemen returning to London'. The management also advertised that they provided a special armed guard, with torches and links, to accompany visitors on the four mile journey to the city, through the dark and dangerous country roads, where thieves and highwaymen lurked, ready to pounce on the unwary.

On 27 July 1702 there was a special 5 o'clock concert, with tickets at half-a-crown, which included 'Instrumental Musick composed by John Eccles for the Coronation of Queen Anne and "several of Mr Weldon's songs, sung by Mr Hughes and the Boy".'

The 1703 season, which opened on 18 May, announced 'Musick and Dancing all day long and so on every Monday all the season,' the opening concert being given for the benefit of Mr Hughs, 'who was to sing the song sung before Her Majesty'; and in addition, there were 'entertainments by Mr Dean and Signore Francesco, three new songs by Mr Hughs, Songs for the Trumpets, Sonata for two Trumpets, and an Extraordinary Entertainment on the Arch-lute'.

During the mid-seventeenth century the first London clubs came into existence, their headquarters established at first in the taverns or newly-established coffee houses. Aubrey defined a club as a 'sodality in a tavern'. Some were social, others political, and one of the most celebrated was the Kit-Kat, the Whig club founded in 1700. Its origins are obscure but it may well have begun as a weekly dinner party given by Jacob Tonson, the distinguished publisher, to his equally distinguished authors, who included Addison and Pope. At its foundation there were thirty-nine members of the Kit-Kat, all of them men of letters and the arts, wits, noblemen or gentlemen of substance, united by a common concern to secure the Protestant Hanoverian succession and put an end to the last hopes of the Stuarts.

From the beginning, Jacob Tonson was the secretary and they met at the Cat and Fiddle in Shoe Lane, the shop of a pastry cook named Christopher Kat. How the club acquired its name has never been settled but Christopher Kat made a particularly good mutton pie, which he dubbed a Kit-Kat, and this seems as good an explanation as any.

Among the members were six Dukes, including Marlborough, Lord Halifax, Sir Robert Walpole, the Earl of Dorset, Congreve, Sir Samuel Garth, the poet physician, Vanburgh, Addison and Steele as well as Godfrey Kneller, who painted for Tonson the portraits of all the members, a collection which Tonson cherished and which has now found its way to the National Portrait Gallery.

Throughout the winter the Club met once a week at Shoe Lane but during the summer months they moved to the Upper Flask on Hampstead Heath. They were a brilliantly gifted group and sat long hours under the famous mulberry tree in the Upper Flask garden, talking, drinking, arguing, debating and drinking again. They ate well and they drank deeply. A Tory lampooner declared that they taught the youth of Queen Anne's day to 'sleep away the day and drink away the night', but they were constructive and their influence was invaluable and far reaching.

Horace Walpole described them as 'the patriots who saved Britain'; and from a minor, more immediately practical point of view, there is little doubt that their presence in Hampstead helped to keep the place fashionable for a few years.

Samuel Garth had no great opinion of the waters, nor of Dr Gibbons' enthusiasm for them, but the doctor was well pleased with business and said that the Wells were frequented by 'as much and as good company as go yearly to Tunbridge Wells in Kent'.

At first the cure consisted only of drinking the waters, but Duffield soon established a bath where sufferers from gout and rheumatic complaints could be totally immersed. In 1705 it was announced that a cold bath had been built in connection with 'one of the best springs on the Heath, lying between the Old Green and New Green, adjoyning to the Spaw-Waters', with 'all convenience for hot and cold bathing', but we hear very little more about it. It obviously never achieved the degree of organisation described by Celia Fiennes at Bath, where the water was so buoyant that two guides had to hold on to you – 'otherwise it will quickly tumble you down', and you were 'pumpt at for lameness and over the head for palsies', wearing for the latter disorder 'a wide brimmed hat without a crown', though one would have thought a crown would have been even more useful than a brim.

Three years later the bath at Hampstead was destroyed by the great frost of 1708. In 1710 Duffield announced that it had been restored and by 1712 it was reported to be 'in better order than usual', which rather implies that it had been in pretty poor shape all along and never used a great deal, for that is the last that was heard of it.

1712 was the year that Steele became, of necessity, a resident of Hampstead for a few months to escape arrest for debt, for with all his brilliance he had no money sense and was too much given to unfailingly optimistic speculation on the most luckless projects. He took a small cottage standing alone among the fields of Haverstock Hill, where Charles Sedley, the playwright and father of James II's mistress Catherine Sedley, had lived during his last, soberer years, repenting the profligacy of his early life during the first years of the Restoration. Steele, writing to Pope on 1 June 1712, said: 'I am at a solitude, an house between Hampstead and London, wherein Charles Sedley died.'

He was engaged with Addison on the production of the *Spectator* at this time, for it ran from March 1711 until December 1712, and

Addison was not his only visitor, for the Kit-Kat members used to call on him and 'take him in their coach to their place of rendezvous'.

Arrests for debt could be made only between dawn and sunset and never on Sundays, so Steele would sometimes slip back to spend the night with his dear Prue, at her lodgings in Bury Street, leaving after nightfall and returning by daybreak. He was a devoted husband and never left her for long. 'Dear Prue,' he wrote one night from Hampstead, 'I am sleepy and tired, but could not think of closing my eyes till I had told you I am, dearest creature, your most affectionate faithful husband, R. Steele.'

The separation did not last for long and within a few months he was able to pay off his debts and return to London, establishing Prue and himself in a new house in Bloomsbury Square.

Nearly everyone played cards during the eighteenth century, often for far higher stakes than they could afford, and gambling and betting of all kinds were the downfall of many a wealthy young man, playing for recklessly high stakes. Soon the card rooms at the Wells were crowded and raffling or betting shops were opened close by. Following in the wake of the betting shops came the sharpers, for Hampstead was very close to London, and those who did not choose to hire a coach or travel by one of the three coaches which by now ran daily from London to Hampstead, found it no great distance to ride or even walk.

The company did not improve but for a few years more it maintained a certain degree of fashion. There were concerts, music and dancing all day but the concerts began to change in character. During the 1706 season there were 'several entertainments of dancing, especially the ladder dance by Mr Robinson'. At another, Scaramouch and other dancing by Mr Layfield was featured and an 'entertainment of Tumbling'. It began to smack of the sort of entertainment offered during the two weeks of junketing at the May Fair in Shepherd Market, where Mr Barnes, the rope-dancer, and the ladder-dancer at Miller's booth had been delighting Londoners for the last ten years. And these were the kind of Londoners who were now visiting Hampstead – no longer the cream of society, but cheerful, noisy day trippers, some innocent enough, others far from it, all of them out for what fun or mischief they could find.

In Baker's comedy *Hampstead Heath*, which was played at Drury Lane as early as 1705, one of the characters remarks shrewdly:

Assemblies so near Town give us a Sample of each Degree. We have Court Ladies, that are all Air and no Dress; City Ladies, that are over-dress'd and no Air; and Country Dames, with broad brown Faces like a Stephney bun; besides an endless number of Fleetstreet Sempstresses, that dance Minuets in their Furbeloe scarfs, and their Cloaths hang as loose about 'em as their Reputations.

Duffield presided over all and established himself in splendid style, in a mansion which he built for himself close by, in 1706, at a cost of £1,000. It stood somewhere between the Vale of Health and the Wells tavern and may, perhaps, have been Foley House, in part of the garden of which the present Numbers 21 to 27 Well Walk now stand.

By 1709 John Macky, in his *Journey Through England* was writing of Hampstead that 'its nearness to London brings so many loose women in vampt-up clothes to catch the City apprentices, that modest company are ashamed to appear here . . . it seems to me to be overstok'd with Jews and sharpers'.

In that same year, in the August number of the *Tatler*, came a sharp reprimand over the goings-on at Hampstead. It ran:

I am diverted from my train of discourse of the fraternity about this town by letters from Hampstead, which give me an account there is a late institution there, under the name of a raffling-shop, which is, it seems, secretly supplied by a person who is a deep practitioner in the law, and, out of tenderness to conscience, has under the name of his maid Sisly, set up this easier way of conveyancing and alienating estates from one family to another. He is so far from having an intelligence with the rest of the fraternity that all the humbler cheats who appear there are faced by the partners in the bank, and driven off by the reflection of superior brass. This notice is given to all the silly faces that pass that way, that they may not be decoyed in by the soft allurement of a fine lady, who is the sign to the pageantry; and at the same time Signior Hawkesley, who is the patron of the household, is desired to leave off this interloping trade, or admit, as he ought to do, the knights of the industry to their share in the spoil.

With the Hanoverian succession of George I in 1714, the Kit-Kats no longer met regularly at Hampstead but dined at Mr Tonson's villa at Barn Elms, and by the late 1720's when many of the leading spirits were dead, the club faded out, for in 1727 Vanbrugh was writing to Tonson that 'both Lord Carlisle and Cobham expressed a desire of having one meeting next winter, not as a club, but as old friends that have been of a club – and the best club that ever met'.

At the Wells the days of high fashion were over. The last straw, perhaps, was the establishment of the Hampstead fair, announced by the *Spectator* in 1712, 'to be kept upon the Lower Flask Tavern, and holds for four days'.

Duffield carried on, hard pressed for money now and making a sub-lease to his backer, Luffingham, who in his turn was raising mortgages and arranging sub-leases in order to keep going. The raffling-shops flourished. Mother Huff, under cover of a respectable tea-garden near the Spaniards, ran a house of assignation and told fortunes, as well as being suspected of witchcraft. The gamblers were still cheated by the sharpers. The Lower Flask tavern became a place where, according to Samuel Richardson, 'second-rate persons' were usually to be found in a 'swinish condition'.

In 1718 the Chairman of the Quarter Sessions, sitting at Westminster Hall, described a recent scandal at Hampstead.

> We sent to inquire lately about the Gaming Room at Hampstead, [he said] and we had an account beought us, That just before our Messenger came, there was a Young Gentleman lost Sixty Guineas to a Sharper of this Town; who went off as soon as he had got his prey: It seems it was the Young Gentleman's All; which put him upon such a Frenzy, that he threw his Hat one Way, his Peruque another; said, He was ruin'd and undone in Body Soul and Estate by Gaming; and having *one* Guinea left, threw that away also, and fell into a Fit of Cursing and Swearing, and Blaspheming the Name of God; Which, I do believe, are the common Effects of losing Gamesters.

The Spa was in fact too close to London to remain exclusive for long. The expense alone of a journey to Bath or Tunbridge Wells meant that the London visitors were relatively wealthy, while Hampstead, being within walking distance or only a short coach ride, quickly attracted day trippers, who in an intensely class-conscious age lowered the tone; and with them came the sharpers and twisters, not to mention the pick-pockets like Jenny Diver, who was eventually hanged at Tyburn.

The affairs of Hampstead and the dwindling fortunes of Duffield were not helped by what was happening at Belsize, down the hill. When Lord Wotton had died, in 1682, the estate and sub-manor of Belsize had passed to his half brother, Philip Stanhope, the second Earl of Chesterfield, who seems to have lived there for a few years and then moved to a smaller house on the estate.

Swift, in a letter to Stella dated 7 September 1710, wrote that his old schoolfellow 'Straford, the Hombourg merchant' had induced him to go to dinner with him at Hampstead, 'among a great deal of ill company, Hoadly being one of them,' but adds that 'I was glad to be at Hampstead, where I saw Lady Lucy and Moll Stanhope', and a week or two later he was reporting that 'he had dined at Hampstead with Lady Lucy'.

The second Earl died in 1713, but although the Belsize estate remained in the Chesterfield family for nearly a century longer, after this reference by Swift there is no record of any member of the family living in Hampstead or even visiting it. By 1726 it had come into the possession of the fourth Earl, who obtained renewals of the lease in 1733 and again in 1751, from the Dean and Chapter of Westminster. He was far too much occupied with his life in Mayfair, the writing of his letters to his son, and the building of his magnificent Chesterfield House, looking on to the future Park Lane, to concern himself with Belsize. The mansion was sub-let, the first tenant being a strange character called Charles Povey, a retired coal-merchant, who moved into Belsize House around 1700 and was soon overwhelmed with the grandeur of his new surroundings. He was a man with a chip on his shoulder and much given to writing pamphlets exposing the evil practices of government agencies, a habit which endeared him to no one. He hated paying taxes and wrote a pamphlet entitled *England's Inquisition; or Money raised by New, Secret, Extinct Law, without Act of Parliament* in which he complained bitterly of unjust extortions on his property and estate by the Commissioners of Excise. At the time of his move to Belsize he was busy with another pamphlet, claiming to be *A discovery of indirect practices in the Coal Trade.* 'The books and pamphlets I have writ exceed 600 in number', he once said.

It was during the early years of the eighteenth century, when the Spa at Hampstead was still high fashion and Povey was settling in at Belsize that we first hear of the Sion Chapel. There is a good deal of uncertainty as to where this chapel was. It has been suggested that it was attached to the tavern and tea gardens in Well Walk, but this may have come about through confusion with the episcopal chapel which was later formed from the old Pump Room.

It seems more likely that it was a venture of Povey's and that he was using the chapel at Belsize House, but no records have survived. The first indication of its existence is an advertisement in *The Postboy* of 18 April 1710.

As there are many weddings at Sion Chapel, Hampstead, five shillings only is required for all the church fees of any couple that are married there, provided they bring with them a licence or certificate according to the Act of Parliament. Two sermons are continued to be preached in the said chapel every Sunday; and the place will be given to any clergyman that is willing to accept of it, if he is approved of.

This advertisement contradicts itself, for if two sermons were already being preached each Sunday, why advertise for a clergyman, and as Belsize was in the heart of the country, who was to form the congregation?

Wherever it was, Sion Chapel was a place for illegal 'Fleet' marriages, performed without banns or licence, and the request that the couple bring a licence with them was an acknowledgment of what should be done rather than what, in fact, was the practice.

Fleet marriages had first been solemnised by underpaid parsons, imprisoned in the Fleet for debt and desperate to make a little money. Women debtors were exonerated from their debts and free to leave prison if they could find a fellow prisoner to marry them, for the debt was automatically assigned to the new husband – a kind of back-handed aspect of women's lib; and if she honoured her obligation she then set about raising enough money, by fair means or foul, to free her husband as well.

There were dozens of reasons, besides this strictly practical one, for people wanting to be married in a hurry, and soon the Fleet parsons established offices for these marriages of convenience in the taverns surrounding Fleet Street. Pennant, describing conditions in the early years of the eighteenth century, said that

> walking along the streets in my youth, on the side next this prison (the Fleet), I have often been tempted by the question: 'Sir, will you be pleased to walk in and be married?' and signs were hung up with two hands joined, and 'Marriages performed within' written below. The parson walked about outside, a squalid, profligate figure, clad in a battered, plaid night gown, with a fiery face – ready to couple you for a dram of gin or a roll of tobacco.

Alexander Keith, who had served his apprenticeship in this trade in the environs of the Fleet, opened his business in illegal marriages at the Mayfair Chapel in Curzon Street in 1730, and prospered for the next twelve years. It was not until 1742, during which year alone he had performed seven hundred marriages, that the rector of St George's, Hanover Square, started a suit against him in Doctors Commons and he was committed to prison, but the trade went on for many more years and generally speaking the Church turned a blind eye.

In 1745 the *Gentleman's Magazine* carried out their own enquiry and described, 'a set of drunken, sweating parsons with myrmidons that wore black cloaks and pretended to be clerks and registrars to the Fleet: playing about Ludgate Hill, pulling and forcing people to some peddling ale-house or brandy shop to be married, and even on Sunday stopping them as they go to Church'.

Even allowing for the verbal excesses of righteous indignation, there was truth in this, and there is no doubt that many a young thing was induced into marriage and deserted after a night or two, only to find that her marriage lines were worthless.

The Postboy for 13 October 1713 announced that Mr Povey at Sion Chapel near Hampstead had 'drawn up a reply to his enemies, who circulated scandalous reports against him, copies of which were to be had at Mr Povey's house at Hampstead, or Mr Bowden's, a Toy Shop, the second house in Chancery Lane, near Fleet Street'.

The following year, 1714, Povey was in trouble with the Chesterfield agents, who complained that he had been committing waste on the estate.

Committing damages and waste upon an Estate, which I have retrieved from utter ruin? [he wrote indignantly] The Mansion House and the outhouses were little more than a Heap of Rubbish; the land was overrun with Briers and Weeds; the Walls tottering and' ready to fall down; but now it is manifest to every eye, that all things are in good repair and order. One complaint against me to his Lordship is, that I have taken away the Leaden Pipes, a pretty Story indeed; Have I wronged his Lordship in exchanging old Lead for new, and adding three times the weight of new Lead to it over and above, which is to be seen on the Flats, and in the new Gutters I have laid? . . . Several Judges as well as Bishops who have done me the Honour of a visit, told me no Nobelman's Estate was ever more beautify'd by a Tenant than my Lord of Chesterfield at Belsize at this time, and other Improvements will likewise be made against next summer.

What these improvements were are not certain but in *Reed's Weekly Journal* for 8 September 1716 appeared yet another notice of Sion Chapel.

Sion Chapel, at Hampstead, being a private and pleasure place, many persons of the best fashion have lately been married there. Now, as a minister is obliged constantly to attend, this is to give notice that all persons upon bringing a licence, and who shall have their wedding dinner in the gardens, may be married in that said Chapel without giving any fee or reward whatsoever; and such as do not keep their wedding dinner at the gardens, only five shillings will be demanded of them for all fees.

This may have been an attempt on Povey's part to achieve respectability, or a further effort to continue the old illegal marriages in more attractive surroundings than the dubious dives surrounding the Fleet, for it was not until 1753 that the Marriage Act became law, making marriages civil as well as religious contracts, for which banns had to be called and a licence granted, and anyone performing a marriage without these requirements was fined £100.

Povey seems to have had no luck with this new bid for a stake in the marriage business. Perhaps his wedding dinners were not up to standard; or the improvements he planned at Belsize were never made. After 1716 'we hear no more of the marriages. He thought about sub-letting, but when the French Ambassador made an offer of £1,000 a year for the mansion, being attracted to it not only by the beauty of the house and gardens, but because of the private chapel, Povey refused, declaring publicly that 'he would not have his chapel desecrated by Popery'.

This was a piece of ill-timed anti-popery propaganda, for with the death of Queen Anne, the last of the Stuarts, the Protestant Hanoverian succession had been secured. George I was on the throne and the agitation against the Roman Catholics had abated. So instead of the approbation for which Povey had hoped from the government, he received a reprimand from the Privy Council, telling him he was an enemy of the new King. And when he suggested recompense for his loss of a high rent and for having kept 'the Romish host' from Hampstead, he received no thanks, and certainly not a penny of compensation.

Povey then offered Belsize to the Prince of Wales – the future George II – for a place of 'recess or constant residence' but the Prince did not even reply.

In high dudgeon and no doubt becoming desperate for some means of disposing of his white elephant, Povey then let Belsize to a man called Howell, who planned to turn it into a pleasure resort to rival and outdo Hampstead Wells. In this he was successful, for Belsize and its lovely gardens became a place of public amusement for the next twenty years, elegant and fashionable when it was first opened in 1720, as Vauxhall had been in Stuart times and as Ranelagh was to be, when it was opened in 1742.

The announcement of the opening of Belsize appeared in *Mist's Journal* of 16 April 1720.

> Whereas that the ancient and noble house near Hampstead, commonly called Bellasis-House, is now taken and fitted up for the entertainment of gentlemen and ladies during the whole summer-season the same will be opened with an uncommon solemnity of music and dancing. This undertaking will exceed all of the kind that has hitherto been known near London, commencing every day at six in the morning and continuing till eight at night, all persons being privileged to admittance without necessity of expense.

A hand-bill announced that

> the park, wilderness, and garden were wonderfully improved and filled with a variety of birds, which compose a most melodious and delightful harmony. Persons inclined to walk and divert themselves, may breakfast on tea and coffee as cheap as at their own chambers. Twelve stout fellows completely armed to patrole between Belsize and London.

The provision of the armed guard was necessary because of the danger from footpads and highwaymen, and later had to be increased to thirty. Similar precautions were taken at the Wells and at Vauxhall, and also at Ranelagh, where the guards were recruited from the Chelsea pensioners.

Howell was successful. He introduced a herd of wild deer into the park and announced that he would, 'hunt one down every Thursday and Saturday through the whole season; and that on these days, for the convenience of single gentlemen, there will be a good ordinary at two o'clock, and for one of the dishes there will constantly be venison'.

The hunt was conducted in fine style, with Howell leading and bugles blowing over the barking of the beagles. Although the grounds of Belsize were no more than a mile in circumference, the hunts were immensely popular for a time. On 15 July 1721, *Reed's Journal* reported that 'Last Saturday their Royal Highnesses the Prince and Princess of Wales dined at Belsize House near Hampstead, attended by several persons of quality, where they were entertained with the diversions of hunting and such others as the place afforded, with which they seemed well pleased, and at their departure were very liberal to the servants'.

Howell, who earned for himself the name of the Welsh Ambassador, was delighted, and on 7 June 1722 the *St James's Journal* reported that 'On Monday last the appearance of nobility and gentry at Bellsize was so great that they reckoned between three and four hundred coaches, at which time a wild deer was hunted down and killed in the park before the company, which gave near three hours' diversion'.

Horse racing and foot racing were also introduced, with the accompanying high betting. In 1721 Howell had offered a plate of six guineas to be run by eleven footmen. The Galloway races were run for a plate of £10, the 'horses to pay one guinea entrance, and to be kept in the stables at Belsize from entrance to the time of running'. Gentlemen paid a shilling entrance on race days, ladies nothing, but dogs were forbidden. 'If any dogs come into the park they will be shot,' announced Howell.

Then he said that 'for the better diverting of the Company he designs to have Duck-hunting every evening; and what will be more extraordinary, the proprietor having purchased a large Bear-dog that will hunt a duck as well as any spaniel in England; and any gentleman may have the liberty to bring his own spaniel to try him'.

This again was like the amusement being offered at the duck pond in Shepherd market, but Howell could go one better, for he had more space and was able to say that 'the expense attending the diversion is met by the payment of sixpence for gentlemen at the time of going into the park; while the ladies are admitted free'; although he adds, as though to imply that he was standing no nonsense, that 'no person will be admitted but who will be thought agreeable'.

Society visited Belsize for a year or two but the fashion soon waned, and when Howell sensed signs of dwindling popularity he made the fatal mistake of announcing 'a part of the house being set aside for the accommodation of the meaner sort'.

There were infinitely more people in London answering this description and they were soon flocking to Belsize, to the cost of Duffield, still struggling along at Hampstead. But while the privileged clients were regaled sumptuously in the elegant coffee room at Belsize, the rest had to be content with a less well appointed room on the north side of the house, although all were free to walk in the grounds. It was an arrangement which could never have worked and very soon:

> Who would at charges be
> Might keep their noble honours company.

By 1722 Belsize was beginning to earn a bad name for itself, as a place of 'dissipation and lewdness'. That year a satire was published in

London, exposing the 'Fops and Beaux who daily frequented the place, the women who made it a place of assignation, the buffoonery of Howell, and the wanton behaviour of the card sharpers who battened on the unwary'.

The law was keeping an eye on Belsize by now as well as on Hampstead, and the *St James's Journal* of 24 May 1772 reported that 'the Courts of Justices, at the general quarter sessions at Hick's Hall★, had ordered the high-constable of Holborn division to issue his precepts to the petty constables and head boroughs of the parish of Hampstead, to prevent all unlawful gaming, riots, etc. at Belsize House and the Great Room at Hampstead,' and a day or two later it was reported that

> On Monday last the High Constable of Holborn Division, with some Petty Constables, having a Warrant sign'd by divers justices of the Peace, went to Bellsize at Hampstead, where they took William Howell, the Proprietor, and several common Gamesters. The said Howell was kept that night in New Prison, and on Tuesday a Bill of Indictment was found against him at the Sessions held in Hick's Hall.

How long he was held is not clear but the occasion called forth yet another satiric verse about him.

> But since he hath obtained his liberty
> By Habeas, the wicked merry be;
> Whom he by advertisements invites
> To visit him amidst his false delights:
> Assuring them that thirty men shall be
> Upon the road for their security:
> But whether one-half of this rabble guard,
> Whilst t'other half's asleep on watch and ward,
> Durst rob the people they pretend to save,
> I to the opinion of the reader leave.

It had very little effect on the popularity of Belsize. Londoners, even if not of the top quality by now, flocked there to amuse themselves,

---

★ Hick's Hall was the Sessions Hall in Clerkenwell which had been built by Sir Baptist Hicks, a square brick house with a stone portico. Close by were the Round House and a pillory, the Round House being the place where highwaymen and other criminals were confined until they were brought before the sitting magistrates and formally committed to prison.

drink claret, Rhenish wine and sack, regale themselves with the renowned venison pasty and lose their money and their virtue.

By 1724 a London guide book was describing Belsize as 'an academy of music, dancing, with a particularly fine ball room and gaming rooms, and play for the diversion of the Ladies,' adding coyly that 'where they are the gentlemen will not fail to be also', but in that same year Defoe was writing of it:

At the foot of this Hill, is an old seat of the Earls of Chesterfield, called Belsize; which for many years had been neglected and as it were forgotten. But being taken lately by a certain Projector to get a Penny, and who knew by what Handle to take the gay part of the World, he has made it a true House of Pleasure. Here, in the Gardens, he entertained the Company with all kinds of Sport, and in the House with all kinds of Game, to say no more of it: This brought a wonderful Concourse of People to the Place, for they were so effectually gratified in all sorts of diversions, that the Wicked part at length broke in, till it alarm'd the Magistrates, and I am told it has been now in a manner suppress'd by the hand of Justice. Here was a great room fitted up with abundance of Dexterity for their Balls, and had it gone on to a degree of Masquerading as I hear was actually begun, it would have bid fair to have had half the Town run to it: one saw Pictures and Furniture there beyond what was to have been expected in a meer Publick House; and tis hardly credible how it drew Company to it; But it could not be, no British Government could be supposed to bear long with the Liberties taken on such Publick Occasions: So as I have said, they are reduc'd, at least restrained from Liberties which they could not preserve by their Prudence.

An anonymous satirist had described the affairs of Belsize more bluntly.

The scandalous lewd house that's call'd Belsize,
Where sharpers lurk, yet Vice in publick lies,
Is publicly become a Rendezvous
    Of Strumpets, common as in common Stews,
. . . Convenient this defiled House is made
To bring the Welsh Ambassador a trade.

Belsize quietened down and in the late 1720s an alternative attraction was created on Hampstead Heath, where races were run on a course laid out near Jack Straw's Castle. By the 1730s Belsize had degenerated into an ordinary popular tea-drinking house, with very mild diversions such as foot-races. On 1 April 1736, the *Grub Street Journal* reported that 'yesterday Mr Pidgeon and Mr Garth ran twelve times round Belsize for £50 a side, which was won with great difficulty by Mr Pidgeon, although Garth fell down and ran ten yards on the wrong side of the post, and was forced to return back; yet he lost by only a foot'.

This was a far cry from the triumphant months of the opening in 1720 and the occasion when the Prince and Princess of Wales and their concourse of attendants had visited the house: and there was nothing now to stop the decline. It stayed open until the 1740s, by which time Ranelagh had opened and quickly became the rage.

The precise end of Belsize as a 'folly house' is not clear but Howell had a long run, even though the greater part was during the years of its decline, and it was probably not until after his death that the old house fell empty again.

In the meantime a similar fate had been overtaking Duffield's Spa and the Great Room, and with frequent visits from the constables, the gaming tables and raffling shops had been declared illegal and one by one had disappeared, leaving only the tavern and a few tea rooms. The original trustees of the Wells Charity were nearly all dead and no one troubled over much that Duffield had never paid any rent. The lord of the manor was no longer a Gainsborough, for in 1707 the family had sold the manor to an absentee landlord, Sir William Langhorne, who had no interest in the Charity.

It was the Overseers of the Poor of Hampstead who took matters in hand. Duffield's twenty-one year lease came to an end in 1722 and he owed £575 arrears of rent. Proceedings were taken against him, in order to preserve the Wells Charity, for with the lessees near bankruptcy, the Gainsborough gift to the poor of Hampstead was fast disappearing. Luffingham and his associates, Dennis Byron, Joseph Rous and William Hoar, were accused of acting 'in such a manner as if they were the absolute owners of the inheritance of the said premises belonging to the said charity'. 'The Trust was wholly obstructed and the poor of the parish knew not of whom to demand either the arrears or growing payment' of the £50 a year rental.

The case dragged on for four years and in the end the debt of £575 was paid and a new lease of the ground was granted to Byron, but by this time the Spa had almost ceased to function, although not entirely.

Dr Gibbons still stoutly proclaimed the virtues of the waters and until his death in 1725 declared that he drank them every day. And people still came to Hampstead to enjoy the peace of the surrounding countryside and the health-giving fresh air, if not for a kind of desperate, lingering faith in the efficacy of the mineral waters.

In 1722 Alexander Pope brought John Gay to Hampstead, to recuperate from the shock of their losses from the South Sea Bubble scandal. Pope had lost a considerable amount of money but poor Gay had lost his entire capital of £1,000, which he had just received from the publication of a book of poems, together with a gift of South Sea stock which was reputed to have been worth £20,000. In 1723 Mrs Pendarves, in a letter to Swift, told him that Miss Kelly was at Hampstead, 'in a very expensive way, with her sickness, her servants, and her horses, high passions, low spirits and a tyrannous father'.

The following year Defoe was at Hampstead, while writing his *Tour Through the Whole Island of Great Britain*. Having given his views on Belsize, he wrote of Hampstead that it,

> indeed is risen from a little Country Village, to a City, not upon the Credit only of the Waters, Though 'tis apparent its growing Greatness began there; but Company increasing gradually and the People liking both the Place and the Diversions together; it grew suddenly Populous, and the Concourse of People was incredible. This consequently raised the Rate of Lodgings and that increased Buildings, till the Town grew up from a little Village, to a Magnitude equal to some Cities; nor could the uneven Surface, inconvenient for Building, uncompact, and unpleasant, check the humour of the Town, for even on the very steep of the Hill, where there's no walking Twenty Yards together, without Tugging up a Hill, or Straddling down a Hill, yet 'tis all one, the Buildings encreased to that degree, that the Town almost spreads the whole side of the Hill.
>
> On the Top of the Hill, indeed, there is a very pleasant Plain, called the Heath, which on the very summit is a Plain of about a Mile every way; and in good Weather 'Tis pleasant Airing upon it, and some of the Streets are extended so far, as that they begin to build even on the highest part of the Hill. But it must be confest, 'tis so near to Heaven, that I dare not say it can be a proper Situation for any but a race of mountaineers, whose lungs had been used to a rarify'd air. . . .
>
> But as there is (especially at the Wells) a Conflux of all Sorts of Company, even Hampstead itself has suffered in its good name; and you see sometimes more Gallantry than Modesty; so that the ladies who value their Reputation, have of late more avoided the Wells and Walks of Hampstead, than they formerly had done.

. . . this place may be said to be prepared for a Summer Dwelling, for in Winter nothing that I know of can recommend it.

Defoe was writing about the last days of Hampstead's first experience as a spa. In 1725 the Pump Room was converted into an episcopal chapel. This idea had first been suggested by Hoar and Luffingham had let it to him for that purpose, but Hoar found he had not enough money to make the necessary alterations. He borrowed from Byron and when he was unable to repay him, Rous stepped in, bought up the interests of them both and completed the work. The chapel was never consecrated, but was used as a chapel of ease for the parish church throughout the rest of the century and the early years of the nineteenth century, while the healing waters were still available for any who wished to take them, bubbling up into the marble bowl close by, as they had for the last twenty years or more.

Well Walk became quiet and decorous, with its chapel and tea garden, attached to the Whitestone Inn, which later was to become the Green Man. Houses were built in place of the raffling shops and even Mother Huff, although she already lived well away from the town, near the Spaniards, now retreated discreetly a little farther north, announcing in *Mist's Weekly Journal* for 31 August 1728, that she had removed from Hampstead Heath, where she had been for over fifty years, to the Hoop and Bunch of Grapes at North End, where cakes and cheese-cakes and the best of entertainment were to be had.

This was the year that John Gay's fortunes revived, with the production of *The Beggar's Opera* at the theatre in Lincoln's Inn Fields; and it also brought success to young William Hogarth.

Hogarth was born in 1693 and he attended classes at Sir James Thornhill's academy in Covent Garden Square, but he was too much of an individualist to tolerate the fashionable method of teaching drawing and painting followed by Sir James, which entailed interminable copying of the masters. He loved life and wanted to depict it as he saw it, and not in any stylised, second-hand manner; and he finally outraged Sir James by eloping with his daughter Jane.

Hogarth achieved his first success when he painted several scenes from *The Beggar's Opera*, and one of his earliest portraits was of Lavinia Fenton, the actress who created the part of Polly Peachum and eventually became the Duchess of Bolton. These were people after his own heart, people whom he knew and understood. E. V. Lucas said of Hogarth that he was 'the first great national British painter, the first man to look at the English life round him like an Englishman and paint it without affectation or foreign influence'.

For a time Hogarth had a country cottage at Hampstead, for here he found ample material for his study of early eighteenth century London life, and his *Road to Finchley* shows both Steele's cottage and Old Mother Huff, but he did not live in the fashionable heart of the town. He chose instead a farmhouse at remote North End, which a few years later was to become the Old Bull and Bush.

Hampstead settled down for a spell into quietness and solitude. It is difficult to tell how much it had expanded during these early Spa days. Defoe's idea of a city was an early eighteenth century one, when populations were small. In 1704 there were probably about 250 houses in the village, including those built on land taken from the Heath, this number being about double that of 1646. By 1720 it has been estimated that the number of houses had increased to about three hundred and the population to somewhere between 1,200 and 1,400.

It was still isolated and the lonely roads approaching it were dangerous, and haunted by highwaymen, who may well have been the inspiration of Gay's opera.

It was many years since Claude Duval had frequented the district, but he was not forgotten. He was a young Frenchman who had come over to England at the Restoration, as a valet in the service of the Duke of Richmond, but he soon took to the road, heading a troop of dangerous highwaymen. He haunted the Holloway Road between Islington and Highgate for a time, and then turned farther west to Hampstead and the Heath. And it was here that on one occasion he stopped a lady's coach, in which, to quote Macaulay, 'there was a booty of £400. He took only £100, and suffered the fair owner to ransom the rest by dancing a coranto with him on the heath'.

Platt's Lane in West Hampstead was originally called Duval's Lane, in remembrance of this performance, which may sound romantic enough in retrospect, but must have been supremely irritating, if not alarming, for the young woman at the time. However, he seems to have been an attractive young man, in some respects, for after he was caught in 1669, at Mother Maberley's tavern, the Hole-in-the-Wall in Chandos Street, Covent Garden, when he was only twenty-six years old, there was said to have been much lamentation. After the trial and his hanging at Tyburn, his body was cut down and brought to the Tangier tavern in St Giles's for a lying-in-state, after which, at dead of night, he was given a splendid funeral at St Paul's, Covent Garden, attended with flambeaux and a long train of weeping women mourners. He is said to have been buried in the central aisle of the Church, with an epitaph which ran:

> Here lies Duval, Reader, if male thou art
> Look to thy purse, if female, to thy heart

but sadly, no trace of it now exists.

The records list dozens of attacks by highwaymen around the Heath, many ending in murder. When Francis Jackson, the highwayman, attacked and murdered Henry Miller at Hampstead his body was strung up on a gibbet made from two elms standing near Jack Straw's Castle, and there it hung in chains for years, from 1673-91, as a grisly warning to fellow highwaymen, but gruesome as the disintegrating skeleton was, swinging on its gibbet elms,* it had little restraining influence, and highway attacks not only continued but increased during the eighteenth century.

Sixteen-string Jack favoured the northern approaches to London for his work. Dick Turpin and Robert King joined forces in 1736, varying their haunts from Epping forest to Finchley Common and the heaths of Hounslow, Putney and Hampstead.

Turpin was said to have come to terms with the landlord of the Spaniards and have in his possession spare keys to the toll gate and to a secret door from the back of the inn to the stables, so that he could make a quick escape at the first sign of danger.

It was he and King who developed the myth of the 'gentlemen of the road', begun by Duval, which seems to have given them a spurious glamour for a time. Even Sir John Fielding, the blind Bow Street magistrate, who was in sole office from the time of his brother Henry's death in 1754 until his own death in 1780, said that:

> robberies on the highway in the neighbourhood of London are not very uncommon; these are usually committed early in the morning, or in the dusk of the evening, and as the times are known, the danger may be for the most part avoided. But the highwaymen are civil, as compared with other countries; do not often use you with ill-manners; have been frequently known to return papers and curiosities with much politeness; and never commit murder, unless they are hotly pursued and find it difficult to escape.

It was a remarkably tolerant view to take and Gay, of course, romanticised them in *The Beggar's Opera*. Nevertheless, many years

---

* The last of the gibbet elms was blown down in a gale, in 1907.

later, towards the end of his time at Bow Street, Sir John seems to have hardened his attitude, for the *Gentleman's Magazine* for 13 September 1773 reported that:

> This day Sir John Fielding informed the bench of justices that he had last year written to Mr Garrick concerning the impropriety of performing *The Beggar's Opera,* which never was represented on the stage without creating an additional number of real thieves; he begged, therefore, the gentlemen would join him in requesting Mr Garrick from performing that opera on Saturday evening. The bench immediately consented to the proposal; and a polite note was despatched to Mr Garrick for that purpose.

With equal courtesy Garrick replied, pointing out the difficulty of altering his programme at such short notice. The run continued and more young men were presumably inspired to follow the ways of Macheath, as ever since, under the far more insidious influence of crime thrillers, films and television, they have copied the ways of crooks and murderers, thieves and thugs. And this aspect of entertainment, first publicly put forward two hundred years ago, has been hotly debated ever since, between the protagonists who insist that realism is the essence of their art and their purpose is to describe life as it is, and those who take Sir John's point of view, the psychologists being about equally divided and therefore contributing remarkably little to the solution of the problem.

Although Hampstead appeared to have failed as a Spa, the doctors did not give up, and in 1734 the waters found a new champion in Dr John Soames, a Hampstead doctor who had been a friend of Dr Gibbons and published his pamphlet *Hampstead Wells; or Directions for drinking the Waters.* He bewailed the fact that they had fallen into neglect, through 'the knavery of some and the folly of others' and extolled their virtues, describing an experiment he had made, in which he had proved the value of their healing powers in 'cutaneous and nervous disorders, as well as those of debility'.

Like Dr Gibbons, he described the attractiveness of the situation of Hampstead,

> situated somewhat romantic, but every way pleasant, on several little hills, on high ground of different soils . . . here persons may draw in a pure and balmy Air, with the Heavens clear and serene, at that Season of the Year that the great and populous city of London is covered with Fogs, Smokes, and other thick Darkness, being

frequently oblig'd to burn Candles in the middle of the Day; while we are here bless'd with the benign and comfortable Rays of a glorious Sun, breathing a free and wholesome Air without the noisome Smell of stinking Fogs, or other malignant Fumes and Vapours, too common in large Cities.

While a few years earlier, Defoe had had little to say about the beauties of Hampstead, apart from the pleasant plain on the top of the hill, and a great deal about the steep hills, which obviously appalled him, Dr Soames expatiated on the magnificent views and lovely surroundings of Hampstead, in a way which no one seems to have done before him. But the waters are his main theme. 'And what adds to the blessings of the place is the salubrious water of Hampstead, which may be justly called the Inexhaustible Fountain of Health' he said, 'for they were as good if not better, than in any parts of Great Britain'.

He described the spring adjoining the chapel, where there

is a bason fixed upon a huge pipe on the declivity of the hill. This pipe is so well stored with water, that . . . it will throw off five gallons of water in four minutes; it has that force, that it may be made to throw the water up in a perpendicular height twelve or fourteen feet at least, there being always a large quantity running to waste.

The waters were, in fact, of no medicinal value and by 1902, when Dr Littlejohn, then the medical officer of health for Hampstead, examined them he reported that the chalybeate water of the Well Walk fountain and a further sample obtained by sinking a shaft 'cannot be used for drinking purposes without danger to health'. Back in the early eighteenth century, before it had been exposed to the later years of contamination, it was no doubt pure enough to drink, but it was probably Dr Soames's proposed regimen and his advocacy of Hampstead's clean and healthy air which revived the popularity of the town, both for visitors in search of new health and also permanent residents, whether they were interested in the cure or not.

In his pamphlet he assures readers that

the chalybeate, though as strong, if not stronger, than that of Tunbridge Wells of the iron mineral, is not at all unpleasant: that if well corked and sealed down, and kept in a cellar for one or two years, when you have drawn the cork it will be most ready to fly, and when poured into a glass, will sparkle and knit up like a glass of champagne or Herefordshire cider.

While advocating the healing properties of the waters, he urged against the drinking of tea as Jonas Hanway was to do twenty years later. Tea, he said, was reducing the stature of the nation, and if it continued it would cause 'the next generation to be more like pygmies than men and women'.

To support his argument he insisted, quite wrongly as it happens, that the non-tea-drinking Romans were far taller than the eighteenth century men and women of England, but he apparently had a grudge against the beverage. Smoking, however, he approved. He was obviously a smoker himself, for he says that: 'They that take tobacco may do it here with all the safety in the World; but let them have a regard not to offend the company, especially the ladies, who cannot well relish that smoke with their waters.'

The best time to take the waters, he said, was between June and Michaelmas, which was clever of him, for this was the fashionable time for visiting any spa. And he suggests that they be taken an hour after sunrise, which must have been a tradition and explains why proceedings began so early in the bad old days of Duffield and Luffingham. He allows sage tea with a little orange peel in it for breakfast, or chocolate, milk, porridge or mutton broth, with bread and butter.

An hour after taking the waters, the patient may drink coffee – but on no account tea – and then, after counselling him to be of a 'merry and cheerful disposition', he recommends a ride of four or five miles, 'because, by the Motion of the Horse, the Stomach and Viscera are thereby borne up and contracted, by which means the Waters will be better digested'.

At the same time he warns against any more strenuous exercise than this, such as 'some of your Country Dances', as they would be a hindrance to the 'due Digestion of the Waters'.

Very soon a new Long Room or Assembly Room was built, on the west side of Well Walk. It was near Burgh House, which had been standing since 1702, and ultimately this building was adapted to become Weatherall House. It is not certain at what date the new Assembly Room was opened after 1734 and until it was ready some old buildings on the site may have been used.

The first person of fame to be found there was Dr Arbuthnot. He was asthmatic and suffering from dropsy. He knew that he was dying but came to Hampstead for a brief respite, taking lodgings in Pond Street.

'I am going out of this troublesome world, and you, amongst the rest of my friends, shall have my last prayers and good wishes,' he wrote to Swift.

Hampstead improved his health for a time, for when he went there he said that he could 'neither sleep, breathe, eat or move' but at the end of a few weeks he was able to ride, sleep and eat again. Yet he knew that it could not last and, being by then sixty-seven, that 'no man at his age could hope to recover'.

'I am at present,' he wrote to Swift, 'in the case of a man that was almost in harbour, and then blown back to sea; who has a reasonable hope of going to a good place, and an absolute certainty of leaving a very bad one'.

Gay had died two years earlier, in 1732, but Pope visited Arbuthnot at Hampstead and wrote to the Miss Blounts that he had spent a whole day with him. 'He was in the Long Room half the morning and has parties at cards every night. Mrs. Lepell and Mrs. Saggione and her sons and two daughters are all with him.'

But in the following March he died. 'Poor Arbuthnot, who grieved to see the wickedness of mankind . . . is dead, to the great regret of everyone who had the pleasure of knowing him intimately,' wrote Pulteney to Swift, who had treasured the friendship of the lovable and witty doctor and writer and had once said of him that 'he has more wit that we all have, and his humanity is equal to his wit'.

V

Hampstead in the Later Eighteenth Century — I

The number of famous names associated with Hampstead during the second half of the eighteenth century is a long one. Some came as visitors but more as permanent residents. Dr Soames's plea for the virtues of the waters was for the most part unheeded and he never succeeded in re-establishing Hampstead as a spa. People came to the little town not for the waters, but to enjoy its charm and seclusion, its country surroundings and the Heath. As London grew steadily more crowded and murky and its terrible winter fogs ever denser, the pleasures of the countryside, still on its doorstep, with its trees and fields and fresh, clean air, were becoming increasingly appreciated. Hampstead became a popular holiday resort, and more important, a desirable place in which to live permanently.

London was still a walled city, for the ancient Roman walls and the massive gates did not come down until the 1760s, but building had spread far beyond the confines of the walls by this time, reaching in the north to Holborn, with a few large mansions in the countryside beyond. Bloomsbury Square had been laid out as early as 1661, with large mansions which disappeared during the later development of the early nineteenth century. In 1704 the Russells had moved from their house in the Strand, on the north side of Covent Garden, to Bedford House in Bloomsbury, a stretch of countryside famous for its peaches and snipe.

When Queen Square was built, early in the eighteenth century, the north side was left open, to afford an uninterrupted view of the Hampstead and Highgate hills.

In 1731 the Russells commissioned Nicholas Hawksmoor to build St George's Square, Bloomsbury, but Bedford Square was not laid out until 1775.

Behind Montague House, rebuilt after the disastrous fire of 1686, and which in 1759 was opened as the British Museum, stretched open country and farmland, including the farm of the Capper sisters, two fierce old ladies who always wore riding habits and men's hats, and expended a vast amount of energy in protecting their land from trespassers. One of them would ride furiously round the boundary on her old grey mare, chasing the boys who flew their kites on Capper land and cutting the strings, while the other one busied herself cunningly in appropriating the clothes of the ones who had dared to steal a quiet bathe in the farm stream.

Beyond the farm stretched the desolate marshy waste of the watercress beds and the lonely duelling ground – the field of the forty footsteps, haunted by the ghosts of two brothers, both in love with the same girl, who are said to have fought each other to the death, while she calmly sat and watched them.

Fields stretched westwards to Lisson Grove and Paddington, eastwards to Battle Bridge and Islington and northwards to Primrose Hill, Chalk Farm, Hampstead and Highgate.

At the northern end of what is now Tottenham Court Road, the old Elizabethan mansion of Tottenham Court still stood, until the end of the century, and beyond it were the Adam and Eve tea gardens. Camden Town was a builder's speculation, on open fields, not begun until 1791, and the only buildings here were a few cottages and the Old Mother Red Cap, the first port of call up the hill after the Adam and Eve.

Old Mother Red Cap, more often known as Mother Damnable, the shrew of Kentish Town, was long since dead but the inn was built on the site of her cottage.

Mother Red Cap had been born some time in the early seventeenth century. Her father was Jacob Bingham, a brick maker, her mother the daughter of a Scottish pedlar, and Jinny was their only child. At fifteen, Jinny had a child by Gipsy George, and they lived together for a time in the Camden Town cottage, which Jinny's father built for them on waste land. Gipsy George came to an untimely end, after stealing a sheep near Holloway, for which he was tried, convicted and hanged at Tyburn. She then lived with a man called Darby for a time, but after a few months of furious, drunken quarrelling, he disappeared, and no one ever know what happened to him. Jinny's parents were accused of killing a young woman by black magic and followed Gipsy George to Tyburn. Jinny then took to her bosom a man called Pitcher, who, after a short time, was found burnt to a cinder in the oven. Jinny was tried for murder, but acquitted after an observant and obliging neighbour had given evidence that Pitcher often hid in the oven, to escape the lash of Jinny's tongue, and his death could have been accidental.

By this time it is not surprising that Jinny found herself alone and shunned by her neighbours, who were mortally afraid of her. How she lived no one knew, but she never left her cottage during the daytime. Only after dark was she sometimes seen, haunting the lanes and hedgerows.

During the troubles of the Commonwealth, she gave shelter to a fugitive, who crept into her cottage one night, begging for a hiding place. The stranger had money and he stayed on with her for several years. From time to time the neighbours heard the sound of quarrelling and fighting, but the strange couple somehow weathered the storm; and when the man died, he left Jinny plenty of money. Rumour whispered that he had been poisoned, but nothing was ever proved against Jinny and she lived on at the ramshackle cottage, a lonely, ill-favoured, cross-grained old woman, whom everyone was convinced by now was a witch, practising the black arts, like her parents before her; and she certainly looked the part, with her large nose and heavy, shaggy eyebrows, her hideous red cap and old grey shawl, and her huge black cat, which seldom left her side.

She is said to have told fortunes and healed strange diseases, but mostly people were so scared of her that they gave her and her cottage a wide berth.

She died alone, sitting by her fire, and later people said they had seen the devil walk into the cottage that night and never come out again. An old pamphlet, printed at the time, said that 'Mother Damnable was found the following morning, sitting before the fire-place, holding a crutch over it, with a tea-pot full of herbs, drugs and liquid'. When some of this was given to the cat, its 'hair fell off in two hours, and the cat soon after died'. . . . 'The old woman's limbs were stiff and the undertaker had to break them before he could get her into the coffin' and 'the justices have put men in possession of the house to examine its contents.'

The first proprietor of the tavern was also an old woman, and she too was called Mother Red Cap, the stories about her having been confused with those of old Mother Damnable, but she was a far less sinister character, and in her youth had been an amiable camp-follower with the Duke of Marlborough's armies. After the Treaty of Utrecht she set up her alehouse here, in Mother Damnable's old thatched cottage, and the inn became a favourite place for soldiers and officers who had known her when she was with the army, for her home-brewed ale was reputed to be excellent.

Yet this part of the world was a grim enough place for many years to come, for in the *Morning Post* of 1776 appeared a notice headed Public Executions, which announced that 'Orders have been given from the Secretary of State's Office that the criminals, capitally convicted at the Old Bailey, shall in future be executed at the cross road near the Mother Red Cap – the half way house to Hampstead, and that no galleries, scaffolds, or other temporary stages, be built near the place'.

The New Road, later known as the Marylebone Road, with its extension the Euston Road, leading to Pentonville Hill and Islington, was made through open country during the years between 1750 and 1760. Within the next few years, building slowly reached up to the south side of the New Road, but to the north, Maida Vale, St John's Wood, and the Crown lands where Regent's Park was to be formed, were woodland and open country, and were to remain so until the early years of the nineteenth century.

So the traveller from London, after passing through the fields and orchards which lined the way from the Adam and Eve to the Mother Red Cap, made his way to Highgate along the country road which led due north through the little hamlet of Kentish Town, or to Hampstead north-westwards past the hayfields of Chalk Farm and up Haverstock Hill and then Red Lion Hill.

The relatively low-lying country of Chalk Farm and the land round Primrose Hill was the Eton College estate of Chalcots and was given over to hay-farming for London's horses. The Lower Chalcot Farm was near the Chalk Farm tavern, the tavern being just outside the parish boundary: and the Upper Chalcot farm was where Eton Road now runs, leading from the foot of Haverstock Hill.

These farmhouses, with one or two cottages and Steele's cottage were the only buildings here as yet.

The Belsize estate was as rural. The Chesterfields leased the two hundred and forty acres of their estate from the Dean and Chapter of Westminster and sub-let it as farmland, the farm standing at the corner of England's Lane and Haverstock Hill.

After the death of Howell, Belsize House, in its forty-five acres of grounds, stood empty and neglected for many years, and it was not until the end of the century that it was rebuilt and used as a private house again. Shelford Lodge had been built some time before 1734 and stood on the northern boundary of the Belsize estate, its drive being where Lyndhurst Road now runs. This was a leasehold property, held on a sub-lease from the Earl of Chesterfield. Just to the north of Belsize House stood a smaller mansion, which was first known as the White House and then as Belsize Court. Lord Paget is known to have had a house near here, too, although all trace of it had disappeared by the early nineteenth century, and by 1734 there were at least nine smaller houses, each set in about half an acre of garden, on the top of Haverstock Hill, where it joined Belsize Lane.

This was the boundary with the Manor of Hampstead and the freehold estate which went with it. It was bought by Sir William Langhorne from the Gainsboroughs in 1707, and by 1777 had descended to Sir Thomas Spencer Wilson, comprising a solid block of three hundred and fifty-six acres stretching from west and south-west of the old town, all of it let as valuable farmland, as well as sixty acres along the east side of the Heath.

The other two large land-owners of Hampstead were Henry Samuel Eyre, whose Hampstead estate, to the west of the Eton College land, adjoined his St John's Wood estate, and John Powell, who held a hundred and seventy acres of land in West Hampstead, along the Kilburn Road and Shoot-Up Hill.

There were other small holdings in the north-west of the parish, which had been acquired by purchase at various times, but these five large estates comprised between them nearly three-quarters of the land, which was profitably let for farming. The little town stood on only one-tenth of the acreage of the parish and it was surrounded by farmland to the south and west and by the Heath to the north and east.

For the people who now wanted to live here, and could afford to build handsome villas or country mansions for themselves – the East and West India merchants, the bankers and City men and rich lawyers, the doctors and publishers – not only was the top of the hill, near the Heath, the most attractive part of Hampstead, but it was, in fact, the only part available to them. In the long term, landowners still reaped a higher return from letting their land for farming than for building, and in some cases the terms of the family trust by which they had inherited forbade their issuing building leases, and the trust could be broken only by a special Parliamentary bill.

It was therefore again on the waste land on the upper slopes of Hampstead Hill, too hilly for farming, that much of the eighteenth-century building of Hampstead took place.

In the heart of Hampstead, around Frognal, there were already a number of old houses, and Frognal House went up in 1740. Close by was Priory Lodge, built about 1746 as quite a small and modest house, although it was later considerably enlarged. In 1745 Henry Flitcroft built houses which are now numbers 103 to 107, Frognal. Frognal Lodge, now number 88, stands in its original high wall, while the Old Mansion, though much altered since it was built in 1700, still stands, sideways on to the road, today numbered 94. Numbers 104 and 106 were built around 1760, numbers 108 and 110 considerably earlier, perhaps at the end of the seventeenth century. Moving up the hill, by the lane leading to Holly Hill and Branch Hill, now called Frognal Rise, there may have been a few smaller houses at one time, but the most important was Frognal Hall, the eighteenth-century mansion where Isaac Ware lived for a time. He had designed many of the houses in Berkeley Square, the Strathmores' house in Bruton Street and Lord Chesterfield's mighty Chesterfield House, but in the end he lost all his money and died in poverty, somewhere near the Kensington Gravel Pits.

Later in the century, the Guyon family were living in Frognal Hall, which stood at the junction of Frognal Lane with the old road leading to the village of West End; and in the late 1790s Lord Chief Justice Alvanley came to live here.

The old Manor farm and farmhouse were where Frognal and Frognal Lane join, and here there was a group of houses, Old Frognal Court being built in 1785 and Maryon House and Maryon Court in 1793.

Nearly all these houses, the homes of rich merchants and prosperous members of the professions, stood in high, enclosing walls, between which ran narrow, intriguing little tree-shaded lanes, leading no-where in particular but making convenient short cuts for neighbourly visits.

To the west of Frognal, the way to West End was by the narrow, leafy West End Lane, winding south-westwards from Frognal Lane through the Kilburn meadows. At the Hampstead end of the lane was a large house called The Ferns, and close by was another called the Manor House, where T. Norton Longman, head of the publishing house, lived, dying here in 1797.

There was a small village at Child's Hill and another at West End, but this stretch of country, running from Child's Hill down to Belsize, along the western border of Hampstead, was some of the best agricultural land in the district and was largely given over to dairy farming.

It was to the east of Frognal that the most intensive building took place. Early in the century the beautiful Church Row was built, running from the old Church due east to a narrow lane which was roughly parallel with the High Street, and today it is regarded as one of the finest surviving terraces of early eighteenth-century town houses not only in Hampstead but in the whole country. Numbers 17 to 28, on the south side, were built about 1720, numbers 5 to 12, on the opposite side, about the same time, and the rest of the street, which was a builder's speculation, was probably completed by the 1740s. The houses vary in size, but most have three principal storeys, with attics and basements; the hooded and pedimented front doors, with their delicate fan-lights, are mainly approached by one or two steps from the pavement and the basements are protected by iron railings. At a first glance, some of the houses look identical, but there are differences in detail, even if it is only in the pattern of the fanlight or the wrought iron lamp bracket over the front railings, which give each house an individual charm, and they all have a neat and well-bred air.

Some were used as permanent residences and others, perhaps, only during the summer months, as holiday homes, when the wife and children moved in for a spell and the husband came down from London each weekend or each night. Although the gardens at the back were fairly spacious, there was no stabling attached, but there was plenty available close at hand in the village, which was necessary, for there was little public transport available as yet. It improved steadily throughout the century but in 1740 there were only two coaches a day running between Hampstead and Holborn or Covent Garden.

Like Well Walk, Church Row was planted with lime trees, and very soon it became Hampstead's fashionable promenade for the Sunday morning Church parade, although the eastern end which now runs straight into Heath Street, was very different in the eighteenth century, being almost blocked by a maze of alleys and courtyards which reached to the High Street, Heath Street ending where it joined the High Street just below Holly Hill.

The main approach to Church Row was by Church Lane, which ran from the High Street, just south of Perrin's Court, and led into a narrow street called Church Place, and it was from here that Church Row led westwards, while the continuation of Church Place to the north, the even narrower Little Church Row, led to Crockett's Court, Banana

Row and Bradley's Buildings, all of which were swept away at the end of the nineteenth century.

In 1745, the old Chapel of the Blessed Mary, being 'quite worn out' as well as too small, was demolished, and, at the expense of the parishioners, the new parish church of St John's was built. Henry Flitcroft, the son of William III's gardener, who had become a protégé of Lord Burlington in his youth, and was now living at number 105 Frognal Grove, had been invited, in competition with other architects, to submit a design for the new parish church, but Flitcroft, known to the world as Burlington Harry, was a busy man. He had rebuilt St Giles-in-the-Fields and St Olave's in Southwark, and was doing a great deal of work for the Duke of Bedford in Bloomsbury, in addition to his work in Frognal, while from 1747 to 1761 he was to be engaged on the rebuilding of much of Woburn Abbey for the Bedfords. He declined the offer and the contract went to a builder-architect John Saunderson, who lived near the Spaniards Inn.

Saunderson soon found himself running short of money, so that he was not able to follow his original design. There is a note which appeared in the trustees records at this time saying that: 'The tower being placed at the eastern end of the church, would be a considerable saving of expense'. So here it was built, behind the chancel, and the chief entrances to the church were at the sides of the sanctuary.

The church was completed and dedicated in 1747, but since that time there have been many alterations. In 1843 the transepts were added, increasing the accommodation from 700 to 1600, and in 1878 there was a great deal of reconstruction, during which the altar and chancel were moved to the west end of the church. At this time there were suggestions for moving the tower, but the residents of Hampstead had grown to love the view from Church Row of the tower and eastern end of the church, and their petition was heeded.

So externally the yellow brick St John's Church looks much as it did when people began to move to Hampstead in the eighteenth century, even to the wrought-iron gates, which were bought at the sale of the Duke of Chandos's possessions at Canons, when the old house was demolished in 1744, at the same time that Lord Chesterfield bought the Canons staircase to install in his new Chesterfield House.

It is a rather squat and sober-looking church, but today it has the composed and well-inhabited air of the Row itself, while the Renaissance interior is a brilliant contrast to the outward appearance, astonishingly light and gay – all pale grey and gold, like the rebuilt St James's, Piccadilly.

There was more close building behind the corner where Heath Street and the High Street met, particularly in the area enclosed by New End, which curves round from Heath Street, just below Elm Row, to the Well Walk end of Flask Walk, while Back Lane, leading from Flask Walk back to Heath Street, as an inner ring to New End, was in existence by 1745. Some of the cottages and houses in New End were built as early as 1700 while New End Square was built for the accommodation of visitors to the Spa. One or two have survived, but many have been altered almost beyond recognition or else demolished. Grove Place, running from New End to Christ Church Hill, was built on the site of White Bear Green and the first White Bear Inn was built here in 1704.

Christ Church Lane, long before Christ Church was built, in 1852, was Green Man Lane, a short cut from the top of the hill to Pond Street, and on the site of Christ Church stood some tea gardens.

Moving northwards up the hill, towards the Heath, the houses of the eighteenth century were larger and more scattered. From the western end of Church Row Holly Walk runs steeply uphill almost due north to Mount Vernon, while Holly Hill running north-east from the corner opposite the meeting place of Heath Street and the High Street, almost meets it at Mount Vernon. Several eighteenth-century houses survive on Holly Hill, as, for example, numbers 16 to 24, while numbers 15 to 19 have been adapted from the old Holly Hill farmhouse. Frognal winds up the western side of Mount Vernon to meet Windmill Hill and then Branch Hill, which mounts up to the Heath. To the east, Holly Hill becomes Holly Bush Hill and then Hampstead Grove, which runs up roughly parallel with Heath Street.

Admiral's Walk leads off Hampstead Grove to the west, running along the north garden wall of Fenton House, and Mount Square leads off to the east. Higher still up the hill, the Grove is intersected by Upper Terrace, and from the western end of Upper Terrace Lower Terrace runs in a south-westerly course to meet Branch Hill.

In Hampstead Grove, opposite Fenton House, is a row of charming cottages, some of which have medieval foundations and are thought to have been the site of lodgings built for the monks of Westminster, when they came to Hampstead to visit the Grange.

Higher up the hill, on the east side, Old Grove House was built early in the eighteenth century and New Grove House not much later, although the Georgian building has been drastically altered and given a Gothic exterior.

Admiral's Walk was originally the carriage drive to the house where

Admiral Barton was living towards the end of the century, an early eighteenth-century house first known as the White House or sometimes as The Grove. In November 1758, Matthew Barton, in command of a ship of Admiral Keppel's squadron, had been cast away on the Barbary coast. Here, with the few survivors of his crew, he had lived for a fortnight on drowned sheep washed ashore from the shipwreck. They had lost all their clothes and were quite naked when they were captured by the Moors and taken into slavery for the next eighteen months. Then the British government paid up the ransom demanded for Barton's freedom and he returned to England, to be court-martialled for the loss of his ship. However, he was honourably acquitted, was appointed to the Téméraire and sent to sea again with Admiral Keppel, to Bellisle. He saw active service for another three years but then his health broke down. He arrived back in England and was paid off in May 1763, after which he found his Hampstead retreat. Here he lived for many more years, getting a lot of fun out of life, even if he was a bit eccentric. He built a railing round the flat roof of the White House, to make it look like the deck of a ship, and installed two cannon there, which he let off whenever the country scored a naval victory, and he lived on until 1795, by which time he was nearly eighty.

Adjoining his house was a farmhouse, today known as Grove Lodge, and while the Admiral was settling himself into his new home, General Charles Vernon was living in Mount Vernon House, near which there were a few cottages, some of which have survived. The General was an aide-de-camp to George III and also governor of the Tower of London, but unfortunately for the prisoners he was said to have had 'the worst temper of any man'.

On Branch Hill there was an old house, Branch Hill Lodge, which Flitcroft redesigned in 1745 for Sir Thomas Clarke, Master of the Rolls, and where Alexander Wedderburn, the future Lord Rosslyn was to live for a time, and beyond this was the Heath.

In Upper Terrace, above the Admiral's house, were some splendid mansions dating from about 1740, including Upper Terrace Lodge and Upper Terrace House, both of which have survived, and the Priory, which was pulled down at the end of the nineteenth century.

Upper Terrace Cottage, where Mrs Siddons was staying in 1804 and part of 1805, seeking a cure for her lumbago, is a charming little Georgian house, long and low, behind its small front garden, and still stands, at the corner of Judge's Walk. It was sometimes called Siddons Cottage but later was re-named Capo di Monte.

In Lower Terrace, running uphill from Frognal, past the western end of Admiral's Walk and cutting across Upper Terrace, were smaller terrace houses, built later in the eighteenth century, while on the southern slopes of Windmill Hill, looking down on to Holly Bush Hill, four large houses have stood from about 1730, in one of which, Bolton House, Joanna Baillie the poetess and playwright lived for many years.

Just opposite this corner is Holly Bush Hill, where several large houses were built towards the end of the century, one by George Romney, in 1797, which he intended for a studio. Round the corner, Holly Mount was a jumble of old alleys and pubs and narrow passages, all at different levels, and a few houses with gardens built over the vaults of the Holly Hill houses.

Much of it survives, still intriguingly haphazard. The Holly Bush tavern was built on the site of Romney's stables and stands today at the top of Holly Bush steps, which lead down to Heath Street, and at the bottom of the steps, just to the right, is Golden Yard, a delightful little courtyard surrounded by white-washed cottages, hidden away behind the shops of Heath Street, which has survived from the sixteenth century, when this piece of land belonged to Henry Goulding.

The west side of Heath Street, like the east side of Highgate Hill, was built up several feet above the roadway, the footpath being reached at intervals by steps. This stretch, known as the Mount, was built early in the eighteenth century, the first house there, now number 6, being called the Mount. Here there was a row of large Georgian mansions, each lying back from the roadway, protected by a high garden wall and large gates, several of which have survived. At the end of the Mount is Money's Yard, with Caroline House, built in the 1750s, hidden away here. Farther up the hill is the eighteenth-century Mount Square, once called Golden Square, on to which look the backs of the houses in Hampstead Grove, and at the top of the hill on this side, where Queen Mary's Maternity Home now stands, was the Upper Flask tavern which the wealthy George Steevens turned into a splendid private house called Upper Heath during the 1750s.

On the east side of Heath Street there were a number of houses, built at varying times throughout the century and Elm Row and Hampstead Square were built about the same time as Church Row.

There were some beautiful elm trees in Elm Row, where building began about 1720, while Elm Lodge was built in 1732. Elm Row, with its dignified terrace of houses hidden behind the high walls of the front gardens, leads from Heath Street to Hampstead Square, which has many early Georgian survivals, including numbers 1 to 3, number 6 –

Vine House, and number 12 – Lawn House. Here also was the Gate Coffee House and it was in Hampstead Square that companies of strolling players used to give their shows.

Stamford Close was built on the grounds of Stamford Lodge, a large house on the site of which the Friends' Meeting House was built in 1907, while the Baptist Church now stands where the Independent Chapel was built in 1775 and Holford House stood at the top of the hill where Holford Road now runs, parallel with the top of Heath Street, due north to East Heath Road.

In the High Street, which was also called Hampstead Street or Hampstead Hill for many years, there were houses, shops and taverns. The parsonage was at number 28, opposite Perrin's Lane, which was the direct route to the Church, while just beyond it, on Rosslyn Hill, which was then known as Red Lion Hill, stood Vane House, where Bishop Butler was living in the early part of the century and where he died, in 1752. The Chicken House was a little lower down on the opposite side. Rosslyn House, farther down still, in Belsize, was known as Shelford Lodge and renamed Rosslyn House when Alexander Wedderburn received his peerage in 1780 and moved there from Branch Hill Lodge.

One or two Queen Anne houses survive on Rosslyn Hill and a chapel for 'protestant dissenters' was built in 1691, near the Chicken House and the present Unitarian Chapel.

Where Shepherd's Walk now runs, named after a local resident called Thomas Shepherd, lay the Conduit fields, stretching westwards to where Fitzjohn's Avenue was to be built a century later, while Pilgrim's Lane, leading from the north side of the hill to East Heath, was named after Charles Pilgrim, who was living in Vane House at the end of the century.

In the district of the Wells, the new Long Room remained a fashionable meeting place for Hampstead residents and visitors for much of the eighteenth century, but when its fortunes flagged it was closed and the contents, including wines and plate, were put up for auction, the sale being advertised in the *Morning Chronicle* in 1794, as the property of Mr Jonas Fox, Vintner, a Bankrupt. Soon after this, the Long Room was turned into a private house, named Weatherall House after Thomas Weatherall, one of its earliest occupants. Gardnor House in Flask Walk was built in 1737 and close by was the beautiful early Queen Anne Burgh House, standing back from Well Walk.

The present Well Road was the lane leading to the spring from which the water for bottling had been obtained and Flask Walk was still approached from the High Street by the archway, which was to remain until 1911. The Lower Flask was still in business and near the fairground were the village stocks and the watchman's hut, with two overnight cells for miscreants built alongside it.

But to the east of Well Walk were watercress beds and then the Heath, while to the south, between Flask Walk and Pilgrim's Lane, stood the late seventeenth century Carlile House, on the ground where Willoughby Road was later to be built.

East Heath Road existed as a track along the edge of the Heath by about 1700 and several mansions were built along it during the following years, including Duffield's Foley House, although the name derived from a later owner, Captain Foley, who was there from 1805 to 1808. East Heath Lodge, South Lodge and Heath Lodge, round the corner in Heath Side, were all built in the late eighteenth century but Gangmoor at the top of the hill, round in Whitestone Lane, was there in the seventeenth century.

Joshua Squire built his mansion Squire's Mount, enclosed in its high, red brick wall, in 1714, and the charming little row of cottages, just round the corner running due north to the Heath and the Vale of Health, was, as we have seen, built about the same time. The Vale of Health itself was an undrained stretch of unhealthy marsh land until 1777, when it was leased to the Hampstead Water Company. The Company drained it and built the pond, after which the Vale became habitable and the first few cottages were built amongst the trees, haphazardly and hidden away in secluded corners. Within the next few years larger houses were built and the spaces between their high brick garden walls make an intriguing labyrinth of narrow, winding lanes, tree-shaded and spilling over with climbing plants and shrubs, which to this day are unnamed.

In Cannon Place, running westward from Squire's Mount, Cannon Hall and Cannon Lodge were built early in the eighteenth century, Cannon Hall being the home of a succession of magistrates.

On the Heath itself, Jack Straw's Castle is first mentioned during the reign of Queen Anne, although there was probably an inn on this site far earlier. Next door, the house now called the Old Court House was built about the same time, although the Manor Courts were held at Jack Straw's Castle and the Old Court House was formerly called Heath View, and at one time Earlswood. This was the house where the absentee Lord of the Manor sometimes stayed, when visiting Hampstead. Close by were two other old houses, Heath Brow Cottage and Heathlands, but they were destroyed during the last war and were never rebuilt, the land on which they stood being incorporated in the Heath in 1950.

At the corner of the Spaniards Road and North End Way, isolated and very dignified, is the splendid Heath House, which in 1790 was bought by Samuel Hoare, the Quaker banker.

Farther north still, beyond Sandy Heath, was the little hamlet of North End, known in Elizabethan times as Wildwood Corner. Here was the seventeenth-century farmhouse which was to become the country home of William Hogarth and later still was to be converted into the Old Bull and Bush.

About 1750 John Turner, a wealthy retired tobacconist from Fleet Street, arranged the building of Sandy Road from the Spaniards to North End, and then south-westwards, just inside the parish boundary, to Child's Hill; and along this road houses in spacious grounds were soon built, including Wildwood Lodge, part of which still stands, and Wildwood Cottage, where Mrs Craik the novelist, lived for a time in 1859, and which has now gone; but the largest of all was North End Place, which during its life, until its demolition in 1952, was known by a number of different names, Wildwood House, Wildwoods and Pitt House. It stood in a short lane running southwards from Sandy Road, and opposite, on the corner with Sandy Road, still stands the gaunt grey mansion once known as Myrtle Lodge or Myrtlewood but later named Byron Cottage, when the wife of the ninth Lord Byron, later to become Lady Houston, came to live here in 1908, although 'cottage' is the most unlikely of terms to describe it.

On the north side of Sandy Road, opposite North End Place, stretched Eton College farmland, which the Wyldes estate bestowed on the college in 1531. In 1785 the land, with its little farmhouse, was leased to the Collins family and was known as Collins farm.

The eastern ends of Sandy Road and the old Spaniards Road, running across the Heath north-eastwards from Jack Straw's Castle, met near the old inn itself, which had been established on the site of the western lodge of the ancient Bishop of London's Highgate chase.

Why it was called the Spaniards no one can say for certain, but the suggestions are legion. A family connected with the Spanish embassy once lived here. The Spanish ambassador to the court of King James I lived here for a time, to escape an outbreak of plague in London. Or a Spanish merchant of the early seventeenth century took up his abode here. Whatever the origin of its name, the little inn perched on the Heath was always loved and has never lost its air of romance.

Almost next door stood Evergreen Hill, where Lord Erskine came to live in 1788 and which later became known as Erskine House. It was almost opposite Ken House, which had come into the possession of Lord Bute from his uncle, the Duke of Argyll, in 1743, but which he sold to William Murray, the future Earl of Mansfield in 1754.

Close by Evergreen House, where the enclave of Spaniard's End has been built, stood John Turner's house, The Firs, which he built in 1743, and of which a small part survives, while The Elms, which stood in several acres of grounds, was built in the 1730s on the site of Mother Huff's tea garden, on the south side of the Spaniards Road, about half way between Ken House and Heath House.

This was Hampstead in the eighteenth century, a little town built on a hill and surrounded by heath or farmlands. It was a mixed community, as any thriving township must be, but there was a far higher proportion of mansions and large houses and wealthy residents than one would expect to find in a town of this size, and the building took place at a time when domestic architecure was at its most attractive. It was then that William Kent was designing his country mansions in the tradition of Palladio, and John Wood and his son were building Bath, which perhaps, in its heyday, was the most beautiful city in the whole of England. Yet over and over again the Victorians, revelling in their Gothic revivals, their turrets and ornaments, expressed their dislike of the beautifully balanced simplicity and austerity of the Georgian houses of their grandfathers.

According to Park, the first historian of Hampstead, by the end of the eighteenth century there were 691 inhabited houses in Hampstead and 47 uninhabited, and the population was 4,343, of whom only 199 were by this time engaged in agriculture. In 1813, about the time that Park was writing his history of the parish, it extended over 2,169 acres, of which between two and three hundred acres were waste. 'Houses stand thick in the town and besides these and the hamlets of West End, Kilburn, North End, Pond-Street, Chalcot and Frognal, houses are scattered occasionally over the greater part of the northern side of the parish,' he said.

Hampstead had its fairs, a full quota of inns and those popular eighteenth- and early nineteenth-century haunts of mild pleasure, the tea gardens.

The green at the bottom of Flask Walk, where the fair was first held in 1712, was far larger than it is today, and the fair continued for many years, but it became so noisy and riotous that in 1746, after repeated protests from nearby residents, the magistrates at Hick's Hall suppressed it. It did not die without a struggle, however, for two years later Thomas Keate of the Lower Flask made his public apology for what must have been a last effort to revive it.

Whereas I published an advertisement on Saturday last, declaring a sale of goods and toys to be held at Hampstead, which advertisement was addressed to persons usually frequenting Hampstead Fair, and occasioned great numbers of loose and disorderly people to resort to Hampstead, under the notion that the Fair suppressed two years since as illegal, would be revived, and held in the Flask Walk. . . . I take this publick opportunity to declare that I am extremely sorry that I should ignorantly be engaged to act in opposition to the Magistrates of the County, in any endeavour to revive a Fair deemed illegal by authority; and I hope this public acknowledgment of my error will satisfy their worships, and declaring that I will desist from any such attempt for the future.

> Thomas Keate.

A year or two later the races on the Heath, behind Jack Straw's Castle, were also suppressed, for although they had been a regular feature of Hampstead since they had first been run, in the early 1730s, as a counter attraction to the races at Belsize, they soon attracted a disorderly mob of tipsters and pickpockets which became difficult to handle.

Here under the village tree, at the top of Heath Street, George Whitfield preached one day in 1739. He took his station, he recorded in his diary, under a tree 'near the horse-course, in Hampstead. He had been invited to preach there, perhaps in an attempt to reach the hearts of the rowdies, but his audience, he said, were 'some of the politer sort'. He preached on the theme of our 'spiritual race' and he confessed that 'most were attentive, but others mocked'.

Two of the last notices of the races appeared in the *Daily Advertiser* in July 1748. On 19 July the paper announced: 'Tomorrow, the 20th inst, will be run for on Hampstead Course, a considerable sum, between two poneys, at the Castle on Hampstead Heath. There are great bets depending. The poneys will be rubbed down at the Castle aforesaid.' And a few days later the paper reported that 'On Wednesday a race was run on Hampstead Heath between a bay poney belonging to Lord Blessington, and a gray poney of Mr Woods, of Jack Straw's Castle, for a considerable sum of money, which was won by the former'

And after that there is no more reference to them.

Hampstead had another fair, which was held on the village green of the little hamlet of West End, just west of Frognal. By 1750 there were only forty houses in West End, but there is a record of this fair as early as 1708, when it was a simple matter of 'swings and roundabouts, penny trumpets, spiced gingerbread, and halfpenny rattles'.

An announcement on 2 July 1744 gave notice that:

> the Fair will be kept on Wednesday, Thursday and Friday next, in a pleasant, shady walk, in the middle of the town. On Wednesday a pig will be turned loose, and he that takes it up by the tail and throws it over his head shall have it. To pay twopence entrance, and no less than twelve to enter. On Thursday, a match will be run by two men, a hundred yards, in two sacks, for a large sum. And to encourage the sport, the landlord of the inn will give a pair of gloves, to be run for by six men, the winner to have them. And on Friday, a hat, value ten shillings, will be run for by men twelve times round the green: to pay one shilling entrance; no less than four to start. As many as will may enter, and the second man to have all the money above four.

By 1786 the fair was still going and had become rather more sophisticated, for in June of that year a bill announced that 'On Whit Tuesday was celebrated . . . a burlesque imitation of the Olympic Games. One prize was a gold-laced hat, to be grinned for by six candidates, who were placed on a platform with horses' collars to grin through.'

Each entrant had to grin by himself for five minutes and then they all grinned together in a row. The proceedings ended with the usual chase for the pig, with its tail shaved and soaped, and anyone who could catch it and throw it over his shoulder could keep it, but on this occasion it was the pig that won, for it led its pursuers such a dance for their money, running for miles all over the Heath, that in the end they gave up and let it go.

By the end of the century the fair had spread from West End Green to a field belonging to General Orde, where West End Lane station now lies, and early in the nineteenth century it was becoming a nuisance, attracting crowds of roughs from London. In 1812 the magistrates tried, unsuccessfully, to suppress it, as a nuisance, and it grew wilder each year. In 1819 some two hundred thugs arrived at the fair ground from London 'who assaulted the men and women with brutal violence, cutting their clothes from their backs', and the Hampstead magistrates had to call in the help of special constables to quell the ensuing riot.

Germain Lavie, one of the local magistrates, thereupon wrote to the Home Office with a renewed plea that the fair be suppressed.

'The getting rid of West End Fair appears absolutely necessary for the public peace,' he wrote. He referred to the earlier request for the ending of the fair and hinted darkly that it would have succeeded if some of the neighbouring residents had not been frightened by anonymous letters.

The extent of the fair had been increased when Harrington, a cow-keeper,

> who occupied a field belonging to Lady Headford at a very considerable distance from the original spot of the Fair presumed to let the Field to be used for additional Booths, Shows, etc.
>
> The outrages then committed were enormous, but notwithstanding, a Bill I preferred against Harrington on the part of Lady Headford and myself under the advice of Mr Gurney was thrown out by the Grand Jury at Clerkenwell, upon the plea that this Field formed part of the original Fair, the Grievance we complained of being merely of the increased nuisance which this occupation of the Field occasioned us.
>
> The Field was in consequence notwithstanding every remonstrance let again by Harrington on the late occasion, and notwithstanding the warning given to the Magistrates the outrages of last year were increased tenfold.
>
> Lady Headford is now determined to get rid by ejectment of this vile Tenant, but if she succeed there are other Fields in the neighbourhood which may and no doubt will be resorted to, and I am convinced that nothing will do but for such proceedings to be adopted as will get rid of the Fair altogether.
>
> The waste on which the original Fair is held is part of the Manor of Hampstead and Sir Thos Wilson, the Lord of the Manor . . . has been accustomed to receive moneis for the erection of the Booths, etc., but which he was ready to give up on the attempt formerly made to suppress the Fair.

He ended the letter by reminding the Government that the fair ground was less than two miles from the north west end of the town, easily approached through the fields from all directions, and he was certain that if it were not suppressed, the troubles of 1819 would be repeated and increased each year.

The same day as Germain Lavie sent this letter to the Home Secretary, the Hampstead magistrates, in support, passed a resolution recommending the appointment of a 'committee of respectable inhabitants to co-operate with them to secure the suppression of the fair', in which they spoke of 'the daring depredations and atrocious outrages committed at the last fair by large gangs of desperate thieves', and the riot and disorder 'productive of drunkenness and debauchery, and the practice of every species of vice and immorality'.

After all that, it was found that the fair was, in fact, illegal, having never been 'sanctioned by charter, special grant, privilege, prescription or otherwise', and it was brought to an end by 1820.

Of the Hampstead inns, a number have survived from the eighteenth century, although several disappeared when the alterations were made in the centre of the town in 1887.

The Green Man had replaced the Whitestone Tavern in Well Walk and the Lower Flask was not to be rebuilt as the Flask until 1874. The Duke of Hamilton at New End had been there since early in the century and the Old White Bear of Grove Place since 1704. In Heath Street there was an old inn, the Nag's Head, where the Cruel Sea was established a few years ago, but it has now taken on its original name of the Nag's Head. In the High Street was the White Hart, which has now gone, although the entrance to the yard, at number 17 High Street, is still there, the main part of the yard being now covered by Gayton Road. The original King of Bohemia was built late in the seventeenth century, named after James I's son-in-law, Frederick the Elector Palatine whose reign as King of Bohemia was so brief and inglorious, and the inn was set in an acre of garden and surrounded by eight acres of pasture land.

On the other side of the street, the King's Head was renamed the William IV, after the King had paid a visit to Ken House in 1835, but several other inns near here disappeared with the reconstruction of 1887. On Rosslyn Hill, then called Red Lion Hill, was the Red Lion, with the Load of Hay on Haverstock Hill: and this is by no means an exhaustive list.

Tea gardens were all the rage during the eighteenth century and there were a number in the rural suburbs of London. In Hampstead the two best known were the New Georgia and the gardens at the Spaniards, but many other old inns had tea gardens attached to them.

New Georgia was a cottage and tea house, with gardens at the back, which Robert Caston built in 1748 in Turner's Wood, close to Turner's house, the Firs, and the Spaniards Inn.

On Caston's two-storeyed cottage, which lay close to the roadway, he inscribed the following notice:

'I, Robert Caston, begun this place in a wild wood, stubbed up the wood, digged all the ponds, cut all the walks, made all the gardens, built all the rooms with my own hands. Nobody drove a nail here, or laid a brick, or a tile, but myself: and . . . thank God for giving me strength at sixty-four years of age, when I began it.'

Like Jenny's Whim in Pimlico, popular about the same time, and the much earlier Spring Garden near Whitehall Palace, fashionable during the reign of Charles I, Caston's New Georgia was full of tricks and practical jokes and 'humorous contrivances to divert the beholder'. Fierce artificial serpents would suddenly rear their heads through the shrubberies as, all unaware, you trod on the spring which released the mechanism, just as at Jenny Whim's 'up started different figures, some ugly enough to frighten you outright – a harlequin, a Mother Shipton, or some terrific animal'.

At New Georgia, Robert Caston described other delights. 'The gentleman is put in the pillory, and the ladies are obliged to kiss him, with such oddities; the building is irregular and low, of wood, and the ground and wilderness is laid out in a romantic taste.'

The Gentleman's Magazine described the chair made à la mode, 'and yet a stranger being persuaded to sit on it, shall have immediately his arms and thighs locked up, beyond his power to loosen them. . . . Put your foot in a slipper and a skeleton rises in front of you.' It wrote of a chair 'of a like kind, but not so innocent, which sinks into the ground on a person sitting on it, whereupon he finds himself amongst figures of apparently animated serpents and vipers'.

It was all very simple and ingenuous, but apparently the sudden appearance of the vipers, which popped up all round a visitor, looking ready to attack, was altogether too much for the nerves of some of the lady visitors and they were removed.

At the Spaniards close by the proprietor, William Staples, offered a counter-attraction when it was announced that his gardens were:

> improved and beautifully ornamented . . . out of a wild and thorny wood full of hills, valleys and sand-pits, [he] hath now made pleasant grass and gravel walks, with a mount, from the elevation whereof the beholder hath a prospect of Hanslope steeple, in Northampton-shire, within eight miles of Northampton; of Langdon Hills, in Essex, full sixty miles east; of Banstead Downs, in Surrey, south; and of Windsor Castle, Berkshire to the west. These walks and plats this gentleman hath embellished with a great many curious figures, depicted with pebble-stones of various colours.

Mr Staples also went in for mechanical tricks and surprises, and the 'curious figures' were inlaid at the sides of the paths which wound between the arbours and little summer houses and included pictures of the Tower of London, the twelve signs of the zodiac, the Colossus of Rhodes, the Pyramids, the Sphinx and similar 'marvels', all reminiscent of Don Saltero's 'knackatory' in Cheyne Walk.

The New Georgia and the Spaniards tea gardens were places of harmless amusement and the woodland surroundings were delightful. New Georgia disappeared, presumably when Robert Paston died, in the 1770s, but the tea gardens at the Spaniards continued long after the mound and the pebble figures had gone, for it was here that, in the early years of the nineteenth century, Mrs Bardell and her friends Mr and Mrs Raddle, Mrs Cluppins, Master Bardell, Mrs Sanders and Mrs Rogers came from the Goswell Road by a Hampstead stage, one sunny summer day, poor Mr Raddle being the only man of the party. And here they regaled themselves on tea and bread and butter, which seems to have been the limit of the menu in nearly all the tea gardens. While they were in the middle of this simple meal, young Mr Jackson, suitably embarrassed, arrived from Dodson and Fogg's in a hackney carriage, accompanied by the sinister, shabby Isaac, with his thick ash stick, and enticed Mrs Bardell back to London, on the plea of urgent legal business, and delivered her, all unsuspecting, into the Fleet prison, for not paying her lawyer's bill. And here, to add to her alarm and mortification, she came face to face with Mr Pickwick.

There was another tea garden near the Kilburn priory, where, early in the century, about the time that Duffield's spa in Well Walk was running into trouble, there had been an attempt to commercialise the healing properties of the waters of the holy well near the old priory. By this time hardly any of the old priory buildings were still standing, the hall, the chamber next to the church, the buttery, pantry and cellar, the prioress's room, the kitchen, larder, brewhouse and bakery, the chaplain's quarters, the confessor's chamber and the church having been left to crumble into ruins, although the orchard and the cemetery were probably still there. The land on which it stood, the copyhold forty-six acres of the Abbey farm, was owned by Richard Marsh, while the freehold farm of Shoot-Up Hill to the north belonged to Arthur Annesley Powell.

The mineral spring near the priory had been known since the sixteenth century, and after the Reformation and dissolution of the priory, a tavern and tea-garden known as Kilburn Wells had been built. By early in the eighteenth century, the spring, which bubbled up to a height of some twelve feet, was enclosed in a brick reservoir, and the waters acquired as great, if as spurious, a reputation as the Hampstead waters, for their curative properties.

14. Angela Burdett-Coutts.

15. Fenton House.

16. Church Row and St John's Parish Church, Hampstead.

17. Downshire Hill and St John's Church, Hampstead.

18. Holly Village.

19. (*Above*) Frognal Priory, 1832.

20. (*Below*) Highgate School.

"He's not much used to ladies society and it makes him bashful. If you'll order the waiter to deliver him anything short, he won't drink it off at once, won't he." only try him"

Page 407.

21. The tea-gardens at the Spaniards, Mrs Bardell being arrested – a famous scene from *The Pickwick Papers*.

22. Assembly and Pump Rooms, Well Walk, Hampstead.

23. The Heath near the Spaniards.

24. Leigh Hunt.

25. Samuel Taylor Coleridge.

Kilburn Water, late discovered (and much approved of for its purgative qualities) be good against all scorbutic humours, blotches, redness and pimples in the face, for inflammation of the eyes, and all impurities of the skin. It is successfully drank in pains occasioned by gravel, and all disorders of the kidneys: drank warm, works off without griping, and leaves no drought after operation, [ran a contemporary handbill, with a footnote added]: By advice of persons of honour and distinction, who have received great benefit by drinking this water, proper conveniences are made for gentlemen and ladies; and attendance is constantly given to deliver to any that shall send for or drink at the Wells.

By the mid-century the popularity of the Kilburn Wells tavern had been eclipsed by that of the nearby Bell, an old inn which had stood since 1600 and was suddenly revitalised by an enterprising landlord. The *Public Advertiser* for 17 July 1773 announced:

Kilburn Wells, near Paddington: The waters are now in the utmost perfection; the gardens enlarged and greatly improved; the house and offices re-painted and beautified in the most elegant manner. The whole is now open for the reception of the public, the great room being particularly adapted to the use and amusement of the politest companies. Fit either for music, dancing, or entertainments. This happy spot is equally celebrated for its rural situation, extensive prospects, and the acknowledged efficacy of the waters; it is most delightfully situated on the site of the once famous Abbey of Kilburn, on the Edgware Road, at an easy distance, being but a morning's walk from the metropolis, two miles from Oxford Street; the footway from the Mary-bone across the fields still nearer. A plentiful larder is always provided, together with the best of wines and other liquors. Breakfasting on hot loaves. A printed account of the waters, as drawn up by an eminent physician, is given gratis at the Wells.

The popularity of the chalybeate waters, selling at the Bell at 3d a glass, did not last long into the nineteenth century, but as a pleasant resort the place was immensely popular and remained so until 1829. About 1863 the Bell, which stood near the corner of Belsize Road and the Kilburn High Road, was pulled down and the brick reservoir demolished, to make way for a new pub.

VI

Hampstead in the Later Eighteenth Century — II

This was the Hampstead about which Samuel Richardson wrote in his novel *Clarissa*, which was published in seven succeeding volumes during 1747 and 1748. His Clarissa Harlowe was abducted by the perfidious Lovelace. With a promise of marriage he lured the innocent Clarissa from her home to a disreputable sponging house in Kentish Town, and then, in company with two of the women living there, had taken her for a drive to Hampstead. 'The coach carried us to Hampstead, to Highgate, to Muswell Hill; back to Hampstead, to the "Upper Flask". There, in complement to the nymphs, my beloved consented to alight and take a little repast.' They went for a walk on the Heath 'to view the varied prospects which that agreeable elevation affords' and then 'home early by Kentish Town'.

But Clarissa was no fool and when she realised what was happening, she managed to escape and found a hackney coach, in which there were only two passengers, both bound for the Upper Flask. She alighted when they did and 'she went into the house and asked if she could not have a dish of tea, and a room to herself for half an hour'. Then she emerged and found lodgings for herself at Mrs Moore's in the village. 'My heart misgave me at coming to this village, because I had been here with him more than once; but the coach hither was such a convenience that I knew not what to do better,' she wrote. However, she was not to rest for long. One of Lovelace's men had been following her and reported on her whereabouts, but before they could catch up with her she had seen them and begged Mrs Moore to help her.

'Let me look out?' she cried, looking desperately from her window. 'Whither does that path lead? Is there no probability of getting a coach? . . . Is that the way to Hendon? Is Hendon a private place? The Hampstead coach, I am told, will carry passengers thither.'

She indeed, went on towards Hendon, passing by the sign of the 'Castle' on the Heath, [wrote Richardson.] Then stopping, looked about her. . . . Then, turning her face towards London, she seemed, by the motion of her handkerchief to her eyes, to weep; repenting (who knows?) the rash step that she had taken. . . . Then, continuing on a few paces, she stopped again, and as if disliking her road, again seeming to weep, directed her course back to Hampstead.

Samuel Stanton was the proprietor of the Upper Flask at that time and in 1750 it passed, by inheritance, to Lady Charlotte Rich. Some years later she sold it to George Steevens, son of a wealthy East India merchant and annotator of Shakespeare, who turned the inn into a large Georgian mansion, known as Upper Heath, and here he lived until his death in 1800. But before this time, Steevens was living in Frognal and it was here that Dr Johnson may have visited him, when he came to Hampstead in 1746. At this time Johnson was only thirty-seven years old, a struggling author and journalist, desperately poor but already making his name and contributing regularly to the *Gentleman's Magazine.* He came to Hampstead for the sake of his difficult and ailing wife, an opium addict who was twenty-three years older than himself, and they stayed at Priory Lodge in Frognal, when it was still a small and modest house.

Johnson seems to have been devoted to his Tetty all his life, although Garrick, according to Boswell, said that 'her person and manner . . . were by no means pleasing'.

Johnson was not able to spend all his time in Hampstead with Tetty, although he visited her whenever he could, but the following year, in 1747, he was commissioned by the booksellers of London to prepare his dictionary, which kept him occupied for the next seven years. In 1748 he moved to his house in Gough Square, where his group of assistants laboured in the large attic. However, it was at Hampstead that he wrote the greater part of *The Vanity of Human Wishes.*

'I wrote the first seventy lines of *The Vanity of Human Wishes* in the course of one morning, in that small house beyond the church,' he said. 'The whole number was completed before I threw a single couplet on paper.'

When Tetty died in 1752 Johnson was heart-broken and he remained a widower for the remaining thirty-two years of his life, yet Boswell wrote:

I have, indeed, been told by Mrs Desmoulins, who before her marriage lived for some time with Mrs Johnson at Hampstead, that she indulged herself in the country air and nice living at an unsuitable expense, while her husband was drudging in the smoke of London, and that she by no means treated him with that complacency which is the most engaging quality in a wife. But all this is perfectly compatible with his fondness for her, especially when it is remembered that he had a high opinion of her understanding, and that the impressions which her beauty, real or imaginary, had originally made upon his fancy, being continued by habit, had not been effaced, though she herself was doubtless much altered for the worse.

And Johnson did once remark that a second marriage was the triumph of optimism over experience.

Living alone in Upper Heath, George Steevens brought out his first edition of Shakespeare in 1766, the year after Johnson after many delays had published his own edition of Shakespeare, which had brought him little credit and about which he himself was ill-pleased. However, in 1773, the year that Johnson set off for the Hebrides with Boswell, appeared another edition in ten volumes – the Johnson and Steevens edition – in which Johnson had given Steevens considerable help. Twenty years later, in 1793, nine years after Dr Johnson's death, Steevens brought out yet another edition of Shakespeare, in fifteen volumes. In this final edition, the volumes of which appeared over the course of eighteen months, he claimed to have 'freed it of servile adherence to the ancient copies' and to have expelled 'useless and supernumerary syllables, and an occasional supply of such as might fortuitously have been omitted'.

Steevens was a strange character, affected, inordinately conceited of his appearance, especially in his younger days, and morbidly offended at any hint of criticism. He was a distinguished classical scholar as well as a student of Elizabethan literature, and was said at one time to be 'lively, varied and eloquent' in his conversation, but after moving to Upper Heath he became increasingly a recluse. While his last edition of Shakespeare was being printed he would, according to Cradock, in his *Memoirs*, set out from his house in Hampstead, with the patrol, and walk to London before daylight. He called up his barber, in Devereux

Court, at whose shop he dressed for the day, changing from the garb of a country gentleman to that of a man of fashion. With him he brought the manuscript and proofs he had prepared the night before, which he delivered to his printer, so that there should be no delay. Then he usually went to the chambers of his friend Isaac Reed in Staples Inn, to read proofs for most of the day, although sometimes, for relaxation, he would attend the morning conversations of Sir Joseph Banks.

Dr Johnson disliked Steevens and said he considered him 'mischievous though not malignant'. He remained a bachelor all his life, his cousin Mrs Collinson and her daughters keeping house for him at Upper Heath, and although he was only sixty-four when he died he had by that time become so eccentric and ill-tempered that he seldom received visitors, and dark stories were told of 'mysterious doings', 'strange noises' and 'deep groans' coming from that elegant house at dead of night.

While Dr Johnson and Tetty were living at Hampstead another odd character, Mark Akenside, the poet-doctor, was living there. He was born at Newcastle in 1721, the son of a butcher, a humdrum origin, the knowledge of which tried him sorely as he rose in the world, as did the lameness he incurred through a childhood accident with his father's cleaver.

He was sent to the Newcastle grammar school, where he did well, and he was writing poetry while still a schoolboy. The Society of Dissenters lent him the money to train for the ministry, but after a year at Edinburgh University he changed his mind, paid back the money and studied medicine. He qualified at Leyden in 1744 and the same year published his long poem *Pleasures of Imagination*, which brought him fame in the world of letters although by no means universal acclaim. He tried his hand at more writing, without much success, started a medical practice in Northampton, which was a failure, and then came to London. Here his wealthy friend of the Edinburgh and Leyden days, Jeremiah Dyson, who later became Clerk to the House of Commons and a Lord of the Treasury, formed a romantic attachment to him, gave him an allowance of £300 a year and set up house with him at Golders Hill. Dyson bought the house in 1747 and it was a later owner, Sir Spencer Wells, who was to rebuild it as Golders Hill House.

Dyson hoped to establish Akenside as a physician to the wealthy and fashionable people of Hampstead. He took him everywhere – to the balls and entertainments at the Long Room, the clubs and the numerous assemblies. But Akenside just did not go down well, either with the men or the women. He was disliked for his cold and condescending manner, his sententiousness and affectation, and his overweening conceit. When the prosperous merchants and city men of Hampstead learned of his humble origins and, despite all his pretentions to superiority, his financial dependence on Dyson, they refused to accept him, and as for the women, he was 'too indifferent to feminine nature to ingratiate himself with their wives and daughters'.

He stayed at Golders Hill for less than three years and then Dyson bought him a house in Bloomsbury Square, presented him with a carriage and maintained the allowance. Akenside began to prosper. He became a Fellow of the Royal College of Physicians, senior physician at St Thomas's hospital and was eventually appointed physician to Queen Charlotte, whereupon, to the annoyance of the Whigs, he declared himself a Tory.

He wrote little more poetry, apart from a few odes, but set about revising and reconstructing his great three-volume poem. In 1757 the first book appeared in its new form, entitled slightly differently, to distinguish it from the first version, *The Pleasures of The Imagination*, and in 1765 the second book appeared, but in 1770 he died.

He was a man of considerable learning, but an affected snob who during his later years at St Thomas's earned the unpleasant reputation of gross carelessness when dealing with the poorest patients.

Among the distinguished and wealthy inhabitants of Hampstead there were some who, neither distinguished nor wealthy, achieved a brief notoriety in their day, among them Moll King, who settled herself on Haverstock Hill in one of the three small houses she owned there, not far from Steele's cottage.

She and her husband Tom had run the notorious Tom King's coffee house in Covent Garden Square, built up against the eastern portico of St Paul's church, at a time when the Finish, on the south side of the square, was the resort of footpads and highwaymen, and Mother Douglas's, on the north side, was where John Cleland's Fanny Hill found herself.

Tom King had been born a gentleman, but he ran away from Eton and married the wrong woman. After his death, Moll ran the coffee house by herself, entertaining the rakes of the town all through the night and providing them with prostitutes. 'The eminent, the eccentric, and the notorious in every walk of life were to be found nightly indulging their festivities within its famous precincts. . . . Moll King would serve chimney-sweeps, gardeners, and the market-people in common with her lords of the highest rank.'

At last the coffee house became so disreputable and scandalous that, in 1739, she was arrested, charged with keeping a disorderly house and committed to the King's Bench prison. By the time she was released, the coffee house had been pulled down and Moll retired to Hampstead, became a regular church-goer and lived in peace and propriety until 1747.

Twenty years later, in 1767, Nancy Dawson, the hornpipe dancer from *The Beggar's Opera*, retired and came to live on Haverstock Hill, in one of Moll King's cottages. Nancy's origins were obscure but her father seems to have been a porter in Clare market, which was close to Covent Garden, and Moll King had given her a helping hand in her early days.

The name of that most elusive of characters, Hannah Lightfoot, has sometimes been associated with Hampstead, although, like so much else about her, there is no real proof of where she may have lived after her disappearance. In fact the very name of Hampstead may have been confused with Hampton, where she is said to have married the young George III, just before his accession, at a time when he was thought to have been deeply in love with Lady Sarah Lennox.

Hannah was born in 1730 near Execution Dock in Wapping, where her father was a shoemaker, but two years later he died and in 1735 Mrs Lightfoot came with Hannah to live with her brother Henry Wheeler and his family, at their drapery business in St James's market, which lay to the west of the Haymarket, round about Jermyn Street, before the whole district was cleared for the building of Regent Street.

Both the Lightfoots and the Wheelers were Quakers and Hannah grew up as a member of the Society, a girl of exceptional beauty. The young Prince of Wales, living at Leicester House with his mother, Princess Augusta, who had been widowed in 1751, used to pass through the market when driving to St James's. He frequently caught sight of the beautiful Hannah and fell in love with her. By some means, perhaps with the co-operation of Elizabeth Chudleigh, the future Duchess of Kingston, who was at this time a maid of honour to his mother and also engaged in amorous dalliance with his grandfather, George II, a meeting was arranged; and in the greatest secrecy, the friendship between Hannah and the very young Prince grew. The Wheelers and the Court nevertheless came to hear what was happening and a hasty marriage was arranged for Hannah with another Quaker, Isaac Axford, which took place at Keith's chapel in Curzon Street on 11 December 1753, when Hannah was twenty-three and Axford nineteen.

For this marriage there is the evidence of the register, but at the chapel door, according to several accounts, Hannah was whisked away from her bridegroom and hustled into a coach, which was driven rapidly away. Axford declared that he set off on horseback, in hot pursuit, but the carriage gained on him, for at every turnpike the driver shouted 'Royal family' and the gates were immediately opened.

Neither he nor Hannah's family ever saw her again, although they advertised for her and made searching enquiries. After more than two hundred years, all must be conjecture, but it is thought that the young Prince of Wales, although he was not yet sixteen, kept her hidden away in some secret place which could have been Hackney or Hampstead or Hampton or Tottenham.

Another piece of definite evidence is that in 1756 Hannah was expelled from the Society of Friends, ostensibly for marrying out of the Society.

By 1759, Axford, assuming that Hannah was dead, or because the marriage had never been consummated, felt free to marry again. By this time the Prince of Wales had come of age, and the strong assumption is that he now married Hannah, since she was no longer legally tied to Axford, and had two children by her; and it was about this time that Sir Joshua Reynolds painted the portrait which is always said to be that of Hannah.

The following year, George II died and the young bridegroom became George III. Under strong persuasion from his mother and Lord Bute, he gave up the woman whom he had declared that he wanted to be queen, Lady Sarah Lennox, and accepted the bride chosen for him, the seventeen-year-old Princess Charlotte of Mecklenburg-Strelitz. Whether Lord Bute or the Queen knew about Hannah is not known. If they did, they ignored the fact, and in any case George was completely dominated by them.

What happened to Hannah? No one knows. There were many stories, one version being that she died in 1765 and was buried under another name in Islington churchyard.

During the King's reign there were many rumours and veiled hints in the press about the marriage to Hannah, the validity of his marriage to Queen Charlotte and the legitimacy of the future George IV and the Duke of York, but it was not until after his death in 1820 that the first detailed accounts, all of them hearsay, began to appear, corroborated by correspondents to the *Monthly Magazine* and *The Gentleman's Magazine*, and the first book on the subject was *The Secret History of the Court of England*, published in 1832 and written by Lady Elizabeth Hamilton, a descendant of his father's mistress, Lady Archibald Hamilton.

Increasingly throughout the eighteenth century, Hampstead became one of the most fashionable and desirable places to live in the vicinity of London. As happened at Highgate, several eminent men of law made their homes here, as they had in the past, from the time when Sir Roger de Brabazon, the Lord Chief Justice, had come to live at Belsize during the reign of Edward II. Judge's Walk, running into Branch Hill, just above Upper Terrace, is, in fact, said to have been the spot where during the Great Plague the judges held their courts under the trees, and it was once known as King's Bench Avenue.

As a student, William Murray, who was to become Lord Mansfield, Chief Justice of the King's Bench, had often stayed at the Chicken House, with fellow students, while it was still a respectable hostelry. He loved Hampstead and knew it well, and with the steady rise in his profession which brought him his peerage, he was able, in 1755, to buy Lord Bute's Ken House, just over the Highgate border, where he lived until his death in 1793.

During the early part of his time there one of his most distinguished neighbours, for some twelve months, though a bitter political opponent, was Lord Chatham, living in close retirement at North End House.

All his life William Pitt had suffered from bouts of a curious malady which was diagnosed as gout, although it was something more than that, for it was accompanied by periods of mental depression and instability which, in 1767, verged on insanity.

The illness attacked him during his schooldays at Eton and again at Cambridge, when ill-health forced him to leave before he had taken his degree.

In 1735, when he was twenty-seven, he entered Parliament as a Whig and quickly developed his gift of powerful and eloquent oratory and the use of a beautiful voice which, like that of an actor, had a wonderful range of tone. 'His words have sometimes frozen my young blood into stagnation, and sometimes made it pace in such a hurry through my veins that I could scarce support it,' said Lord Lyttelton.

Yet for years Pitt remained a back-bencher and by the time he was in his mid-forties, still a bachelor, he was a disappointed man, often crippled with gout, and thinking seriously of retirement from politics.

However, in 1754 he married Lady Hester Grenville, who was devoted to him. Not only did his fortune change but his health improved noticeably. In 1756 the Duke of Newcastle resigned office as Prime Minister and his successor, the Duke of Devonshire, appointed Pitt as Secretary of State and leader of the House of Commons. The

Seven Years' War had broken out and things were going badly for England. Pitt, with supreme self-confidence, said to his Prime Minister: 'My Lord, I am sure that I can save this country, and that nobody else can.'

The Duke of Devonshire was no leader for the crisis in which England found herself and resigned office, the Duke of Newcastle returning as First Lord of the Treasury and Prime Minister, while Pitt, as Secretary of State, had sufficient power to put his plans into operation. He was a brilliant war leader and planned the campaign in North America which, under the generalship of Amherst, Lawrence and Wolfe, and culminating in Wolfe's capture of Quebec, systematically reduced the French to total capitulation, laid the foundations of the British Empire and made England the most important country in the world and mistress of the high seas.

Before the war was over, George II died and the young George III came to the throne. Pitt was perhaps the most popular figure in the country at this time, and virtually Prime Minister. 'England has at last brought forth a *man*,' declared Frederick the Great, and Edmund Burke acclaimed him for the magnitude and greatness of his designs. But the new king set about removing Pitt and appointing his old friend and mentor, Lord Bute, as Prime Minister, and for the next five years Pitt was out of office.

Bute made himself so unpopular that, in 1763, he was forced to resign. The Rockingham ministry was even more disastrous and in 1766 the King was obliged to recall William Pitt, to form a ministry. At last he was the Prime Minister, but he was a sick man again and had been spending much of his time at Bath, desperately seeking a cure. He appointed his ministers but gave to himself the office of Lord Privy Seal, which involved his move to the House of Lords with the title of the Earl of Chatham.

He was no longer the 'Great Commoner'. His friends were dismayed, his enemies delighted. 'He has had a fall upstairs and has done himself so much hurt that he will never be able to stand upon his legs again,' wrote Lord Chesterfield to his son.

The accepted explanation for the move is that the new Lord Chatham, aware of his failing health and strength, wanted to spare himself the strain of the stormy debates of the Commons.

During the Christmas recess of that year, 1766, he went to Bath again and when Parliament met in the middle of January, 1767, he did not appear, remaining in Bath and too ill to travel. The cabinet met in consternation. News from the East India Company was disturbing, that from America even more alarming. They needed a man of Chatham's strength and vision to form a guiding policy. Word came that he had travelled from Bath to the Castle Inn at Marlborough, on his way back to London, but then there was silence again.

Charles Townshend, the Chancellor of the Exchequer, reimposed duties on American imports, including the fatal tax on tea which led to the final rebellion, and he also increased the land tax. The Opposition was up in arms and secured a defeat for Chatham's government. Chatham, with a supreme effort, managed to reach London, to reprimand Townshend, but before he had dismissed him, he was overcome once more with his malady. He was unable to discuss any affairs of state, retiring to North End House, which was then in the tenancy of Lord North, seeing no one and suffering a complete mental breakdown.

'Lord Chatham's state of health is certainly the lowest state of dejection and debility that mind and body can be in,' reported Grenville's secretary, after consulting with Lady Chatham. 'He sits all day leaning on his hands, which he supports on the table; does not permit any person to remain in the room; knocks when he wants anything; and, having made his wants known, gives a signal without speaking to the person who answered his call, to retire.'

For nearly a year he remained like this, spending most of his time in a small room, little more than a closet, on the third floor of North End House. There was an opening in the wall, about eighteen inches square, giving on to the staircase, with a door on either side of the wall, the inner door being padlocked. When meals or messages were taken to him, the messenger knocked on the outer door and placed them in the recess, and not until the Prime Minister heard the outer door shut again would he unlock the inner door, take them and lock himself up again.

Occasionally he would be driven about the lonelier parts of the Heath, in a carriage with drawn blinds, and there were probably very few, if any, people in Hampstead who knew who the occupant was.

Once, in a period of sanity, he offered his resignation to the King, but the King would not accept it, telling him that his name alone helped the government to steer its difficult course. By October of 1768 he was sufficiently recovered to move to Hayes in Kent, and here he finally resigned office, being succeeded by the Duke of Grafton. During the summer of 1769 the malady left him and apart from the severe gout in his foot he was normal again. In January of 1770 he re-appeared in the House of Lords, as vigorous as ever in his condemnation of the policy being adopted against the American colonies and the treatment of Wilkes, though grievously changed in appearance.

The Duke of Grafton resigned and Lord North became Prime Minister. Emaciated and crippled, Chatham continued to attend the House when he was able. In 1776 the American War of Independence, which he had tried so hard to avert, was declared. He was ill again and for the next two years was incapacitated, nursed by his devoted wife. Then he recovered sufficiently to appear again, protesting against the conduct of the war and declaring his 'eternal abhorrence of such preposterous and enormous principles'.

On 7 April 1778, he again attended the House of Lords, his eighteen year old son, William, and his son-in-law supporting the dying man. He rose to speak. Gradually a spark of the old grandeur came into his failing voice. 'Shall this great kingdom now fall prostrate before the House of Bourbon? If we must fall, let us fall like men!' he declared.

As the Duke of Rutland rose to reply, Chatham was seen to fall. He was carried to Downing Street and then back to Hayes, but a few weeks later he was dead.

For many years the room in North End House, where Chatham had endured his strange spell of mental disorder, was preserved, and the house, later known as Pitt House, or Wildwood House, or simply as Wildwoods, survived until 1952, when it was demolished, and two modern houses were built in the grounds. There is a plaque on the garden wall, commemorating the tragic year, and to add to the melancholy story is the legend that the garden was haunted by the ghost of a maid servant who, some time during the eighteenth century, was murdered by the butler in the summer house.

In 1788, the year that Lord Mansfield resigned office as Chief Justice of the King's Bench, to spend his remaining years in retirement at Ken House; Lord Erskine, the Lord Chancellor, came to live close by, at Evergreen Hill.

He was born in 1750, the youngest son of the impecunious Earl of Buchan, and because the family could afford nothing else for him, he became, at the age of fourteen, a midshipman on the *Tartar*, a man-of-war under the command of Sir David Lindsay, a nephew of Lord Mansfield. When his father died, he managed to buy his way into the 1st Regiment of Foot as an ensign, married, when he was only twenty, a niece of Sir John Moore, and spent the next two years in Minorca. But all the time his heart was in the law, and he had a profound contempt for many of the professional, aristocratic officers he met, 'these apes in embroidery,' who rise 'almost universally over the heads of officers grey with fatigue and rough with scars – whose courage and abilities yet preserve the honour of the English name – who, without money and without interest, languish in the subaltern ranks, unknown and unrespected'.

Back in London, he became a friend of Dr Johnson and was befriended by Lord Mansfield. With very little money to support himself and his family, he resolved to become a barrister. He sold his commission, entered Lincoln's Inn in 1775 and Trinity College, Cambridge in 1776, to keep his terms and eat the requisite number of dinners. For three years the family lived in lodgings in Kentish Town, subsisting mainly, he later declared, on cow heel and tripe. He was called to the bar in 1778 and less than six months later he achieved a success with his first case, which was so outstanding that his future career was assured. This was the affair of Captain Baillie, Lieutenant Governor of Greenwich Hospital, who had found many abuses there, but when he made them public he was suspended from office, at the instigation of Lord Sandwich, and sued for libel. Erskine won the day for Captain Baillie and the case was dismissed with costs.

Another of his famous cases was the trial of Lord Keppel on a charge of incapacity and misconduct at the battle of Ushant, in 1778, not long after Admiral Byng had been shot, after being found guilty on a similar charge.

Keppel's trial lasted for thirteen days. As it was a court martial, Erskine could not speak for Keppel, but he wrote his speech for him, with such force and clarity, that the Admiral was acquitted.

In case after case where men had been accused of high treason for the exposure of some clearly reprehensible abuse, he succeeded in obtaining an acquittal. In 1783 he entered the House of Commons as member for Portsmouth and with the famous trials of Hardy, Horne, Tooke and Thelwall, all of whom he defended successfully, he reached the heights of national popularity.

Yet in his private life he was a very simple man, happy with his family and his new home at Hampstead. Sir Egerton Brydges wrote,

At that time it was a very small place, and though commanding, from its elevation, a most extensive and splendid prospect, was entirely shut out from it by banks and hedgerow timber, so as to possess no beauty or interest whatever. The improvement and decoration of this spot has been the amusement of many years, and though attended with very considerable expense, by great additions to its extent, and by cultivation and ornament, has amply repaid its possessor, being now a most delightful retreat, though within an hour's distance of any part of London. It is so entirely shut out from the road between Hampstead and Highgate by walls and plantations, that no idea can be formed of it by a stranger to the place. Lord Erskine having ornameted it with evergreens of different descriptions, has lately given it the name of Evergreen Hill.

'Of this house we see little but its end, and a simple portico leading into it from the road,' wrote William Howitt, in his *Northern Heights of London.* 'A high wall shuts in what little of garden it has on that side, and another high wall shuts out from view the spacious gardens and grounds formerly belonging to it on the other side of the road.' These adjoined Ken Wood and were approached by a tunnel under the road, but they were later incorporated in the Mansfield estate. Howitt continued:

There is no grace of architecture about the building. It is simply a bald, square house, shouldered up against by another house at its back. We see, however, the tall windows of its large drawing-room on the second floor, commanding a splendid view over Caen Wood and some part of Highgate. Yet this was the house inhabited by Thomas Lord Erskine, contemporary with both the law lords, his neighbours, Mansfield and Loughborough. Here he converted the place from a spot of no account into a very charming residence. . . .

Lord Erskine was very much a family man and found time to relax with his wife and children and to superintend the alterations to his gardens.

'I am now very busy flying my boy's kite, shooting with a bow and arrow, and talking to an old Scotch gardener six hours a day about the same things, which, taken altogether, are not of the value or importance of a Birmingham halfpenny, and scarcely up to the exertion of reading the daily papers,' he wrote to a friend from Evergreen Hill, but he also gave gay and brilliant parties here, which included the Duke of Norfolk, Lord Grenville, Lord Grey and Lord Holland. On these occasions, politics were hardly mentioned and all parties were welcomed. Lord Byron, Fanny Burney, Lady Morgan, Hannah More and Anna Seward were his friends and also Edmund Burke, until, frightened by the French Revolution, Burke turned Tory, but just before he died he came to Evergreen Hill to make his peace with his old friend.

Lord Erskine was a man of many parts, a great orator on the side of liberty and truth, with a beautiful voice and compelling personality. He loved animals and in addition to his dogs, had a favourite goose which followed him about the grounds, a macaw and two pet leeches which had once saved his life and which he called Howe and Clive.

In 1806 he became Lord Chancellor, and this was the year that both Lord Chatham's son, William Pitt, and Charles James Fox died. With the ministry of Lord Grenville which followed, Lord Erskine lost the Chancellorship, but still exerted his influence for the promotion of human freedoms. He advocated concessions to the Catholics and in 1809 was bringing in the first bill for the prevention of cruelty to animals, at a time when dog-fighting, cock-fighting, bear-baiting and bull-baiting were acceptable and popular. Neither this attempt nor the second was successful, but his work and enthusiasm for the cause of animals led, before long, to the foundation of the Royal Society for the Prevention of Cruelty to Animals.

His wife died in 1805 and some years later he sold Evergreen Hill, which was to become known as Erskine House, transferring the copyhold to the second Lord Mansfield. He bought an estate in Sussex and also had a town house in Pimlico. As late as 1820 he was defending the persecuted Queen Caroline in the House of Lords, against George IV, demanding for her a list of all the witnesses against her, and resisting at every stage the 'Bill of Pains and Penalties' against her; and he was successful in having it thrown out.

By this time he had made a second marriage and dissipated a large part of his fortune, but in 1823, at the age of seventy-two, he died.

Alexander Wedderburn, the Scottish lawyer who was to become Lord Chancellor and the Earl of Rosslyn, and was living in Hampstead at the same time as Lord Mansfield and Lord Erskine, was a very different character. Like his father and grandfather, he was trained for the law, and after leaving Edinburgh University he came to London, to enter the Inner Temple. He was ruthlessly ambitious, and to rid himself of his Scottish accent and develop his powers of oratory, he studied under Dr Sheridan, the father of Richard, and Charles Macklin.

Wedderburn had little success during his first years in London, but he assiduously cultivated the right people and joined the right clubs and eventually made himself known to Lord Bute; and when, with the accession of George III, Lord Bute became Prime Minister, he brought Wedderburn into Parliament as member for Rothesay and Inverary. With the fall of Lord Bute three years later, Wedderburn astutely changed his politics and became a staunch Whig, but in supporting Wilkes he went too far and lost his seat. However, with the help of Lord Clive he was soon back in Parliament, as member for Bishops Castle, and was advocating the liberty of the Press and sympathising with the American colonists.

During the next session he changed his politics again, whereupon Junius declared that 'there was something about him that even treachery could not trust'; but nevertheless, to the fury of the Whigs, he was made Solicitor-General. His conduct, said Lord Campbell, was 'one of the most flagrant cases of *ratting* in our party annals'.

Even Wedderburn was embarrassed by the contempt of his allies and for the next few years he behaved with propriety and urged several obviously needed reforms. The right of reporting Parliamentary debates was established. He asserted the copyright of an author to his work and advocated the right of laymen to be admitted to the universities without religious qualifications. In 1773 he successfully defended Lord Clive, during the investigation of his conduct in India. This was the year that he married a rich Yorkshire heiress and established himself amongst the aristocracy in Lincoln's Inn Fields, and to add to his rising prosperity and grandeur, Lord Clive, as a token of his gratitude, presented him with a country house at Mitcham.

The following year Wedderburn caused a sensation which was to have far-reaching results. Benjamin Franklin, the political agent in England of the American colonies, had acquired some private correspondence between the Governor and Lieutenant Governor of Massachusetts and the private secretary of George Grenville, in which the American governors recommended that England should send a military force to America, to quieten the tax rebels.

Franklin applied for the removal of the governors from office, but Wedderburn, for the Privy Council, defended them, accusing Franklin, in a tirade of scathing contempt, of stealing Grenville's correspondence. Franklin's case was declared 'false, groundless, vexatious and scandalous', and Franklin departed from England, vowing never to return.

When the American War of Independence broke out, two years later, Wedderburn supported England's resistance with all his powers of compelling oratory, and, more than any other man, deepened the bitterness between the two sides. And the dying Lord Chatham was powerless to oppose him and try to heal the breach.

About this time Wedderburn moved to Branch Hill Lodge, where so many lawyers had lived before him, among his predecessors being Sir Thomas Clarke, Master of the Rolls, the third Lord Macclesfield, grandson of Lord Chancellor Macclesfield, who had incurred a fine of £30,000 and a term of imprisonment in the Tower for corruption, and Thomas Walker, a Master in Chancery.

In 1780 Wedderburn was made Chief Justice of the Common Pleas and elevated to the peerage, with the title of Lord Loughborough, Earl of Rosslyn. This was the year of the Gordon riots and he was merciless in his punishments, ordering the execution of scores of the rioters. Burke protested that in his address to the jury Wedderburn had prejudged the case and Lord Brougham said his conduct of the trial was a 'denial of whatever could be alleged in extenuation of the offender's conduct, without reference to age or degree of culpability'.

Yet nothing seemed to curb the steady course of his career. In 1782, the year of his second marriage, he was made Commissioner of the Great Seal, and in 1788, during the King's first serious bout of insanity, he urged the right of the Prince of Wales to become Regent. Over this, he was defeated by Pitt's government, whereupon he joined forces with Charles James Fox and the Prince of Wales's circle. However, Pitt wooed him back from Fox and in 1797 he realised his ultimate ambition and was made Lord Chancellor. In this year he bought Shelford Lodge, which he renamed Rosslyn House. It stood on Red Lion Hill, which soon became known as Rosslyn Hill, and was on the Chesterfield estate of the Dean and Chapter lands of Westminster.

Lord Rosslyn was a hated man, as ruthless as ever Judge Jeffreys had been, and was merciless to the poor, even denying them the right to glean in the cornfields after the harvest. As late as 1769 there had been a hundred and sixty offences for which the penalty was death or transportation, and the number was reduced only very slowly. He condemned children of fourteen to be hanged for the smallest offences and George Selwyn, who never missed a hanging if he could help it, said that he 'never saw boys cry so much in his life'.

Yet at Shelford Lodge he lived in princely splendour. It was originally a square house with a high-pitched roof in the centre and square turrets with pyramidal roofs at each corner, rather like a small French château, but he blurred the basic design of the house by adding a large ballroom, some thirty-four feet long, to the west side of the house, with a large room above it. Here he entertained the Prince of Wales and leaders of the Whig party, including Charles James Fox, Sheridan and Burke on occasion, but also, when the moment was favourable, the Tory leaders Pitt, Windham and the Duke of Portland.

His style of living was most splendid, wrote Lord Campbell.

Ever indifferent about money, instead of showing mean contrivances to save a shilling, he spent the whole of his official income in official splendour. Though himself very temperate, his banquets were princely; he maintained an immense retinue of servants, and, not dreaming that his successor would walk through the mud to Westminster, sending the Great Seal thither in a hackney coach, he never stirred about without his two splendid carriages, exactly alike, drawn by the most beautiful horses, one for himself, and another for his attendants. Though of low stature and slender frame, his features were well chiselled, his countenance was marked by strong lines of intelligence, his eye was piercing, his appearance was dignified, and his manners were noble.

During the Napoleonic wars he seemed to exult in the most stringent anti-Jacobin measures, suggesting the Traitorous Correspondence Bill, which would have meant hanging, drawing and quartering for anyone corresponding with a Frenchman. He urged the suspension of the Habeas Corpus act, strenuously opposed any suggestion of Parliamentary reform and any peace with France, and when, in 1801, Pitt drew up his plan for Catholic emancipation, despite all that had gone before, he urged the King to reject it, reminding him of his coronation oath.

Pitt was forced to resign, but that same year the King dismissed Lord Rosslyn and appointed Lord Eldon in his place.

Although Lord Rosslyn moved to a house near Slough, in order to be near the Court at Windsor, he never recovered his influence and shortly afterwards he died. When the King heard the news, he said: 'He has not left a greater knave behind him in my dominions!' and Lord Brougham described him as a man of,

shining but superficial talents, supported by no fixed principles, embellished by no feats of patriotism, nor made memorable by any monuments of national utility; whose life being at length closed in the disappointment of mean and unworthy desires and amidst universal neglect, left behind it no claim to the respect or gratitude of mankind, though it may have excited the admiration or envy of the contemporary vulgar.

Before Lord Rosslyn departed so ingloriously from Hampstead another lawyer, destined for high office, was living close at hand. This was Sir Spencer Perceval, son of the second Earl of Egmont. Born in 1762 he had married, in 1790, Jane, daughter of Sir James Spencer

Wilson, Lord of the Manor of Hampstead, still an absentee landlord, living at the family seat at Charlton.

For many years after the death of Howell, in about 1742, Belsize House had stood empty and neglected, gradually falling into ruin. At some time it was restored and partially rebuilt. There are no records to say when or by whom this work was done, but prints of the house at this period show it as a handsome, plain Georgian mansion, with three storeys above a basement, two short wings and a simple, pillared portico, approached by a shallow flight of steps. There seem to have been several occupants of the house after its restoration, and in 1798 the Percevals moved in, with their already large family. Sir Spencer had entered Parliament two years earlier, as member for Northampton, and was a staunch Tory all his life, respected and admired by both Pitt and Addington.

From Belsize he would ride every day, over the fields of Chalcots, to Westminster, a simple family man of probity, in contrast to his flamboyant neighbour, Lord Rosslyn. In 1801 Addington appointed him Solicitor-General, and he remained in office when Pitt succeeded; but after Pitt's death, he refused to serve under the Whig Lord Grenville. In 1807 the Tories were back in power and the Duke of Portland appointed Perceval his Chancellor of the Exchequer and leader of the House of Commons. The Percevals, with their eleven children, left Belsize House for Downing Street. In 1809, Sir Spencer became Prime Minister, but only two and a half years later he was murdered in the lobby of the House of Commons, shot through the heart by the assassin Bellingham, who had a grievance against the government not remotely concerned with Perceval.

Bellingham freely confessed that he had nothing against the Prime Minister personally, and he was undoubtedly mad, but he refused to plead insanity and was duly tried, condemned and hanged within a week of the murder.

While these great political figures were living in their splendid eighteenth-century mansions, and the merchants and bankers in a style almost as grand, there were many lesser men of the law, barristers and solicitors, as well as the other professions, living in Hampstead during these years, in the smaller terrace houses of the old town.

In 1775 the people of Hampstead waxed indignant over the affair of Mrs Lessingham, an actress from Covent Garden who was 'under the protection' of Mr Justice Addington. Mrs Lessingham had a fancy to build a house for herself on the waste of the Heath, where so many had built before her. She applied to the Lord of the Manor, who, with the consent of the copyholders, had the right to grant his permission for her to build, and it was duly given, although it would appear that, on this occasion, the formality of seeking the consent of the copyholders had been omitted.

Building began on the house which Wyatt had designed for Mrs Lessingham, on the north-west side of the Heath, but the copyholders and commoners of Hampstead suddenly took exception, protesting that Mrs Lessingham was not a copyholder and therefore had no right to enclose any part of the Heath. Not only did they protest to the Manor Court, but in no uncertain way took positive action, by demolishing the work of the bricklayers as they began building operations.

'A battle of a very sanguinary nature is reported to have taken place between the bricklayers and the constables,' recorded Park.

George Steevens, installed in Upper Heath, was a protagonist of Mrs Lessingham, for his own house had been built on the waste, but the copyholders took the case to the Court of Common Pleas. The court action which followed is interesting, because of the mid-nineteenth century agitation in regard to the rights of enclosure and ownership of the Heath.

Before the copyholders' case was heard, Mrs Lessingham was advised to make herself a copyholder, by buying a small copyhold cottage. This she did, but, nothing daunted, the copyholders brought their case against her for encroachment and injury to their rights of pasturage. They were on uncertain ground, for they and their predecessors had been guilty of just such encroachment for generations. The Judge declared that the grant of the land was 'a reserved right of the Lord of the Manor' and the jury found that the land was of no value in any case, and the plaintiffs had suffered no loss. So Mrs Lessingham won the day and the building of Heath Lodge and the enclosing of the garden proceeded, but the real issue of whether the Lord of the Manor had, in fact, the right to grant the land without the consent of the copyholders remained unchallenged.

Mrs Lessingham lived at Heath Lodge until her death in 1783, which was the same year that a far less distinguished Hampstead resident also died, and was buried in Hampstead churchyard. This was Miss West, said to have been the most accomplished pickpocket of her day. She had been compared with Jenny Diver, but was far luckier than Jenny, for she had been spared to end her days in peaceful retirement in Hampstead; and when she died, she left £3,000, 'the fruits of her industry'. This she bequeathed to her two children, one of whom had been born in Newgate Prison, where Miss West was spending a year, for picking a pocket in a room over the Exeter Exchange, while the body of Lord Baltimore was lying there in state.

Dr Johnson, his health fast failing, visited Hampstead again for a brief spell in 1784, a few months before his death at the end of the year, and in 1785 Mrs Barbauld and her husband Rochemont came to live at number 8, Church Row.

Although she is never read today and her books have been long out of print, Anna Letitia Barbauld was much read and esteemed in her day, for her poetry and essays and her books for children, amongst her admirers being Queen Charlotte.

She was born in 1743 at Kibworth Harcourt in Leicestershire, where her father, the Reverend John Aikin, kept a boys' school, and here she received the same classical education as the pupils and her brother John. In later years she claimed that she could just remember, although at the time she was only two years old, the excitement and alarm in the family at the news that the Jacobite army had entered England, for Kibworth was on the main highway to London.

In 1758 Dr Aikin became classical tutor at the new Dissenting Academy opened at Warrington and here Anna lived for the next fifteen years, devoted to her father, although there was little sympathy between herself and her mother.

The Academy lasted for less than thirty years, not surviving the death of Dr Aikin in 1781 and several of the other tutors, who had been there since the beginning, but in its day it was an intellectually stimulating place, and amongst its interesting visitors was John Howard. His education had been left to parsimonious guardians who had put him into the care of a schoolmaster so incompetent that all his life John Howard was never able to write English correctly, and he brought his manuscripts and proofs up to Warrington, for young John Aikin to correct and revise.

In 1773 Anna published her first book of poems, which was well reviewed, warmly praised and ran into four editions in the first twelve months. She received dozens of letters from both friends and strangers, amongst them one from Mrs Montagu in Hill Street, warm and friendly, if somewhat impertinent in parts: '. . . I made many enquiries into your character as soon as I was acquainted with your works, and it gave me infinite pleasure to find the moral character returned the lustre it received from the mental accomplishments.'

The following year Anna published another volume of poems and essays, in collaboration with her brother John, entitled *Miscellaneous Pieces in Prose*, by J. and A. L. Aikin, which proved just as successful,

but it was at this time that she made the false step of marrying
Rochemont Barbauld. He was a young Frenchman descended from a
family of fugitive Huguenots, and had been sent to the Warrington
Academy to train for the ministry. Although he had decided by this
time that the ministry was not for him, and he had neither money nor
prospects, he proposed to Anna and was accepted.

> Her attachment to Mr Barbauld was the illusion of a romantic fancy –
> not of a tender heart, [wrote her niece, Lucy Aikin, in later years.]
> Had her true affections been early called forth by a more genial home
> atmosphere, she would never have allowed herself to be caught by
> crazy demonstrations of amorous rapture set off with theatrical
> French manners, or have conceived of such exaggerated passion as a
> safe foundation on which to raise the sober structure of domestic
> happiness. . . . She was informed by a true friend that he had
> experienced one attack of insanity, and was urged to break off the
> engagement on that account. 'Then' answered she, 'If I were now to
> disappoint him, he would certainly go mad.'

Poor Mr Barbauld was an amiable enough man when he was sane,
but he was subject to fits of ungovernable temper and insane jealousy,
which made Anna's life increasingly miserable; yet she maintained an
amazingly courageous and calm front to the world, even when people
asked her why she had given up writing her poetry, and few knew the
real state of affairs.

The young couple moved to Palgrave in Suffolk, where Rochemont
opened a boys' school and also accepted the charge of a dissenting
congregation. The school was very successful in the first few years and
Anna herself took charge of the teaching of the youngest boys. Finding
that there were very few books published yet for little children and their
elementary instruction, she set about writing some herself, for her
young pupils and also her small nephew Charles, whom she had
adopted.

She began by publishing a volume of devotional pieces compiled
from the Psalms and *Hymns in Prose for Children*. Many of her friends
were disappointed. Dr Johnson remarked:

> I hate by-roads to education. Education is as well known, and has
> long been as well known, as it ever can be. Suppose they have more
> knowledge at five or six years old than other chilren, what use can be
> made of it? . . . Too much is expected of precocity, and too little
> performed. . . . Miss Aikin was an instance of early cultivation, but in

what did it terminate? In marrying a little Presbyterian parson, who keeps an infant boarding-school, so that all her employment is 'to suckle fools and chronicle small beer'.

However, these books filled a long-felt need for parents and those engaged, as she was, in teaching the very young, and they sold in thousands and went through many editions.

The Barbaulds spent each winter holiday in London, and in January of 1784 Anna was writing to her brother of a party she had attended at Mrs Chapone's, and of a visit to the theatre to see Hannah More's new play *Percy*. ★ She says that Mrs Montagu, 'not content with being the Queen of literature and elegant society, sets up for the Queen of fashion and splendour. She is building a very fine house . . . and I am afraid will be as much the woman of the world as the philosopher.'

'. . . Miss Burney is the object of public curiosity,' she wrote. 'I had the pleasure of meeting her yesterday. She is a very unaffected, sweet and pleasing young lady. . . .'

Sad to relate, Fanny Burney did not feel the same about Mrs Barbauld and spoke of her 'set smile, her air of determined complacency and prepared acquiescence, also of a sweetness which never risks being off guard'.

Dr Johnson had recently died and the Barbaulds were 'reading in idle moments, Boswell's long-expected life of Johnson. . . .' 'Johnson, I think, was far from a great character,' Anna wrote to her brother. 'He was continually sinning against his conscience and then afraid of going to Hell for it.'

In 1768, having stayed in Hampstead for a few months, they settled at number 8 Church Row, where Rochemont kept a small school for boys and also became pastor of the Dissenting Chapel on Red Lion Hill.

Hampstead is certainly the pleasantest village about London, [Anna was writing to her brother that year]. The mall of the place a kind of terrace, which they call Prospect Walk, commands a most extensive and varied view. . . . Hampstead and Highgate are mutually objects to each other, and the road between them is delightfully pleasant. . . . On observing the beautiful smoothness of the turf in some of the fields about this place, I was told, the gentlemen to whom they belonged had them rolled like a garden plot.

'. . . I pity the young ladies of Hampstead,' she wrote, on another occasion, 'there are several very agreeable ones. One gentleman in

★ A tragedy, first produced by Garrick at Drury Lane in 1777.

particular has five tall marriageable daughters, and not a single young man is to be seen in the place, but of widows and old maids such a plenty.'

'Hampstead was then even more secluded than its distance from town seemed to warrant, the hill apparently being considered almost inaccessible,' wrote her niece, Anna Le Breton, in her Memoir of her aunt, and she quotes from Rochemont's diary, in which he frequently spoke of being prevented from going to town because of the bad state of the roads, while the stage coach passengers always had to alight and walk up the hill.

Anna Barbauld wrote some of her prose essays while living in Church Row and also contributed to her brother's famous talks for children *Evenings at Home*. She met Samuel Hoare and his family, who in 1790 were established at Heath House, and also the young Joanna Baillie, who was about to move from Church Row into Bolton House, with her sister, after the death of their mother. She corresponded with Hannah More and met again Samuel Rogers, who was an old friend of the Aikin family. In October, 1788, Anna was writing to him.

> Your visit was so short that we wish to think of anything which may induce you to make a longer, and as we are to have an assembly at the Long Room, on Monday next, the 2nd, which they say will be a pretty good one, I take the liberty to ask whether it will be agreeable to you to be of our party, and in that case, we have a bed at your service. . . . Our dinner hour, if you can give us your company to dinner, is half after three.

She also corresponded with Maria Edgeworth and in London met Sir Walter Scott.

In 1798 her brother, Dr Aikin, had a severe illness and had to give up his London medical practice and retire to Stoke Newington. Rochemond Barbauld was growing more difficult each year. He and Anna left Church Row and lived for a few months at Heddon House, on the west side of Rosslyn Hill, a house 'standing in the high road at the entrance of the village, quite surrounded by fields,' but his condition grew steadily worse, and in 1802 Anna persuaded him to move to a house in Stoke Newington, near her brother.

Rochemont's insanity increased. One day at dinner he grabbed a knife from the table and chased Anna round the room, and she escaped with her life only by climbing out of the window. He was moved to a house close to her nephew's, in the charge of a keeper, but one day in

1808 he bribed the man to allow him out alone, and some time later his drowned body was found in the New River.

Anna Barbauld lived on at Stoke Newington until 1825, surviving her brother by four years, and during this time of her widowhood she turned to more philosophical writing, including critical essays on Akenside and Collins, four editions of their works, and a life of Richardson, as well as editing a collection of British novelists, with an introductory essay and biographical and critical notes: and she also wrote many more poems.

Fanny Burney had published *Evelina* in 1778, and it had won her instant acclaim from Dr Johnson, Mrs Thrale and their illustrious friends. Four years later she published *Cecilia*, and not long afterwards, during a visit to Mrs Delaney at Windsor, she was introduced to the King and Queen, with whom she quickly became a favourite. At the time that Anna Barbauld met her, in 1786, Fanny had just accepted the post of second keeper of the robes to Queen Charlotte, an appointment which she grew to detest, mainly because of the disagreeable behaviour and jealousy of Mrs Schwellenberg, with whom she shared her court duties.

In *Evelina*, Fanny Burney gave a description of a public ball at the Long Room at Hampstead, which must have been a very different affair from the assembly to which Mrs Barbauld invited Samuel Rogers ten years later.

Evelina had not the slightest wish to go to the Hampstead ball, but Mr Smith pressed the tickets on her and her grandmother, Madame Duval, who insisted that they went. Mr Smith had hired a hackney coach for the occasion, and Evelina hated every minute of the evening. Both Mr Smith and Madame Duval were vulgarly over-dressed, Evelina considered, and the old lady was wearing far too much rouge. The Long Room, she wrote later to Mr Villars, 'seems very well named, for I believe it would be difficult to find any other epithet which might, with propriety, distinguish it, as it is without ornament, elegance, or any sort of singularity, and merely to be marked with its length'.

To the relief of Evelina and the chagrin and frustration of Mr Smith, Madame Duval insisted on dancing the first two dances with him. Then she told him to ask the master of ceremonies to arrange a minuet, and invited a complete stranger to dance it with her, cutting such an odd figure that everyone laughed at her. 'Mr Smith,' said Evelina, 'was so ill-bred as to laugh at her openly, and to speak of her with as much ridicule as was in his power'.

Then there were more country dances and Madame Duval pounced on Mr Smith again, leaving Evelina alone. When a young man asked her to dance with him she refused politely and 'very much rejoiced at being relieved from this troublesome young man; but scarce had I time to congratulate myself, before I was accosted by another'. He bruised Evelina's susceptibilities by begging 'the favour of hopping a dance with her'. She said firmly that she did not dance at all. Several other young men spoke to her, 'of whom the appearance and language were equally inelegant and low-bred' and she soon found her situation both disagreeable and improper. Relief came when Madame Duval at last tired of dancing and announced that she would retire to the card tables and Evelina could dance with Mr Smith. But Evelina was prepared, and to Mr Smith's fury she said demurely that, as she had already turned down several offers to dance, it would not appear seemly for her to dance now with Mr Smith. And she spent the rest of that disastrous evening standing behind her grandmother's chair in the card room, until it was time to return to London in the coach.

Joanna Baillie was born in 1762, at her father's manse at Bothwell, in Lanarkshire. It was a dour and cheerless household, where 'repression of all emotions, even the gentlest and those most honourable to human nature, seems to have been the constant lesson,' but after her father's death in 1784, Joanna, her elder sister Agnes and their mother came to London, living for some years in Church Row: and it was at that time that Anna Barbauld, by then in her forties and already a literary figure, would sometimes meet the two shy young Baillies, both still in their twenties, during their walks on the Heath.

In 1790 Joanna published her first volume of verse, anonymously. It had a modest success, but her renown came with the appearance of the first volume of her *Plays on the Passions*, in 1798, the best of which *De Montfort*, was presented at Drury Lane in 1800 by John Kemble, Kemble playing the part of De Montfort and his sister, Sarah Siddons, that of Jane de Montfort.

Mrs Barbauld, writing to a friend at this time, said:

I have received great pleasure lately from the representation of *De Montfort* a tragedy, which you probably read a year and a half ago in a volume entitled *A Series of Plays on the Passions*. I admired it then, but little dreamed I was indebted for my entertainment to a young lady of Hampstead whom I visited, and who came to Mr Barbauld's Chapel all the while with as innocent a face as if she had never written a line.

Sir Walter Scott was a great admirer of Joanna Baillie and her plays and made a point of calling on her when he visited London. This was in 1806, the year that Mrs Baillie died and Joanna and Agnes moved to Bolton House, on Holly Bush Hill at the foot of Hampstead Grove. They lived there for the next forty or fifty years, until Joanna died in 1851, at the age of eighty-eight, and Agnes ten years later, when she was over a hundred.

In 1802 the second volume of *Plays on the Passions* appeared, and four years after the move to Bolton House, Joanna wrote the Scottish tragedy *The Family Legend*, which was staged in Edinburgh with a prologue written by Scott and with Sarah Siddons again in the lead, and later it had a London production.

Although Scott admired Joanna Baillie's work so much and hinted that it had in it a suggestion of Shakespeare's 'inspired strain', and although Byron once said that she was the only woman who could write a tragedy, her plays were essentially literary exercises and not really acting plays. All too often the plots were obvious from early in the first acts and there was not enough light and shade or dramatic tension. When *De Montfort* was revived, in 1821, with Edmund Kean playing De Montfort, he admitted as much, although he said the play was a fine poem.

Nevertheless, Joanna Baillie, who was an unassuming and charming person, had a devoted following in her day, and at one time had two plays running in London at the same time, *Separation* at Covent Garden and *Henriquez* at Drury Lane. She also wrote many songs and short poems. Sir Walter Scott said that her society was one of the chief pleasures which a visit to London had in store for him, and amongst the circle of distinguished friends who made their way through the large iron gates and up the garden path to the tall, Georgian house were Wordsworth, Sir David Wilkie, Crabb Robinson, Jeffrey of the *Edinburgh Review*, Marie Edgeworth and the Baillies' next door neighbours, John Merivale, a barrister and writer, and his wife, who were also close friends of the Longmans.

With the outbreak of the French Revolution a number of refugees, fleeing to England, settled in Hampstead. At one time there were said to be about two hundred, amongst them the Abbé Morel, who had been connected with the Grand Seminary at Bourg and reached Hampstead in 1796. He conducted services in French for his fellow exiles, first at Fenton House and then at Oriel House, which then stood at the end of Church Row, with its large oriel window looking westwards towards the Church, the back of the house giving on to Little Church Row.

There was another distinguished arrival in Hampstead in 1796, while Joanna Baillie and Anna Barbauld were still living in Church Row. This was George Romney, at the end of his career, lonely and in ill-health, who moved into a house on Holly Bush Hill, at the bottom of Hampstead Grove, for a time.

Joshua Reynolds, Thomas Gainsborough and George Romney were the three great English portrait painters of the eighteenth century. Reynolds and Gainsborough were rivals all their lives, until the final reconciliation, when Gainsborough was dying, but Romney never exhibited at the Royal Academy and would have no dealings with Reynolds, who was its first president.

Romney was born in 1734 of a poor Lancashire family and had little formal education, but when he was twenty he met a second-rate artist, Christopher Steele, who earned a living by travelling through the countryside, painting inexpensive portraits. Seeing Romney's gift for portraiture, Steele accepted him as an apprentice and took him with him on his journeys, but shortly afterwards Romney fell ill and Steele had to go on without him. Romney was tenderly nursed by his landlady's daughter, a maid servant, Mary Abbott, who probably saved his life. In a fit of youthful, impetuous gratitude, he married her: but he had no money, and when he was well enough, he had to leave her and join Steele again, while Mary returned to domestic service.

After a few years, Romney managed to buy his freedom from apprenticeship and took Mary to Kendal for a time, where he earned a living by painting portraits at two guineas at time. By 1762 he had saved £100 and decided to try his fortune in London, leaving Mary with £70 for herself and their two small daughters and taking the remaining £30 for himself.

His first work in London was a historical picture – 'The Death of Wolfe' – for which a prize had been offered by the Society of Arts. At first he was awarded the prize of fifty guineas but later the decision was reversed and given to John Hamilton Mortimer, a friend of Reynolds and Richard Wilson, Romney receiving the consolation prize of twenty-five guineas. Romney never forgave Reynolds for this, but he quickly found success and by the 1770s was making more than £1,000 a year as a portrait painter. He visited Mary from time to time and kept her and his family in comfort, but he never brought her to London, knowing that she would have been out of her element in the circles in which he was now moving. After a visit to Italy, for a year of intensive study, he took a house and studio in Cavendish Square and set himself up as a fashionable portraitist in competition with Reynolds, who now recognised him as a serious rival.

Romney never achieved the high earnings of Reynolds, but he was well satisfied with his rewards and became increasingly absorbed in his work and its techniques. In 1782, at the age of forty-eight, when he was at the peak of his powers, the beautiful Emma Lyon, then a girl of twenty, came to him to have her portrait painted, and he was so fascinated by her loveliness, her exuberant vitality and generous heart, that he often refused wealthier sitters in order to paint her in a number of different characters – as Miranda, Magdalene, Calypso, Cassandra, St Cecilia and many others. Emma at this time was the mistress of Charles Greville, but in 1786 Greville, finding himself short of money, sent her out to Naples, to his widowed uncle, Sir William Hamilton, the English ambassador. Romney was undoubtedly in love with Emma, but all the malicious gossip was of little account. He produced some magical portraits and after she left for Naples he saw her again only once, when she returned to England with Sir William for their marriage.

Another of Romney's beautiful sitters was Perdita Robinson, the actress who in the early 1780s became the mistress of the future George IV and whom he abandoned so callously in 1785.

Romney's health and spirits were failing. He was growing tired of London and turned to Hampstead for a breath of country air. At first he took lodgings near a nursery garden on the Kilburn Road, known as Pineapple Place, and journeyed each day to Cavendish Square, but soon he decided to live permanently in Hampstead. In 1796 he bought an old house and stable on Holly Bush Hill, opposite Bolton House, where Joanna Baillie and her sister were to move ten years later. The following year he bought two more plots at the back of the house, where he built his studio and gallery. Then he let the original house and concentrated on building a studio, gallery and house on the new land he had acquired, and while the building was in progress he lived at The Mount, above Heath Street. He was his own architect and produced a strange and inconvenient dwelling, about which both he had his friends had increasing misgivings. His friend Haley described it as 'a singular house . . . the painting room and gallery had been nobly planned, but all domestic conveniences overlooked'.

The story goes that he moved in to his new house too soon, before the paint was dry, and 'never enjoyed a day of good health afterwards'. Ill and with the consciousness that his powers as an artist were failing, he lived there for only a year or two, and in 1799 made his way back to Kendal and the wife whom he had not seen for years. She received him with the love and forbearance which she had always given him and nursed him devotedly for the last four years of his life, as he 'sank gently into second childhood and the grave'.

This was in 1804. The house he had first taken on Holly Bush Hill and let, was bought by the tenant, Mrs Rundell, who subsequently sold it, while the studio and new house at the back being 'wholly without domestic accommodation, and the gallery and painting room out of all proportion for family requirements', became the Hampstead Assembly Rooms, bought by the first trustees of the Assembly Room Committee. A few years later, they were enlarged and for the next sixty years these Assembly Rooms were a valuable social centre in Hampstead. The Hampstead Literary and Scientific Society, formed in 1833, held their meetings here, and many famous people lectured to them. After the formation of the Conversazione Society, in 1846, paintings and drawings were exhibited and there were countless other meetings, lectures, exhibitions, balls, receptions and bazaars.

VII

Highgate in the Eighteenth and Early Nineteenth Centuries

Highgate was very much smaller than Hampstead, and although the two villages were so close, Highgate was even more inaccessible because of the steeper hill approaching it from London. In bad weather, heavily loaded wagons were known to take all day to negotiate the stiff climb, but the little village at the top remained a delightful retreat for the wealthy and privileged.

In 1700 Highgate had ninety houses and by 1793 there were still only two hundred and sixty-four, the rapid increase in building taking place during the nineteenth century, for there were nine hunded and three houses by 1846 and one thousand, one hundred and thirty in 1886.

At the foot of the hill were a few cottages and shops, but higher up stretched the mansions of the rich in their walled gardens, amidst the surrounding farmlands and commons.

As late as 1714, in a preamble to an Act for erecting turnpikes and making other improvements to the roads about Islington and Highgate, it is stated that the highways were very ruinous and almost impassable for five months of the year.

Half way up the hill, where later the St Joseph's Retreat was to be built, stood the Black Dog Inn, used by the drovers to help them on their way. On the east side was the Old Crown, with its tea gardens, and above it, Hornsey Lane, cutting across to the east, an old cross-road forming the boundary between Highgate and Islington and leading to the hill which, early in the nineteenth century, was to become known as the Archway Road. Highgate proper began above it, at the foot of the High Street, with Winchester Hall on the northern corner of Hornsey Lane and adjoining it Cromwell House. Ireton House and Lyndale House, with their segment-headed windows, today numbers 106 and 108, were once one large house, built in the early eighteenth century, and number 110, attached to it, was a smaller house, with straightheaded windows, of about the same date.

Just opposite number 110, in the wall beyond Lauderdale House, is the tablet commemorating the spot where Andrew Marvell's cottage stood until the mid-nineteenth century.

On the Bank, where the footway is built up above the road, two early nineteenth-century houses still stand, probably on the site of earlier houses, and beyond the Channing School, at the top of the hill, where the Bank ends and Highgate High Street begins, are a pair of later eighteenth-century houses, Ivy House and Northgate House. Where Cholmeley Park now runs, leading from the north side of the High Street, stood Sir John Woolaston's country home and here, early in the eighteenth century, Sir Thomas Abney was living, the nonconformist who was one of the founders of the Bank of England. He became Lord Mayor of London in 1700 and the following year member of Parliament for the City of London; and Dr Isaac Watts came to live with him in Highgate in 1712, remaining with the household when they moved to Abney Park.

There was another large house on the site of Bisham Gardens, a few yards up the hill on the opposite side, and the grounds of Bisham House stretched back to Swain's Lane. Little is known of the early tenants, but amongst the later ones was Captain Hayward, who had been a midshipman on the Bounty at the time of the mutiny.

Farther up the High Street, and round to the left, where it is joined by Swain's Lane, was the house of Sir John Hawkins, a descendant of the Elizabethan sea-dog. Sir John was a musician and student of the history of music, and at his Highgate home he gave concerts from time to time to his wide and illustrious circle of friends, which included Handel, Sir Joshua Reynolds, Dr Gibbons, Oliver Goldsmith, Horace Walpole, Jeremy Bentham, Mrs Clive, John Wilkes, Lord Mansfield and Dr Johnson. His history of music was published in 1776.

He married a Highgate girl and their daughter recalled an entry in her mother's diary, written during her girlhood. From the windows of her father's house, which looked across the pond down the North Road, 'she saw the troops march towards Scotland at the rising of 1745, and was particularly struck with the number of sumpter mules which carried the baggage of the Duke of Cumberland . . .'. The rumour spread that the Highlanders had been victorious, that they were marching south and had already reached Dunstable. Highgate was in a panic. Her mother fainted away and her grandfather, a dour Presbyterian, dug a hole in the garden and buried his silver and two hundred guineas.

Later, when the Jacobite prisoners were being brought back to London, she saw the perfidious Lord Lovat, who had escaped once but had been recaptured, as he was hiding in a hollow tree. The cavalcade halted at Highgate and Lord Lovat alighted from his coach at the Angel Inn, on the corner of the High Street and South Grove, for a meal. Afterwards he paced up and down in front of her house, and Hogarth arrived to make a sketch of him.

Her future husband, Sir John Hawkins, then still in his twenties, managed to acquire a seat to watch the beheading of Lord Lovat on Tower Hill, but at the 'get ready' signal, Sir John fainted away and missed the final act.

After the death of Lauderdale, in 1682, the house passed into the hands of a succession of owners, being a boys' school for a time. By the end of the eighteenth century it was looking very different from when Lauderdale had lived there and Pepys had visited it, for it was greatly altered and had taken on the appearance of a late Georgian stuccoed country villa, but a very spacious one, considerably deeper than its frontage. The house was extensively renovated in 1893, but in essentials looks much as it did at the end of the eighteenth century, with its pillared porch, two deep sash windows to the left and four to the right. On the first floor are five sash windows, the central one being surmounted by a triangular pediment above a hemispherical sash window. The back of the house has a similar triangular pediment over a hemispherical attic window, with five deep sashes on the first floor, but the four ground floor windows open on to a long, pillared portico which overlooks a small, square lawn, surrounded by the remains of a low red brick wall from gaps in which shallow flights of steps lead down to the main pleasure grounds, which are now Waterlow park. There are more remains of the old wall to the north of the house and there are still traces of sixteenth-century masonry in one of the ground floor rooms, but in 1965 the interior was severely damaged by a disastrous fire and still awaits renovation.

Walking along the High Street it is easy enough to feel what it was like in the eighteenth century, for so much has survived. Number 10 is a little eighteenth-century house and opposite, from number 17 to number 23, is a terrace of small houses, their little front doors approached by steep flights of steps. Numbers 17 to 21 were built about 1723 and number 23, wider and lower, is even earlier, a Queen Anne house dated 1710.

The short remaining stretch of the High Street consists mainly of shops, but above them are many traces of the eighteenth-century buildings from which they have been adapted.

At the top of the High Street, leading off to the left, is the triangular stretch which once formed the nucleus of the old village. South Grove runs south-west from the High Street until it meets the Grove, which runs due north into Hampstead Lane, the third side of the triangle being the top of the High Street and the right-angled bend into Hampstead Lane, with the Gate House Tavern on the corner.

This triangle includes the little Pond Square, which is not a square at all, but another triangle, where the hermit once built his pond, and beyond it is Highgate Green. Here much of the eighteenth-century building and atmosphere have been beautifully preserved. Walking down South Grove, the eastern part of which faces on to Pond Square, the early Georgian houses stand back in little courtyards, protected by a low wall or privet hedge, neat, symmetrical and demure-looking. Russell House, with its elaborate window frames and hooded doorway, has been there since the early eighteenth century, and next to it the larger Church House is neat and precise as a Queen Anne's doll's house. Beyond the low, white stucco, flat-fronted Literary and Scientific Institute, which was founded in 1839, and the Congregational Church, is number 14, Moreton House, a three-storeyed, early Georgian house of 1715, with an Ionic doorway, and number 17 is the magnificent Old Hall, a red brick mansion built in 1691, standing back behind its beautiful, wrought-iron entrance gates.

On the north side of the square is a row of toy, red brick cottages, a few of which have today been colour-washed. One or two of these cottages have only one window on the ground floor, with two above, but others are considerably larger, and Rock House has an attractive oriel window.

The square itself has been covered with asphalt, but it is well planted with plane trees, so that it still has a leafy, rural air, and on the eastern side are some old shops, including the Highgate Book Shop and an entrance to the narrow high back of the Prince of Wales pub, both of which are approached by narrow flights of wooden steps.

At the southern end of South Grove, where it joins the Grove, West Hill curves southwards, along the edge of Parliament Hill Fields, and on the corner of West Hill and the Grove the neo-William and Mary mansion, Witanhurst, still has, in its west wing, part of the original house, which was built about 1700.

In the Grove, which is the finest terrace in Highgate, the late seventeenth- and early eighteenth-century houses, which were built on the site of Dorchester House, are still there. They are large, red brick houses, set back behind paved courtyards and low railings, some with handsome wrought iron gates, and they look on to a wide elm-shaded footpath, with the Green beyond, while almost opposite, on the far side of the Green on the corner of Pond Square, stands the ancient Flask Inn, with two or three crazy-looking cottages, approached by steep flights of steps, built on to the back of it so that they face the Old Hall.

From the northern end of the Grove ran the drive to Fitzroy House and its adjoining estate, the house having been built by Lord Southampton in 1780.

Sir William Ashurst's mansion and seven acres of garden and orchard were to the south of South Grove and to the west of Swain's Lane, where the cemetery now lies. It was a beautiful old house, with tapestry hung rooms and a chestnut wood staircase, said to have been designed by Inigo Jones. Towards the end of the eighteenth century, Sir Alan Chambre, one of the Justices of the Common Pleas, was living here, and he was one of the last residents, although it became a school for a few years. It was deserted and haunted for a long time, and in 1830 it was pulled down and St Stephen's Church built on the site.

Swain's Lane was still a narrow country lane. The steep and winding West Hill, running down to meet the end of Swain's Lane, was made about 1700, a secluded, leafy lane, the whole of the eastern side, once the grounds of Dr Sacheverell's South Grove House, being the boundary of the grounds of Hollybush Lodge, which stretched over the wide sweep of Highgate Rise, and this house was bought early in the nineteenth century by Thomas Coutts and renamed Holly Lodge. On the western side of West Hill were a few houses set in large gardens, secluded in front by large shrubberies and at the back reaching down to Millfield Lane and Parliament Hill Fields, and here, just above the entrance to Millfield Lane, stood the mysterious Hermitage. A larger, three-storeyed house, where William and Mary Howitt lived for a time, was built alongside it, but the original Hermitage was much older, a tiny place with a thatched roof comprising one small low room, with a room above it approached by an outside staircase. It was entirely covered with ivy and almost hidden by great elm trees and how it came to be there in the first place or who built it no one knows, but the ceiling of the ground floor room was painted with 'naked figures in the French style', and there were dark stories of orgies being held there, as well as deep drinking and high gambling. At one time Sir Wallis Porter owned it and here the Prince Regent was a frequent visitor, until Sir Wallis, playing too high, lost all his money and at last shot himself, beneath the smiling, heartless, painted ladies.

A few years later, in 1824, Henry Fauntleroy, the banker, took refuge here when he was being sought for the embezzlement of £170,000 of Bank of England stock, which he had appropriated in order to save the credit of his own banking house, but he was found, brought to trial and executed later that year.

The old Hermitage together with the adjacent house, known as The Hermitage, were pulled down in 1860 and St Albans Villas built on the site.

The old gateway across the top of Highgate Hill did not come down until 1769 and the laundress living in the rooms over the archway lost her home. The old chapel still stood on the corner of Southwood Lane and was to remain there until the rebuilding in 1833, while the school was sadly neglected, like so many similar grammar schools, through-out the eighteenth century. In the *Account of Public Charities*, published in 1828, it was reported that the forty boys in attendance were at that time taught no classics and that although the reader of the chapel was officially in charge of their education, he was a pluralist who had appointed the sexton as his deputy, to do the teaching for him. However, as we shall see, within a few years matters were put right.

On the south side of Southwood Lane, opposite the school and at the corner with the High Street, a row of eighteenth-century town houses still stands, and beyond the site of the Old Presbyterian Chapel, founded in 1662, which later became the Baptist Chapel and is now a photographic studio, is a delightful terrace of small Georgian houses, some of which have iron balconies on the back ground-floor rooms, with a superb view across London to the Surrey hills.

On the opposite side of the lane, the Woolaston-Paunceforth almshouses are still there, rebuilt by Edward Paunceforth in 1722, when he added six more of his own foundation.

Southwood Lane, leafy and winding, runs due north along the side of the hill, the ground rising steeply to the west and falling away sharply to the east, and in places the roadway is several feet below the level of the footpath, which is protected by a railing.

Many of the eighteenth-century houses which lay scattered along the lane have survived, the spaces between now filled in with Regency,

Victorian and Edwardian houses, as well as some twentieth-century blocks of flats, but the leisurely air of the eighteenth century has somehow persisted and there is no feeling of disharmony when one comes across a weather-boarded cottage amidst the newer buildings. Southwood House was built by General Wade, on the site of an older house, in 1745, after his success during the '45 rebellion, and behind it, in Jackson's Lane, was the house of Squire Jackson.

Southwood Lane meets the Archway Road at right angles and on the opposite far corner stands the old Woodman tavern. Across the road, the lane continues as the Muswell Hill Road, still running due north, dipping and rising again, with the ancient Highgate Woods soaring high above the roadway on the left and the Queen's Wood sloping steeply down on the right, towards Crouch End. The woods are dark and dense and the pilgrims who once threaded their way along this ancient route, now deepset and a true hollow-way, must have needed all their courage, at times, to face its hazards.

To the north of Highgate village, the North Road was cut through the Bishop's Park in Elizabethan times, giving a direct route to the north, in place of the old winding route through Crouch End and Friern Barnet. This North Road was widened in 1767. Many of the old elm trees were cut down, the old foot causeway was removed and the road levelled. Soon after this, villas and cottages were built along the west side, at the southern end, with the Red Lion, which became an important coaching inn, and the Bull Inn farther towards Finchley.

From the Gate House, Hampstead Lane ran then, as now, due west along the crest of the hill, passing on the right the Bishop's Wood and on the left Ken House, and continuing on to Hampstead and the Heath.

This was the extent of Highgate, with fields and farms and common land to the north of the High Street and on either side of Southwood Lane, fields and countryside to the west, and to the south the private parks of the great mansions separating it from Parliament Hill Fields and the Heath.

Highgate had its fair and there were several tea gardens along the approaches to the village. There was morris dancing on the green at Whitsuntide and the fair advertised on 2 July 1744 was very like those held in Hampstead.

This is to give notice that Highgate Fair will be kept on Wednesday, Thursday and Friday next in a pleasant walk in the middle of the town. On Wednesday a pig will be turned loose, and he who takes it by the tail and throws it over his head, shall have it, to pay twopence entrance. On Thursday a match will be run by two men a hundred yards in two sacks for a large sum, and to encourage sport, the landlord of the 'Mitre' will give a pair of gloves to be run for by six men, the winner to have them. On Friday, a hat value 10s will be run for by men twelve times round the Green, to pay one shilling entrance, no less than four to start; as many as will may enter, and the second man to have all the money above four; no one to be entitled to take the hat that ever won that value.

Hogarth would often walk over from Hampstead, to drink at the Flask and watch the fair, while later in the century, George Morland, dissipating his talents and drinking himself to death, lived for a time at the Bull on the North Road, before his miserable end when he was still only forty-one years old, in a debtors' prison.

One of the nearest tea gardens on the way to Highgate was at Kentish Town, where there was an assembly house by around 1725, if not earlier. This was a large inn, with a skittle alley and a delightful garden, and a Long Room for balls was built on the south side, entered from the outside by a covered stairway. This inn became very fashionable and later in the century Kentish Town itself was a favourite summer resort, where visitors often took lodgings.

Another popular spot was Copenhagen House, which stood isolated, on rising ground, in fields alongside Maiden Lane, which was the old way from Battle Bridge, at the foot of Pentonville Hill, to Highgate and the North. This was a seventeenth-century house but, like the Spaniards, the origin of the name is a mystery. Some said that the Danish ambassador had stayed there during the plague, others that it had been built during the 1620s by some Danes, who had come to London in the train of the King of Denmark, when he had visited James I and his sister, King James's Queen Anne, in 1606, and settled here.

It was at Copenhagen House, in the 1780s, that the game of fives was first introduced to London from Shropshire and the first London fives courts were built. The story goes that the assistant to the manageress at this time was a young woman from Shropshire. She became friendly with a Highgate butcher from the same county, and together they played the game and made it popular.

There was also a cricket ground attached to Copenhagen House, and early in the nineteenth century, when there was still nothing but fields between here and Highgate, it was a favourite tea garden, especially in summer time during the hay harvest, for Londoners on a Sunday afternoon.

It lasted until 1852, when the Corporation of the City of London bought the house and grounds and the seventy-five acres of fields attached to it and built here the Islington cattle market, to replace the sordid slaughter houses of Smithfield. With it moved what was left of the old St Bartholomew's fair, which became known as the Caledonian market, and here they remained until the outbreak of World War Two in 1939, when they were closed and never re-opened.

The Highbury Barn tavern opened about 1740 as a small cake and ale house, a favourite resort of templars and literary men, including Goldsmith and his friends, who used to walk from the Temple, to enjoy a dinner of two courses and pastry for 10d, which included the penny tip for the waiter.

Towards the end of the century, when Mr Willoughby was the landlord, he added a bowling green, a trap-ball ground, a hop garden and brewery. He enlarged the pleasure garden which became a popular Sunday tea garden and established an Assembly Room, adapted from the Long Barn of the neighbouring farm. Here monthly assemblies were held, and it was also a place for large public charity and club dinner parties. In early Victorian times, a later proprietor turned the Highbury Barn tavern into a place for public dancing. He built a large dancing platform and laid out five acres of gardens, charging sixpence admission. By 1865, in addition to the entertainments in the gardens, which included Blondin, the tight-rope walker, the Siamese twins and the man-frog, the Alexander theatre was opened in the grounds, but by 1871 it was decided that the place had become too noisy and rowdy. It was closed, and within a few years the site had been covered with new buildings.

The Devil's House in Holloway was on the Hornsey Road, only two fields away from the Holloway turnpike. Originally it had been a moated timber house, Old Tollington House, which had been the manor house of Highbury manor, but with the passing years it had become an ale house. There was a tradition that during the seventeenth century it had been a favourite retreat of Claude Duval, when he was haunting the northern approaches to London, and the Hornsey Road was at one time called Duval's Lane, like the lane in West Hampstead which later became Platt's Lane. During the 1760s, the Devil's House became a public house and tea garden, much frequented by anglers, where the landlord offered 'tea and hot leaves, ready at a moment's notice, and new milk from the cows grazing in the pleasant meadows adjoining', and it lasted until 1849.

Closer still to Highgate village was Hornsey Wood House, a 'genteel tea house' standing by the entrance to Hornsey Wood, and immensely popular in the mid-eighteenth century. It was kept by two elderly sisters, both widows, and the pleasures they offered were unsophisticated and simple – tea drinking, a walk in the wood, and lovely views. On Whit-Sundays it was particularly popular with visitors from London, and from nine or ten o'clock in the morning the long room was crowded with 'men, women and children eating rolls and butter and drinking of tea at extravagant prices'.

Towards the end of the century, when both the old ladies were dead, the new proprietor built the Hornsey Wood tavern, enlarged the tea gardens and made a fishing lake; and it remained a popular resort for Londoners until it was pulled down in 1866, for the formation of Finsbury Park.

Throughout the eighteenth century, Highgate, like Hampstead, had a far higher proportion of handsome villas and mansions than was usual for a place of this size, for it was as much favoured as Hampstead as a place of residence for rich merchants, bankers and legal men, book-sellers, doctors and men of letters.

It was quiet, secluded and rural, its only drawback compared with Hampstead being that it was less accessible, and its remoteness meant that it had more than its fair share of highway robberies, many of which are listed in the Middlesex County Records.

On 9 April 1766, for example, 'two footpads robbed a lone rider on horseback of a considerable sum and his watch, but returned him 2s to pay his expenses to London'. In August, 1770, the Chester Mail was robbed at the foot of Highgate Hill. In 1777 three footpads attacked a gentleman riding back to London from Highgate, stripped him quite naked and left him in a ditch.

On 20 December 1753, a young couple eloping to Scotland were 'stopt by the lady's relations at Highgate, and after a struggle brought back to town'.

But the most intriguing of the records is for 6 June 1762. 'This morning between twelve and one a past-chaise in which was a lady was drove through the town very furiously by two postillions, and attended by three persons who had the appearance of gentlemen, from which she cried out, Murder! save me! oh, save me! till she was almost spent; but there was no possibility of relief, and they hastily drove towards Finchley Common'.

And no one ever knew what happened to her.

Highway robberies became so frequent towards the end of the century that Highgate and Hampstead took steps to protect themselves.

A newspaper of 1782 reported that:

> the number of robberies lately committed on the roads near the metropolis, some of which have been marked with cruelty and murder, prevent many from travelling in the evening, however pressing their occasions may be, and create a general alarm. To exterminate these desperate wretches who infest all parts of the roads round London, requires resolution and vigilance.
>
> It is much to be wished that the laudable example of the gentlemen of the Highgate and Hampstead trust may be followed by the trustees of the other neighbouring roads; they have employed a considerable number of horses and foot patroles, well armed with powder and ball, with instructions to apprehend robbers, so stationed and under such regulations that the traveller may pass unmolested.
>
> While the public are protected, there cannot be any who would not cheerfully pay the toll.

The most important house in Highgate during the eighteenth century was Ken House, the woods of which reach out to Hampstead and the Heath. The house had remained in the Bill family until 1790, when they sold it to the Brydges family, and it seems probable that it was William Brydges who altered the old Jacobean house and built the main structure of the existing house. He sold it in 1704 and it then passed through several hands, but by 1715 had come into the possession of the second Duke of Argyll. He sold it to his brother Lord Ilay and his brother-in-law, the second Earl of Bute, and they, in their turn, sold it, in 1720, to an upholsterer named William Dale, who fancied he had made his fortune in the South Sea Company, but when the bubble burst Dale had to mortgage the house to Lord Ilay. Dale could not pay, Lord Ilay foreclosed, and the house reverted to the Argyll family. Lord Ilay succeeded his brother as Duke of Argyll and in 1746 disposed of his interest in Ken House to his nephew Lord Bute, the third Earl, who was already a friend of Frederick, Prince of Wales, and destined to become Prime Minister for a brief time.

He was born in 1713, succeeding to the earldom when he was only ten, after which he was sent to Eton. In 1736 he married Mary, the daughter of Lady Mary Wortley Montagu. It was a runaway match, said Lord Chesterfield, 'notwithstanding which they lived very happily together; she proved a very good wife. . . . He proved *a great husband*, and had thirteen or fourteen children successively by her, in as little time as was necessary for their being got and born, though he married her without a shilling, and without a reasonable probability of her ever having two'.

The year after his marriage, Lord Bute retired to the Isle of Bute, which was his personal property, and here he remained for the next eight or nine years, living 'in a frugal and prudent manner' . . . applying himself 'to the study of agriculture, botany and architecture, the employments more of an industrious than of an elevated mind'.

Lord Shelburne, who was to know him well, said that in the Isle of Bute he lived 'with as much pomp and as much uncomfortableness in his little domestick circle as if he had been King of the Island, Lady Bute a forlorn queen, and his children slaves of a despotick tyrant'.

However, in 1746, the year that he came into possession of Ken House and the surrounding woods and park of some 280 acres, he returned to London. Wraxall, in his *Historical Memoirs*, describes how the impecunious Lord Bute met Frederick, Prince of Wales and Princess Augusta at the Egham races and how a warm friendship sprang up between the Royal couple and the obscure Scottish aristocrat. He was invited to Leicester House and, says Lord Chesterfield, 'he soon got to be at the head of the pleasures of that little, idle, frivolous and dissipated Court'.

In the meantime, Lady Bute and the children were installed at Ken House, and in 1749 Lady Mary Wortley Montagu was writing to her daughter: 'I very well remember Caenwood House, and cannot wish you a more agreeable place. It would be a great pleasure to me to see my grandchildren run about in the gardens. I do not question Lord Bute's good taste in the improvements round it, or yours in the choice of furniture.'

The scandalmongers were already whispering about the close relationship between the Princess of Wales and Lord Bute, and after the death of the Prince, in 1751, the gossip spread. Horace Walpole said he was certain that they were lovers, but Wraxall, writing a generation later, by no means supports the suggestion.

Yet Bute remained at Leicester House after Prince Frederick's death, supervising the education of the young Prince George, and when George II died and the Prince became George III, Bute was admitted to the Privy Council, and by 1762 had become Prime Minister, only to resign the following year. But by this time he had left Ken Wood, having sold it to William Murray, the future Earl of Mansfield, in 1754, to pay his steadily mounting debts.

In 1761, however, after the death of his father-in-law, Edward Wortley Montagu, followed by that of Lady Mary, only a few months later, he inherited a large fortune, for they had disinherited their only son.

This young man, to whom Lord Bute made a generous recompense for his loss of the inheritance, had been a trouble all his life and at this time was living in the East, having taken to eastern dress and declared himself a Moslem, but shortly afterwards he choked himself on a partridge bone and died. Lord Bute set about building the magnificent Bute House, off Berkeley Square, which was later to be known as Lansdowne House, but he was already heartily disliked for his conduct of the last phases of the Seven Years' War and his influence over the young King, and with the unpopular Treaty of Paris in 1763, at the end of the war, he was accused, probably quite wrongly, of having raised the money for his new mansion by accepting a bribe from the French. He resigned office, and before Bute House was even completed, he sold it to Lord Shelburne, the future Marquess of Lansdowne.

Lord Bute kept his house in South Audley Street, for his London home, and bought the medieval mansion of Luton Hoo, which he commissioned Robert Adam to transform, with a new exterior, about the same time that Adam was working for Lord Mansfield at Ken House.

William Murray, the 'Great Lord Mansfield', was born in 1704, the fourth son of the fourteen children of the Jacobite Lord Stormont of the Castle of Scone. Despite their aristocratic lineage, the family was desperately poor and after a few years at the Perth grammar school, he was sent to Westminster School. His could not afford the coach fare, so young William made his way south by pony, a journey which took him two months.

He was a brilliant scholar and from Westminster he went to Oxford and then to Lincoln's Inn, being called to the Bar in 1730. As a student, when he used to visit Hampstead, staying with his friends at the old Chicken House, he became a close friend of Alexander Pope and, as Dr Johnson remarked, 'drank champagne with the wits'.

Like Lord Erskine, he had a beautifully modulated speaking voice which, with his mild manner and incisive intellect, helped his steady rise to distinction. He became Solicitor General in 1742 and in 1745 was called upon to appear as Government prosecutor against the Scottish rebel Lords, including old Lord Lovat, whose cause he and his family had once so ardently supported. He condemned them and 'only once was he seen to flinch, when Lord Lovat complimented him on his prosecution speech, but added "I do not know what the good lady your mother will say to it, for she was very kind to my clan as we marched through Perth to join the Prince".' William Pitt, Lord Chatham, his bitter adversary, was never to let him forget that occasion. Nevertheless, his career continued, unchecked. By 1754, at the age of forty-nine, he succeeded Sir Dudley Ryder as Attorney General and two years later, when he was fifty-one, he was made Lord Chief Justice and created Baron Mansfield. He remained in office for the next thirty-two years and came to be regarded as the greatest lawyer of his day.

In some respects he was, like Wilkes, a 'friend of liberty', for he advocated free trade and religious toleration and was the first to decree that no slave could remain a slave on English soil, declaring that the state of slavery was odious, an echo of the Elizabethan resolution, two centuries earlier, that 'England was too pure an air for a slave to breathe in'.

He gave literary copyright to authors and, on technical grounds, reversed the judgement of outlawry against Wilkes, yet in many cases he was despotic and hated for his heartlessness. He did not support the freedom of the Press, opposed Pitt over the question of the taxation of the American colonies, upheld the press-gangs and insisted on the hanging of all forgers, including the unhappy Dr Dodd. And during his years of office he grew immensely rich through monopolies, for he had a 'keen appetite for emoluments'.

After the death of Pope, he seems to have been a solitary man, married but childless. Lord Campbell, in his *Lives of the Chief Justices*, says,

> A more serious defect was his want of *heart*. No one had a right to complain of him; he disappointed no just expectation of favour; and he behaved with kindness to all within the sphere of his action; but all that he did might have been done from a refined, calculating selfishness, with a view to his own credit. He had no warmth of affection; he formed no friendships; and he neither made exertions nor submitted to sacrifices purely for the good of others.

For the first ten years after he had bought Ken House, Lord Mansfield used it only as a holiday villa and for occasional entertaining, but in 1764, when Robert Adam was at the height of his career, he asked him to remodel the house. When he had bought it from Lord Bute it was a plain, early-eighteenth century, two-storey brick house with stone quoins and an orangery along the west side. Adam added a storey to the main block and, to make the south front symmetrical, added the boudoir leading to the orangery and on the east side built the beautiful library and ante-room. On the north side he built the entrance porch, with its startlingly impressive four columns rising the full height of the house and surmounted by a pediment, and the whole building was encased in stucco.

The library today is regarded as one of Adam's finest interiors, with its tunnel vaulted ceiling and semi-circular recesses at both ends, screened by its great columns. Adam said that Lord Mansfield 'gave full scope to my ideas' and that the library 'was intended both for a Library and a room for receiving company. The circular recesses were therefore fitted up for the former purpose, and the square part, or body of the room, was made suitable for the latter.'

The book cases are recessed at either end of the room, therefore, in the apses, and on either side of the fireplace in the north wall are arched recesses opposite the five tall windows which look out on to the gardens. The ceiling is most beautifully decorated with panels of scenes illustrating classical allegories, painted by Zucchi, and the painting of the ceiling of the rather low entrance hall was for a long time attributed to Angelica Kauffman. The story went that in the perfect setting of Ken House she and Zucchi fell in love. Sadly for romance it is now established that the little painted panel on the entrance hall ceiling was by Biagio Rebecca. Nevertheless, Angelica and Zucchi often worked together, as, for example, at Luton Hoo and Mrs Montagu's house in Portman Square, they did fall in love, and, after the end of Angelica's disastrous marriage to the bogus 'Count Frederick de Horn', who fleeced her of nearly all her money, while he still had a first wife living, she did marry Zucchi.

Ken House, for all its splendour, has a feel of domestic comfort. The boudoir, the tea-room and the breakfast room are small and intimate, with an air of quiet informality.

Lord Mansfield superintended much of the landscaping of the gardens and introduced the little imitation bridge at the eastern end of the string of lakes, a ridiculous, if fashionable folly with no function, for there is no footway and only one parapet, yet it has a charming effect when seen from the right angle. A good deal more was done to the gardens, with the help of Humphrey Repton, during the time of the second Earl.

Shortly before the Gordon riots, Lord Mansfield had roused the wrath of the anti-Catholics by directing the jury, in accordance with his belief in religious toleration, to find a verdict of Not Guilty against a Roman Catholic priest who had been informed against for celebrating Mass; and when, in 1780, Lord George Gordon led the rioting mob through London, they attacked Lord Mansfield's home in Bloomsbury Square and burnt it to the ground. Everything was lost, including his valuable library, and his records and private papers accumulated over fifty years, many of which he had hoped to publish. He and Lady Mansfield escaped with their lives, only by managing to slip away, unobserved, from the back of the house. The mob then turned north to attack Ken House. Lord Mansfield was, of course, no papist, but the rioters had long forgotten their main purpose. Excited by their first successes, they were ready to attack any great mansion, particularly one belonging to a man like Lord Mansfield, whom they must have known would ultimately be sitting in judgement on them.

Horace Walpole, in a letter to the Countess of Ossory written on 7 June 1780, said that Lord Mansfield's house in Bloomsbury was in ashes and that George Selwyn had just told him that five thousand men were marching on Ken Wood, and that six thousand of the Guards had gone after them.

It was Giles Thomas, the landlord of the Spaniards, who saved Ken House. As the mob approached he went out to meet them, showed sympathy for their cause and invited them into his house and cellars, for free drinks and a rest before they set about storming the gates and burning down the beautiful Ken House. It was a blazing hot day, they had had a long walk and needed no second invitation. Free beer had seldom come their way before, and as they sat around drinking and congratulating themselves on their good luck, Thomas sent messages to the steward of Ken House, John Hunter, for more supplies of beer, and to the barracks for a detachment of horse guards. Hunter ordered up barrels of beer from the Ken House cellars, which were emptied into tubs ranged along the roadside. William Weatherall, another member of Lord Mansfield's staff, addressed them. Giles Thomas kept them drinking. And soon, under-nourished at the best of times, they were all rip-roaring drunk, so that when the guards arrived soon afterwards the mob 'instantly abandoned their intentions, and returned to the metropolis in as much disorder as they quitted it'.

Lord Mansfield, by this time an old man of seventy-five, never forgot the timely action of Giles Thomas and he bore the loss of his Bloomsbury house and its valuable possessions with remarkable fortitude and lack of rancour. A few weeks later he had to sit in judgement, with his fellow judges, on Lord George Gordon, who was defended by Lord Mansfield's near neighbour, Lord Erskine. Lord Erskine, while admitting that Gordon had excited the mob by his cries of 'No Popery', denied the charge that he had intended to 'compass the

King's death and levy war against his person', and argued so persuasively that Lord George was exonerated.

With the house in Bloomsbury Square gone, Lord and Lady Mansfield now lived permanently at Ken House. The adjoining estate to the east was Fitzroy Park, in which the mansion, Southampton House, was not built until this year of the Gordon riots, 1780.

This land had originally been part of the manor of Tottenham Court, owned by the Dean and Chapter of St Paul's Cathedral. In 1768 the manor was conveyed by Act of Parliament and the payment of some £18,000 to Charles Fitzroy, brother of the Duke of Grafton. It was a piece of land stretching northwards from Oxford Street and comprising a large part of the parish of St Pancras, Camden Town and Highgate, including its copses and woods. This was an astute move on the part of the Fitzroy family, for London was slowly spreading northwards. Charles Fitzroy kept only 23 acres for his own use and the rest, a three mile stretch, he sold for building land, made £1,500,000 on the deal and acquired the title of Lord Southampton.

Southampton House was built on the site of Derrick's Hole farm and the grounds stretched from the lower corner of Millfield Lane up West Hill to behind the Grove and round Hampstead Lane to where Millfield Lane enters Hampstead Lane.

Mrs Barbauld, writing to her brother in 1787, said that Lady Mansfield at Ken House and Lady Southampton in her *ferme ornée*, were both admirable dairywomen, and 'so jealous of each other's fame in that particular, that they have had many heart-burnings, and have once or twice been very near to a serious falling-out, on the dispute which of them could make the greatest quantity of butter from such a number of cows'.

Lady Mansfield died a few years later and Lord Mansfield, having resigned office through increasing years and infirmities, lived on at Ken House, an increasing recluse, cared for by his two nieces until his death in 1793 at the age of 88.

While he was living in retirement, another old man of nearly the same age, was preaching in Highgate. This was John Wesley, who in December 1788, in his 85th year, wrote in his diary:

In the evening I preached at Miss Teulon's school in Highgate. I think it was the coldest night I ever remember. The house we were in stood on the edge of the hill, and the east wind set full in the window. I counted eleven, twelve, one, and was then obliged to dress, the cramp growing more and more violent. But in the morning, not only the cramp was gone but likewise the lameness which used to follow it.

Mrs Teulon had begged him to sit to Romney for his portrait and a few weeks later he was saying that 'Mr Romney is a painter indeed. He struck off an excellent likeness at once; and did more in one hour than Sir Joshua (Reynolds) did in ten'.

Towards the end of his life, Lord Mansfield was bedridden, and at this time Fanny Burney and her father were on a three day visit to Mrs Crewe, the beautiful Whig hostess, at her 'small but commodious villa on Hampstead Hill' the exact location of which has long since been forgotten; but, recorded Fanny,

> Mrs Crewe took my father and myself to see the Hampstead lions. We went to Caen Wood, to see the house and pictures. Poor Lord Mansfield had not been downstairs, the housekeeper told us, for the last four years; yet she asserts he is by no means superannuated, and frequently sees his very intimate friends, and seldom refuses to be consulted by any lawyers. He was particularly connected with my revered Mrs Delaney, and I felt melancholy upon entering his house to recollect how often that beloved lady had planned carrying thither Miss P. and myself, and how often we had been invited by Miss Murrays, my Lord's nieces. I asked after these ladies and left them my respects. I heard they were upstairs with Lord Mansfield, whom they never left. . . .
>
> We spent a good deal of time in the library, and saw first editions of almost all Queen Anne's Classics; and lists of subscribers to Pope's *Iliad*, and many such matters, all enlivening to some corner or other of the memory.
>
> We then drove through Lord Southampton's park, and some other beautiful grounds in the neighbourhood.

It was the Murray sisters' father, David Murray, the sixth Viscount Stormont, nephew of Lord Mansfield, who succeeded to the title and now became the owner of Ken Wood. He had been ambassador to Vienna and to Paris and was a highly cultured man, although his manner was said to have been 'cold, haughty and ungracious'.

When he came into the property he at once set about enlarging the house one more, employing George Saunders, a follower of Henry Holland, to add the two white brick wings to the north front, on either side of the entrance, which contain the dining room to the east and the music room to the west. He also built the service block, the stables and farm buildings and altered the line of the Highgate-Hampstead road, so that Ken House, instead of standing only a few feet from the road, was now far more secluded, being approached through trees and shrubberies and a wide stretch of lawn, by two curving carriage ways.

The second earl died in 1796, his son, the third earl, making little alteration to Ken House during his life time. He had a reputation for parsimony. It was during his years of ownership that William IV and Queen Adelaide paid their visit and Fanny Gascoyne-Cecil, the 2nd Marchioness of Salisbury, recorded in her diary for Thursday, 23 July 1835:

> The breakfast at Ken Wood. The road was crowded with people all the way anxious to see the King. A triumphal arch was erected on Hampstead Heath, and in most of the houses by the side of the road there were preparations for illuminations. I heard the King was extremely well received by the crowd, and the Duke (Wellington) still more so. We did not arrive till some time after them. It was a beautiful day. The grounds are excessively pretty, and if there had been enough to eat, it would have been perfect. . . . The King and Queen and all the Royalties seemed extremely well pleased: the King in particular trotted about with Lord M. in the most active manner, and made innumerable speeches!

The Marchioness was at Ken House again two years later, on 11 July 1837, and had much the same complaint. 'Breakfast at Ken Wood. No men, and few eatables; very dull.'

The third Earl died in 1840 and was succeeded by his son, the fourth Earl, who lived on until 1898, but like his father before him, he spent most of his time in Scotland, at Scone the family seat.

Fitzroy House had a very short life. By the time Fanny Burney was driving through the grounds, the Southamptons had departed. The Earl of Buckingham lived there for a few years, until 1811, and then Mr Robarts the banker, but in 1828 the house was pulled down and in 1840 the estate was auctioned in lots. On the west side of West Hill many of the existing houses were built, as well as the villas of Fitzroy Park.

Living at Moreton House in South Grove during the early years of the nineteenth century was Mr James Gillman, a surgeon, and his family, and here in 1816, Samuel Taylor Coleridge came to live, remaining with the Gillmans for the next 18 years, until his death in 1834.

Coleridge was born in 1772, at Ottery St Mary in Devon, the son of the parish vicar. He described himself as a 'poetic child, a devourer of fairy-tales, a weaver of day-dreams, at odds with his playmates,' but delighting in long conversations with his learned father. However, when he was only nine years old, his father died and Samuel was sent up to London, to enter Christ's Hospital.

Conditions at the school were harsh for a sensitive small boy. He was lonely and unhappy at first, as well as ill-fed, but his extraordinary talents were soon apparent, and in later life he said that he owed his faculty as a writer and poet to the 'severity of his fierce but painstaking master, James Boyer, who forced him to use his brains and control his fancies'.

Among his lasting friendships at Christ's Hospital was that of Charles Lamb, two and a half years younger than Coleridge, who, in the early days, looked up to him as 'elder and superior'.

In his essay on Christ's Hospital, Lamb later described some of the rigours of school life. On whole-day holidays, the boys 'were turned out for the live-long day' with no food; and boys who, like Coleridge, had no pocket money, and could not buy any, had to go without through the entire day.

One day, when he was about 17, Coleridge in a fit of youthful exuberance, swam across the New River fully clothed and remained in his wet clothes all day. The result was that he had to spend the next five or six months in the sick ward of Christ's Hospital, suffering from jaundice and rheumatic fever.

It was during these months of illness, with 'seas of pain waving through each limb', that the seeds were sown of the ill-health and suffering which were to be with him all his life.

When he was well enough to leave the sick ward, he had his first love affair, falling in love with the blue-eyed sister of a schoolfellow, Mary Evans. She was his 'phantom of delight', but she had other ideas and married someone else.

He won a scholarship to Cambridge but soon fell hopelessly into debt. In 1793, in despair, he enlisted in the Dragoons, but his brother, a commissioned officer, heard of his plight, bought him out of the army and returned him to Cambridge. On a walking tour during the next long vacation he met Robert Southey, with whom he discussed eagerly his first ideas of socialism. They ended the tour at Bristol, where he met Southey's future wife, Edith Fricker, and himself became engaged to her eldest sister, Sara.

Coleridge spent only one more term at Cambridge and left without taking a degree. He went to London for a few weeks, writing sonnets for the *Morning Chronicle* and 'sitting late, drinking late' with Charles

Lamb, at the Cat and Salutation in Newgate Street, but soon he was back in Bristol with Southey, where the two friends lodged together and tried to make a living by lecturing on politics, history and theology. A few months later they parted, Southey being the first to realise that Coleridge's particular brand of socialism, which he called Pantisocracy, was not workable.

Coleridge married Sara and settled happily in a 'myrtle-bound' cottage at Clevedon for a while, but they were soon back in Bristol with Sara's mother. He continued to scrape a living, writing poetry, issuing, with the help of patrons, short-lived political periodicals, and then, with his wife and baby, moved to Nether Stowey, where he decided to try his hand at market gardening. At this time his health was indifferent and he was often in great pain, which he alleviated with opium.

The market gardening idea came to nothing, but it was here that he wrote many of his greatest poems, including 'The Ancient Mariner' and the first part of 'Christabel': and it was also here that he met William Wordsworth, two years older than himself, and his sister Dorothy, and that Wordsworth and he composed the *Lyrical Ballads*, the first volume of which was published in 1798.

Coleridge was interested in theology and metaphysics as well as poetry. He renewed his friendship with Southey and explored the Lake District with Wordsworth. After another spell of journalism in London, during which he contributed regularly and brilliantly to the *Morning Post*, he moved with his wife and family to Greta Hall, a newly built and partly furnished house near Keswick, not far from the new home of William and Dorothy Wordsworth, who in 1799, the previous year, had taken possession of Dove Cottage, on the shores of Lake Grasmere.

But the dampness of the Lakes was bad for Coleridge's gout and heart condition, his marriage was unhappy, and he came to rely more and more on opium and laudanum for relief from the incessant pain he suffered.

Coleridge's wife was a good woman, intelligent and quick-witted, but she had little sympathy with her husband's imaginative temperament. 'She could not share his dreams, nor laugh away his fears, nor make the cheerless cottage warm'. 'Home was no home for him,' said Wordsworth. They 'stood apart' and there was no love between them or to find again 'with tears'.

After 1803, although Coleridge continued for some years to make occasional visits to Greta Hall, he and his wife were virtually separated; and about this time Southey, the future poet laureate, already married to Edith, joined their sister at Greta Hall, Southey, for long periods, maintaining the Coleridge family and remaining at Greta Hall until his death in 1843.

Amongst the Wordsworths' circle of friends at Dove Cottage were two sisters, Sarah and Mary Hutchinson. Coleridge fell desperately in love with Sarah, and William, less rapturously, with Mary. To Dorothy's grief and despair, William and Mary became engaged and married, but Coleridge returned to London.

Between 1804 and 1816 his story is a melancholy one. He travelled abroad – to Malta, Sicily, Naples and Rome – in a vain search for renewed health, but back in England with the Wordsworths in 1807 he was writing of his sense 'of past youth and manhood come in vain'.

In London he wrote a number of essays and earned a subsistence by giving courses of lectures on philosophical and political subjects and on Shakespeare and Milton. He kept in close touch with Wordsworth and sent all the money he could muster to his family at Greta Hall, but his health was deteriorating and by 1814 he was 'wrecked in a mist of opium', very poor and very unhappy. He made valiant but hopeless efforts to cure himself of his addiction, and in a pathetic letter to Joseph Cottle at this time he said: 'Had I but a few hundred pounds, but two hundred, half to send to Mrs Coleridge and half to place myself in a private madhouse, where I could procure nothing but what a physician thought proper . . . then there might be hope. Now there is none!'

He declared that he had never loved evil for its own sake, nor ever sought pleasure for its own sake, 'but only as a means of escaping from pains that coiled round my mental powers as a serpent around the body and wings of an eagle! My sole sensuality was not to be in pain'.

In 1816 his fortunes improved. Byron, although hard pressed for money himself and just about to leave England, never to return, lent him £100 and also recommended his poem 'Christabel', at last completed, to John Murray.

Murray agreed to publish the poem and a few weeks later, on the recommendation of Dr Joseph Adams, a relative of one of Coleridge's Bristol friends, he was received into the house of Mr Gillman, as a patient and boarder. From the moment they met, James Gillmann was delighted with Coleridge. 'His manner, his appearance, and above all his conversation were captivating,' he later wrote. And not only Mr Gillman, but his wife, their children and the four maidservants all came to love him deeply.

Despite many stories to the contrary, the Gillman family maintained that during the years Coleridge lived with them at Highgate he overcame the opium habit. Mrs Gillman's granddaughter, in a letter to the *Spectator* of 8 November 1884, said that her grandmother had assured her that Coleridge had '*freed* himself from the *habit* of taking opium while under her roof, and that he took it when prescribed for him by my grandfather (with the concurrence of another medical man) to relieve the most agonising pain'.

And although he admittedly had one or two very occasional lapses, it is true to say that by a tremendous effort of will and with the sympathetic discipline of Mr Gillman and the faithful maid-servant, Harriet Macklin, who was deputed to be his attendant and nurse, he was able to keep the addiction well under control.

Only three weeks after Coleridge arrived in Highgate, 'Christabel' was published, together with 'Kubla Khan' and 'The Pain of Sleep' and very soon distinguished visitors began to call.

C. R. Leslie, the American artist living in Hampstead, wrote in his Autobiography on 3 June 1816:

> Mr Coleridge . . . has just published his poem of 'Christabel'. He lives at Highgate (about three miles from us) in a delightful family. He requested me to sketch his face, which I did out there, and by that means became acquainted with Mr and Mrs Gillman, who are the sort of people that you become intimate with at once. . . . There are some beautiful scenes about Highgate and I shall in future make it my resort for landscape studies. . . .

A few weeks later, Crabb Robinson was visiting Coleridge and reporting that he had never seen him look so well. He was working steadily at this time, having been commissioned to write his *Lay Sermons*, at a time when there was great distress in England and widespread unemployment, much of it caused by the demobilisation of the army at the end of the Napoleonic wars.

He also took to heart the cause of the child factory workers, particularly in the Lancashire cotton factories, and wrote compellingly in support of the Parliamentary Bill of 1818, which shortened their working hours.

About two years after his arrival at Highgate, the Gillmans moved to number 3, the Grove. 'Our new home is and looks comely, and of an imposing respectability', wrote Coleridge to a friend. 'The views from the garden-side are substitutes for Cumberland, especially from the attic in which I and my books are installed; Mr Gillman has shewn much taste in smart-smoothing and recreating the garden – a gloomy wilderness of shrubs.'

Coleridge had first been given a room on the second floor of the house, but going up one day to the attic, he was so enchanted with the view over Ken Wood that he asked to be moved up there. One side of the room was completely covered with book shelves, and eventually the room was rebuilt, so that the original sloping ceiling was squared. He also had another room in the house, where he worked, dictated and entertained his friends.

Coleridge loved the Gillmans, and was ever grateful for their goodness to him. In a letter to Mrs Gillman, sent when he was away on one occasion, on a brief holiday, he wrote: 'I feel more and more that I can be well off nowhere away from you and Gillman. May God bless him! For a dear friend he is and has been to me. . . . God bless you both! my most dear friends.'

Coleridge delighted in the little garden at the Grove, with its steps leading down from the verandah at the back of the house, its neat lawn and winding paths, and he loved to stroll under the lime trees and elms in the Grove, and down the surrounding lanes to Millfield Lane. 'It was in company with Coleridge that I first heard the nightingale', wrote Leslie. 'It was in a lane near Highgate, where there were a number singing. . . . He even told me how many there were.'

Coleridge left a note amongst his papers: 'Heard the nightingales in Widow Coutts' Lane. The gardener (N.B. so deaf that I was forced to holloa in his ear) had heard them he said two days before!'

Widow Coutts' Lane was probably West Hill, for Thomas Coutts, the elderly banker who had bought Holly Lodge, had died in 1822, leaving his widow, the former Harriet Mellon, the Drury Lane actress, the whole of his vast fortune.

Highgate was a rare place for nightingales. In a letter of 1826, a friend of the Gillmans was writing to them: 'Years have passed since I heard the nightingales sing as they did that evening in Mr Robart's Garden Grounds'; and this was a reference to Fitzroy Park, where Mr Robarts was living in the 1820s, just before the house was demolished.

Another of Coleridge's favourite walks was to the Scotch fir grove, on the Sandy Road, near John Turner's old house, The Firs, and here, whenever Mrs Gillman saw him becoming depressed and discouraged, she would walk with him, to watch the sunset.

In 1817 Wordsworth came to London and made his first visit to Coleridge at Highgate. Later that year, in order to raise the money to send his second son, Derwent, to the University, Coleridge prepared a prospectus of a course of lectures which were begun in January 1818, at the Philosophical Society, off Fleet Street. The following year he prepared a set of fourteen lectures on the history of philosophy and another course on six selected plays of Shakespeare, which were delivered at the Crown and Anchor in the Strand.

From about 1821, Coleridge held receptions every Thursday afternoon and evening at the Grove, when he received a distinguished circle of friends which included C. R. Leslie, Judge Talfourd, Basil Montagu, Hookham Frere and Lord Hatherley. Charles and Mary Lamb were sometimes there, but more often they preferred to visit Coleridge on less formal occasions. Sometimes they stayed the night, and if the house were full, they would sleep at the Gate House. Other visitors included Southey, Hallam, Hazlitt, and, in the later years, Leigh Hunt.

Coleridge was a magnificent conversationalist, Lord Hatherley saying that he 'poured forth all the riches of his prodigious memory and all the poetry of his brilliant imagination to the listener'.

Most of the time he was in great pain and discomfort, but, as James Gillman said, in these later years, he seemed to acquire the extraordinary power of apparently overcoming and drowning his sufferings, 'as it were in fervid colloquy'.

It was at this time, during the 1820s, that he wrote his *Aids to Reflection* and his *Confessions* and also prepared a history of logic, but from about 1830 his health declined and his sufferings increased. He was forced to spend much of his time in bed or in his room, although he had brief intervals of recovery. By this time his wife was living with their daughter Sara in a cottage in Downshire Hill. Sara had married her cousin, Henry Nelson Coleridge, and Coleridge was well enough to be driven over, in Mr Gillman's coach, to the christening of their daughter, Edith, his first grandchild.

He died on 25 July 1834, and in due course he was acclaimed as the greatest religious, moral and critical philosopher in England since the days of Bacon. He was buried in the old Chapel at Highgate, and when the new St Michael's Church had been consecrated, the memorial tablet which the Gillmans had placed in the Chapel was moved to the new Church, while in 1961 his remains were removed from the vault in the school chapel and re-buried under the central aisle of St Michael's Church.

VIII

Poets and Artists

Living in Hampstead Square during the 1780s was the Hunt family. Mr Hunt, who was born in Barbados and had been trained for the law in Philadelphia, had been arrested during the American revolution for his loyalty to England, and had escaped tarring and feathering and a long term of imprisonment only by bribing his gaoler and making his escape, first to Barbados and then to England, where his wife and four small boys were not able to follow him until nearly two years later. He was a handsome, gallant and feckless young man, with very little money and no facility for making any, still less for keeping such that came his way.

He could find no work in London as a lawyer, so he made use of his beautiful speaking voice by becoming ordained, like his father and grandfather before him, and setting up as a popular preacher. Thus socially, if not financially, the family maintained the level they had held in America: and he became particularly in demand for delivering charity sermons, for he had a good deal of the actor in his make-up and could wheedle a shilling from the flintiest heart.

Hearing him preach at Southgate one Sunday, the Duke of Chandos, who had a country seat close by, invited him to become tutor to his nephew. So the Hunt family left Hampstead Square for Southgate, and here their fifth son, Leigh Hunt, was born in 1784, the year that Dr Johnson died.

The family prospects now seemed bright, for to be tutor in a ducal family often led to a bishopric, but Mr Hunt was soon in trouble again.

He fell into disfavour for defending a young American artist, John Trumbill, who had served in the Republican army under Washington, but had come to England to study painting under Benjamin West, Mrs Hunt's uncle, with whom the family had stayed for a time when they first arrived in London. The government suspected Trumbill of being a spy. He was arrested and only by the exertions of both Benjamin West and Hunt was he set free. But it did Hunt no good, and the bishopric was not forthcoming.

The Duke of Chandos, who might have been his patron, died in the oddest of circumstances. One day the Duchess, who adored him, but was of 'great animal spirits', pulled his chair away as he was about to sit on it. The fall killed him and the Duchess went mad with grief and remorse; and the Hunt family went back to Hampstead for a time, hopelessly in debt and with few prospects.

Leigh Hunt says in his autobiography that the first room he remembers was one in the King's Bench prison, where his father was committed for debt – and one of the inmates who impressed him most was Stoney Bowes, who arrived there in 1790, having been committed for cruelty to his wife, the Countess of Strathmore, in the course of which he had run a needle through her tongue.

Benjamin West at last secured a pension of £100 a year from the Loyalist Pension Fund for the Hunt family, and a wealthy aunt came over from Barbados with more money for them. Mr Hunt struggled on, usually in debt and often committed to the King's Bench, but always planning new schemes which never materialised. 'I believe he wrote more titles of non-existent books than Rabelais,' said Leigh Hunt, although he always spoke of his father with indulgent affection. They moved to Finchley for a time, still proud but desperately poor. Somehow or other, the eldest four boys were educated and apprenticed and in 1792, when he was seven years old, Leigh was sent to Christ's Hospital in Newgate Street. Coleridge and Charles Lamb had both left the school a year or two before he arrived, and Coleridge he did not meet until many years later, but Lamb often came back to visit his old masters and friends while Hunt was still a pupil: and during these years of his early childhood he grew to love the countryside north of London – Southgate, Enfield, Highgate, Hampstead and Finchley – and recalled his walks with deep happiness.

Towards the end of his life, he wrote that,

the walks across the fields from Highgate to Hampstead, with ponds on one side and Caen Wood on the other, used to be (and I hope is still, for I have not seen it for some years) one of the prettiest of England. *Poets'* (vulgarly called Millfield) *Lane* crossed it on the side next to Highgate, at the foot of a beautiful slope, which in June was covered with daisies and buttercups; and at the other end it descended charmingly into the Vale of Health, out of which rose the highest ground in Hampstead.

Leigh Hunt was born into a world which was changing very quickly. The flames of the American Revolution had not long died down and the fires of the French Revolution were already being kindled. He was only five years old when the revolution broke out and during his schooldays England was fighting against Napoleon. In England the leisurely elegance of the eighteenth century, so enviable for the few and so disastrous for most of the rest of the people, was slowly disappearing, although not without a struggle, and throughout the Napoleonic wars and for some years afterwards the new spirit of freedom and realism which was seeping into the thinking and writing of so many English men and women was regarded by the Tory government with alarm and distrust.

In the world of the arts, Joshua Reynolds and Horace Walpole had had their day, Reynolds dying the year that Leigh Hunt entered Christ's Hospital and Walpole five years later, in 1797. Sheridan had rebuilt the old Drury Lane theatre in 1791 and Sarah Siddons and her brother John Kemble were at the height of their popularity. Fanny Burney's play *Edwin and Elgitha* was produced at the new theatre in 1795, with Sarah Siddons playing the lead, but audiences were becoming more discerning, and when the dying heroine was brought out from behind a hedge at the back of the stage, to die in front of the audience, and was then carried back again, the house was convulsed with laughter.

The glories of Ranelagh were fading and as well as beginning to think differently, men and women were different in appearance. Women's saques and hoops and their ridiculously elaborate high head-dresses were going out of fashion, although Leigh said he remembered his mother describing the misery of 'having her hair dressed two or three stories high, and of lying in it all night ready for some visit or spectacle the next day'.

Men were taking to pigtails and smaller wigs, and soon the tricorn hat was to give way to a hat with a round crown and broad, turned-up brim.

Leigh as a child was taken to both Houses of Parliament, and could remember seeing Pitt, the first Lord Liverpool and Charles James Fox, round and jovial, wearing a broad-brimmed round hat. And yet, by the time Leigh died, in 1859, Bernard Shaw was already three years old.

His time at Christ's Hospital was happy enough and before he left, in 1799, he had already written a few poems, for all his life he dreamed of being a true poet, an ambition which was never fulfilled, for it was as an essayist that he made his mark and that his name has lived.

For the first few years after he left school, his story is vague. He thought seriously of becoming an actor. Despite his liberal views, he was very class conscious and was at pains to point out in his autobiography that in those days the theatre was a favourite diversion of all social classes, the nobility, the gentry and citizens. The nobility married theatre people, the gentry wrote for them and princes not only enjoyed talking to them but frequently lived with them. Sheridan was a member of parliament as well as a theatre manager, and actors and actresses, such as the Kembles and Garrick, with their beautiful voices and keen intelligence and culture, were received everywhere, in the highest social circles.

Hunt published two books of indifferent poems and wrote one or two amateurish plays while he was still very young, but in later life he became endearingly critical of his early literary efforts. His essays for the evening paper *The Traveller* were more successful, and in 1805 Leigh joined his elder brother John, who had become editor of a new paper called *The News*, writing mainly theatre criticism: and he went to live with him in New Brydges Street.

Three years later, John and Leigh established their own weekly paper, *The Examiner*, becoming joint partners. This paper aimed at airing its honest opinions, free of party influence or any breath of corruption, an ideal to which Leigh Hunt clung all his life; but since the paper advocated the much needed Parliamentary reform it was soon associated with the Reform Party and aroused the suspicions of the Tories. They regarded it as standing for Bonapartism, republicanism and disaffection from the Church and the State. The Napoleonic wars were at their height, Napoleon was undefeated and the Jacobin panic was spreading. But Leigh Hunt was still only twenty-four and his political convictions went no farther than a sentiment that the working masses of the population had a good case to answer and that, out of human kindness and common justice, they should be given a better life. He was no republican, for he disliked the commercialism of the young America, and he had no great admiration for Napoleon, whom he regarded as a good soldier but with no more than an average intellect.

Violence he hated and he had abhorred the cruelty of the French Revolution.

He had much of his father in him, including, unfortunately, his total lack of business sense and ineptitude in handling money, but his literary gifts were considerable and he had a courageous integrity, a selfless admiration of the work of his contemporaries and an engagingly frank appraisal of his own writing, which was to make him an invaluable entrepreneur.

During these early years, he met many of the great names of the day, Thomas Campbell, Theodore Hook, Charles Matthews, Horace Smith, Fuseli, Godwin, several of them at the Friday night parties given by Rowland Hunter, the bookseller of St Paul's Churchyard, and in 1809 Leigh married Hunter's stepdaughter, Marianne.

The following year his father died, his spirit broken at last by his dreary life of unfulfilled dreams and eternal debt.

The Examiner uncovered the scandal of Mary Ann Clarke and the commissions she had been selling, while mistress of the Duke of York, who was Commander-in-Chief of the Army, and steps were taken to prosecute the paper, but when Colonel Wardle demanded a full scale investigation in Parliament, the prosecution against *The Examiner* was dropped.

Although Hannah Lightfoot's connexion with Hampstead is so tenuous, Mary Anne Clarke's is substantial. She lodged there for a time and two of her descendants were distinguished residents.

Mary Anne was probably born at Oxford in 1772, the daughter of a journeyman printer named Thompson, but while she was still an infant the family moved to London – to Bowl and Pin Alley, off White's Alley, Chancery Lane. Her father died when she was still very young, perhaps killed while fighting during the American War of Independence, and her mother married again shortly afterwards. Her new husband was Robert Farquhar, a compositor, and the family moved to lodgings in Black Raven Passage, off Cursitor Street, Chancery Lane. The surroundings were crowded and squalid and Mary Anne was both attractive and witty, extremely intelligent and overflowing with good spirits and a zest for living. Her step-father taught her to read and write and she very soon decided that she was destined for something better than life in a city slum. When she was fifteen she eloped with Joseph Clarke, the son of a prosperous builder. Joseph was apprenticed to a stone-mason, with premises close by, at the corner of Cursitor Street and Chancery Lane, and the young couple set up housekeeping, first in Pentonville and then in Charles Square, Hoxton. After their second child was born, by which time Mary Anne was seventeen, they decided to marry, Robert Farquhar giving his consent.

Joseph Clarke had completed his apprenticeship by now and his father had died, leaving, it is said, £80,000, but to Joseph he left only an annuity of £50, and as Joseph disliked work and did none at all for the first two years of the marriage, they were soon hard pressed for money.

They moved to Aldersgate and he then tried to set up business as a stonemason, but he spent too much time in drinking and playing skittles, and the venture ended four years later in bankruptcy.

By this time there were three children and Mary Anne insisted on their moving to Craven Place, near the Kensington Gravel Pits, to try and make a fresh start, but Joseph drank more heavily than ever and soon disappeared.

Mary Anne took the simplest course open to her. She became a courtesan. Her early affairs were short-lived, but she learnt a great deal of the ways of life in high society and ended up in a house in Tavistock Place, where her mother, now separated from Farquhar, joined her and helped to take care of the children.

How she came to meet the Duke of York has never been made clear, but by 1803 he had rented a furnished house for her in Park Lane and shortly afterwards established her, with her three children, in a splendid house at number 18 (now number 62), Gloucester Place, off Portman Square.

Mary Anne was twenty-eight, the Duke forty, twelve years married to Princess Frederika, daughter of the King of Prussia and with no children. The Duchess lived in seclusion at Oatlands near Weybridge, devoted to her forty or more dogs, as well as her parrots and monkeys, loved by the villagers in whom she took a practical interest, but having little more than a dutiful affection for the Duke.

Mary Anne was a complete contrast to the Duchess, warm and lively and revelling in her new-found luxury, her score of servants, her carriages and her lavish furnishings. It all went badly to her head. She spent wildly and grew increasingly extravagant.

The Duke had been Commander-in-Chief of the Army since 1795 and although he was drinking and gambling heavily and was always disastrously in debt, he took his army work seriously, and despite many of the disasters of the Napoleonic Wars for which he was held responsible, he worked hard and conscientiously.

He had a town house in Portman Square, as well as at the Albany, but spent most of his time during the week at Gloucester Place, though returning to Oatlands each weekend.

During the day time, when he was working at the Horse Guards, Mary Anne was free to enjoy herself as she pleased, and in order to acquire even more money than the Duke could allow her, she was soon receiving people anxious for preferment in the army or some other remunerative office, cajoling the Duke to make the appointments and receiving handsome rewards from the people who had importuned her.

Nevertheless, she had no money sense and seldom paid the enormous bills she incurred during her brief spell of grandeur. Two and a half years later, in the summer of 1805, a man called Turner summoned her for debt and informed the Duke of York that he intended to sub-poena him as a witness. The Duke hurriedly paid the debt, but warned Mary Anne that matters could not continue in this way, and under pressure from his advisers, he at length decided to end the affair, sending his representative to break the news to her. The Duke gave her the lease of the Gloucester Place house, which she sold for £4,400, along with most of the furniture, but nearly all this money went in settling her outstanding debts. He also promised her an annuity of £400, although this was paid at very irregular intervals. She moved from one address to another, desparately trying to keep up appearances on very little money.

Only a few months later, there were an increasing number of queries in the House of Commons and in the Press, as well as *The Examiner*, about the unfairness in the treatment of army officers and their promotions, echoing the criticisms which Lord Erskine had made a generation earlier. Soon it became openly accepted that Mrs Clarke had been inducing the Duke of York to grant commissions to anyone who applied to her, and accepting payment for her services.

Mary Anne was living in Exmouth by this time, but to escape her creditors and the prospects of a debtors' prison, and also to try to obtain more instalments of her annuity, she returned hastily to London with her children. In October 1897, she took lodgings with William Nichols in Heath Street, on the corner of New End, but by June of the following year, penniless and with eight months rent owing to Nicholls, she was on the move again, this time taking lodgings in Holles Street, off Oxford Street.

Nicolls, seeing the folly of throwing good money after bad, did not sue her, but he had acquired something of great value. During her stay in his house, Mary Anne had recklessly sent down a sackful of old letters, to be burnt, and Nicholls, glancing through them, saw that many of them were from the Duke of York and took possession of them.

Once more in fear of arrest for debt, Mary Anne retreated again to Hampstead. Her problems, she said, 'obliged me to conceal myself at different times under the roof of a Mrs Andrews at Hampstead, a worthy woman, who has been twenty years resident in that village'. Here she was run to earth by Pierre M'Callum, who said he had been directed 'to call on Mrs Andrews . . . who resides in a yellow cottage on Haverstock Hill, where I might hear of the celebrated harlot'. He had begun investigations for Colonel Wardle and reported maliciously that Mrs Clarke 'was forced to chum with Mrs Andrews in a wretched hovel behind the cottage, into which Mrs Andrews retired in times when the cottage was let. From Mrs Andrews I learnt that she was indebted to her from day to day for a scanty subsistence which they divided between them.'

However, she had moved to Westbourne Terrace off Sloane Square (now renamed Cliveden Place). Here M'Callum found her and arranged her first interview with Colonel Wardle. She had no scruples in implicating the Duke in the scandalous allegations and in January 1809 he was publicly indicted.

As a peer, he could not be brought to the Bar of the House of Commons, but Mary Anne was called and appeared willingly and cheerfully. She wore for the occasion 'a light blue silk gown and coat, edged with white fur, and a muff. On her head she had a white cap or veil, which at no time was let down over her face to hide it'.

She frankly admitted having accepted bribes to use her influence with the Commander-in-Chief to obtain army commissions or coveted appointments, and 'the whole attention of the country was drawn to the strange spectacle of a laughing, impudent woman, brought to the bar of the House of Commons, and forcing them to laugh in their turn at the effrontery of her answers'.

William Wilberforce, Richard Sheridan and Arthur Wellesley were amongst those who questioned her and Sir Francis Burdett, son-in-law of Thomas Coutts of Holly Lodge, Highgate, had seconded Colonel Wardle's motion for the investigation. Spencer Perceval, at this time Chancellor of the Exchequer and Leader of the House, bore the full responsibility of defending the Duke, since the Prime Minister, the Duke of Portland, was old and ill and about to retire, and it was about this time that Perceval moved from Belsize House to Downing Street.

The examination of Mary Anne began on 1 February 1809 and was long and searching. Letters were produced which incriminated her over and over again and caused appalling embarrassment to dozens of people. Nicholls produced the Duke's love letters. Mud was slung in all directions and the lampoonists and satirists had a field day. It was shown that Wardle had paid Mary Anne for information. It was suggested that the Duke of York had made certain appointments in order to discomfort and thwart the Duke of Kent, with whom he had a long-standing dissension.

Yet there was no absolute proof that the Duke had connived at Mary Anne's practices and many years later Leigh Hunt wrote: 'My own impression at this distance of time, and after a better knowledge of the Duke's private history and prevailing character, is, that there was some connivance on his part, but not of a systematic nature, or beyond what he may have considered as warrantable towards a few special friends of his mistress, on the assumption that she would carry her influence no farther'.

The enquiry ended on 23 February, and in the Parliamentary debate which followed Spencer Perceval's resolution that the Duke should be acquitted was carried, but in the meantime he had resigned. At the same time he dismissed Mrs Carey, the actress, who had succeeded Mary Anne as his mistress. Two years later he was re-instated as Commander-in-Chief, and held the position until his death in 1827.

Mary Anne had expected money from Colonel Wardle, but it was not forthcoming. She wrote her memoirs and offered them to Sir Richard Phillips, the radical bookseller whom she had met while living in Hampstead, but he refused them. They were accepted by another publisher, but before they could be circulated the government stepped in and arranged to buy from her and the publisher all the copies of the book and all the manuscripts and letters relevant to the case for a down payment of £10,000 and the restoration of her annuity of £400, which was to be paid to her two daughters on her death. They also indemnified the publisher.

She signed the agreement, but back in Westbourne Place she found herself friendless and alone and bitterly regretting the loss of her papers and letters, which she felt would, in the long run, have produced far more than the £10,000 she was fast spending.

She published a bitter attack on William Fitzgerald, a Lord of the Treasury, and his father, who had been her legal adviser. The reason for this was mainly because Fitzgerald had destroyed a letter to her from the Duke, in which he had promised her son an army commission. She was accused of publishing a libel and committed to the Marshalsea prison for nine months, where conditions were so appalling that she soon became ill. However, the Duke kept his promise, and while she was in

26. Flask Walk.

27. John Keats.

28. Keats' House, Wentworth Place.

29. Highgate Cemetery in the 1860s.

30. Heath Street, Hampstead in 1924.

31. Holly Bush steps, from Holly Mount leading down to Heath Street.

32. Stanley Spencer.

33. (*Above*) 1976 – Carnival time in Pond Square, Highgate.

34. (*Below*) Highgate village – with many eighteenth-century buildings surviving above the modern shop fronts.

35. (*Above*) Highpoint Flats, Highgate.

36. (*Below*) Kingswell Shopping Centre, Heath Street.

37. (*Above*) Swiss Cottage Library.

38. (*Below*) Royal Free Hospital, Hampstead.

prison she received the news that her son George had been appointed, 'without purchase', a Coronet in the 17th Lancers.

She left prison in November 1814, and embarked for France with her two daughters. Here her daughter Ellen married the scientist Louis-Mathurin Busson du Maurier, and their eldest son George du Maurier, coming to England to finish his education became both artist and author. About 1877 he settled in Hampstead, first in Church Row and then in New Grove House, while his son Gerald, the actor-manager, lived from 1916 until his death in 1934 at Cannon Hall, and Gerald's daughter Daphne has achieved equal distinction as a novelist.

Mary Anne died in Boulogne on 18 June 1852, at the age of seventy-four, poor and alone. The French edition of *The Times* said: 'We hear that she has lived in Boulogne for many years, with the necessaries, but few of the comforts of life' and the entry on her death certificate was 'indigent'.

It is almost impossible to hold an independent view on social and economic matters without being given a political label, and after the Mary Anne Clarke scandal of 1809 the Hunts' *Examiner* was associated with the group of younger Radicals, who were becoming known as Liberals.

In 1811, during the last phase of George III's illness, the Prince of Wales was at last appointed Prince Regent. He thereupon forsook his Whig principles and his old Whig friends and kept all his father's Tory ministers in office. His debts, his ostentatious way of living and his cruel treatment of his mistresses had already aroused the anger and contempt of a large section of the public, and when a particularly sycophantic eulogy of the Regent appeared in a Tory paper, Leigh Hunt replied, in *The Examiner*, by saying that this 'Adonis in loveliness' was a corpulent man of fifty! 'In short, this delightful, blissful, pleasurable, honourable, virtuous, true and immortal prince is a violater of his word, a libertine overhead and ears in disgrace, a despiser of domestic ties, the companion of gamblers and demireps, a man who has just closed half a century without one single claim on the gratitude of his country, or the respect of posterity.'

It voiced the feelings of nearly all the country, except the Regent's new Tory friends.

Leigh Hunt was at this time living with his young wife in a cottage in West End, Hampstead. Both he and his brother were arrested and brought to trial. They were committed to separate prisons for two years and each fined £500. At the last minute, they were offered a bribe which would have saved them from prison, if they promised to refrain from any further criticism of the Regent or the Government, but they refused, and on 3 February 1813, they were despatched, in separate hackney coaches, each accompanied by two tipstaves, John to Coldbath Fields and Leigh to the Horsemonger Lane prison in Newington Causeway.

Horsemonger Lane was a prison for common felons and Leigh Hunt, sensitive and mortally depressed despite his gallant bearing, heard the rattle of their chains with horror, and then the turn of the key which was to shut him away for two years from the fields and trees, the skylarks and nightingales of his beloved Hampstead.

Nevertheless, he was soon to have special privileges, for he had many sympathisers. He was allotted a ward on the ground floor of the infirmary which had a small room leading from it, and here his wife and their five small children came to live with him.

I turned it into a noble room, [wrote Hunt.] I papered the walls with a trellis of roses; I had the ceiling coloured with clouds and sky; the barred windows I screened with Venetian blinds; and when my bookcases were set up with their busts, and flowers and a pianoforte made their appearance, perhaps there was not a handsomer room on that side of the water. . . . Charles Lamb declared there was no other such room, save in a fairy tale.

But I possessed another surprise, which was a garden. There was a little yard outside the room, railed off from another belonging to the neighbouring ward. This yard I shut in with green palings, adorned it with a trellis, bordered it with a thick bed of earth from a nursery, and even contrived to have a grass-plot. The earth I filled with flowers and young trees. There was an apple tree, from which we managed to get a pudding the second year. As to my flowers, they were allowed to be perfect. Thomas More, who came to see me with Lord Byron, told me he had seen no such heart's ease. . . . Here I wrote and read in fine weather, sometimes under an awning. In autumn, my trellises were hung with scarlet-runners, which added to the flowery investment. I used to shut my eyes in my armchair, and affect to think myself hundreds of miles off.

And here, in this strange prison, Leigh and Marianne Hunt's sixth child, Mary Florimel, was born.

No one writing of the Hunts has ever had a good word to say for Marianne, except her own husband. He had fallen in love with 'this good daughter, who completed her conquest by reading verses better than I had ever yet heard', he said; and writing in 1850, seven years before her death, he declared that she still read beautifully and was also an accomplished artist. Yet she has been described as a slattern, a drug addict, a drunkard, a feckless housewife and inveterate borrower.

Perhaps she was all or some of these things, but Hunt, far more than many people today, was always sensitive and reticent about private and personal matters, and never gave an inkling of this side of her character. She was only twenty-five when she joined him in prison and had already had five children. She was far from strong and had been brought up in a prosperous household. She must have endured dire privations during her sixth confinement, within the prison, yet she had never a word of reproach for her husband, and he wrote with deep gratitude of her loyalty.

Leigh studied and wrote in prison and received many visitors, both old friends, including Charles and Mary Lamb, and new ones whom he had not met before, among them William Hazlitt, Byron and Tom Moore, the aged Jeremy Bentham and Cowden Clarke.

Cowden Clarke was a master in his father's Nonconformist Academy at Enfield and was a great admirer of the Hunts' radical *Examiner*. It was a good school, where the sixty or seventy boys were taught, in addition to the Classics of the public schools, history, geography and French. It was a converted house, in rural surroundings, and the boys slept in small dormitories which had a homelike atmosphere. The boys were each given a garden plot to cultivate. There was no flogging and Cowden Clarke had a special concern for character training as well as a formal education.

Here in 1803, arrived little John Keats, aged eight, and his younger brother George, from the busy Swan and Hoop, the inn which their parents ran in Moorgate. A few months later their father was killed in a fall from his horse, and within two months their mother married again. John and George remained at school, but the two younger children, Tom and Fanny, were sent to live with their mother's parents at Edmonton.

Then the grandfather died. He left money for his widow and a little for the children, but their mother, whose second marriage was disastrous, began a long lawsuit contesting the will. The loss of their father and the estrangement from their mother were devastating for the children. They knew nothing of their father's family, and were thrown very much on each other's company, an affectionate and very closely-knit quartet, cared for by their ageing grandmother to the best of her ability.

The lease of the Swan and Hoop fell in. Shortly afterwards their mother's second husband, Rawlings, died, and their mother, with no money of her own, became reconciled with the grandmother and joined the little family at Edmonton. John in particular was overjoyed at the reunion, but she was a sick woman and only two years later she died of consumption.

That year Keats left school and the trustees of his small estate raised the money for him to be apprenticed to a doctor at Edmonton, with a view to his becoming a surgeon apothecary.

John had had a sad childhood. 'I scarcely remember counting upon any happiness', he once said. But Cowden Clarke was kind to him and recognised the unusual quality of his mind. Twice a week John would walk from Edmonton to Enfield to visit him and receive further lessons from him in the Classics as well as English literature and poetry, in which he became increasingly absorbed. Clarke introduced him to *The Examiner* and made him a radical, and when Clarke visited Leigh Hunt in prison and their friendship developed, John's imagination was fired.

George left school to become a city clerk. In 1814 the grandmother died. John continued his apprenticeship with Doctor Hammond, but no longer lived under his roof, taking lodgings with George. Tom was still at school and Fanny, also at boarding school, spent her holidays with her guardian and trustee Abbey and his family, at Walthamstow.

John began to write his first poetry – sonnets to Byron and Chatterton, and then a poem 'To Leigh Hunt on Leaving Prison'. Cowden Clarke encouraged him and in 1815, when the time came for him to take his year's training at Guy's and St Thomas's hospitals,* his mind was nearly as full of poetry as medicine, but he worked hard at his medical studies, moving to lodgings in the Borough. George left his clerk's apprenticeship that same year. He was a gregarious soul and began a gay, Bohemian life, living mainly in the region of the Goswell Road and Oxford Street, with a circle of minor poets who were mainly the sons and daughters of prosperous tradespeople, given to family concerts, dances and parties, but John, living in the sordid slums of the Borough, with their squalor and poverty, their bear gardens and body-snatchers, saw a grimmer side of life.

These were the days when surgical operations were performed without anaesthetics and the body snatchers were busy securing corpses, either stolen from their death-beds or from the graveyards, for the anatomists to study. Some of the surgeons achieved remarkable

* Students attended both hospitals at this time.

speed and dexterity during their operations but John became dresser to one of the worst, who had a horrifying lack of skill and was considered by his fellow surgeons to have pursued a career of butchery.

Keats began to read Wordsworth who, until 1815, was little known, and had been sharply criticised by Hunt in *The Examiner* for becoming a Tory. As a student at Cambridge, Wordsworth had visited France during the early days of the Revolution, and fired with romantic enthusiasm for the ideology of the revolutionaries, had declared himself a Jacobin, but when he returned the following year, ostensibly to improve his French, he became disillusioned by the behaviour of the revolutionaries and suffered a change of heart. He returned to England when the war with France seemed imminent, leaving behind the French girl he had promised to marry and their child, but his family dissuaded him from the marriage, and just before war was declared he made another quick journey to France, to break the news to her that the marriage would not be taking place.

It was after this that he and Dorothy moved to the Quantocks and he met Coleridge. The *Lyrical Ballads* made no great impact at first and certainly little money, but after Wordsworth's marriage he wrote much of his finest poetry, and by the time his collected edition of poems was published in 1815 he was regarded as one of the finest poets in the country, even by Hunt.

Keats was inspired by him and Hunt, just released from prison, began to publish Wordsworth's sonnets in *The Examiner*, as well as some of Byron's work.

In the summer of 1814 Hunt and his family were all ill. Mrs Hunt left the prison and took the children to Brighton to recover, but Hunt had to remain for the full term, being freed on 3 February 1815. He had very little money and the fine had still to be paid. Lodgings were found for them all in the Edgware Road, near his brother, and Hunt said that as his coach drove along the New Road (the Marylebone Road), from which there was a clear view of Hampstead and Highgate, he saw again 'the old hills of my affection standing where they used to do and breathing me a welcome'.

Gradually, despite his ill-health, Leigh Hunt took up the reins again. He visited Lord Byron at his mansion in Piccadilly, in return for the visits Byron had paid him in prison. Byron was 28 and had already earned a name for himself as a Regency rake of the worst type, although he probably pretended to far more wickedness than he ever committed. After several unimportant publications and an extended grand tour, which he could ill afford, he suddenly achieved romantic fame with his publication of *Childe Harold* in 1812. It also brought him much needed financial success, although not nearly enough for his tastes, for he was an inveterate gambler. He was a radical and a Bonapartist and with his friends Samuel Rogers and Tom Moore, who were already part of the Hollands' circle, became a welcome visitor to Holland House, and it was here that he and Caroline Lamb met, to begin their strange, brief love affair.

For a year or two Byron was the idol of all the romantic young women in London society. In 1815 he married Anne Isabella Milbanke and at the end of the year their daughter was born, but the marriage was unhappy and a few weeks later Lady Byron returned to her family with the baby and never returned. The charges against him were never exactly specified, but the rumours were all dark and lurid, and overnight his popularity vanished, only true friends like Lord Holland, Samuel Rogers and Tom Moore remaining loyal to him.

When Hunt visited him in Piccadilly 'the separation had just taken place, and he had become ill himself', he recorded. Byron 'felt the attacks of the public severely; and to crown all, he had an execution on his house'. There were, in fact, nine executions on the house in twelve months, which may well have been one of the reasons why his wife felt she could take no more, and at the end of 1815 Byron had to sell his library.

It was very soon after this that he left England, and by the spring of 1816 the Hunts were back in Hampstead, living in the house of Mrs Hunts' step-father. The Hunts had many homes throughout their chequered lives, but this Hampstead house has been identified as Vale Lodge in the Vale of Health, standing behind its large garden and high hedge on the very edge of the Heath. It was no doubt not so large then as in the days when Edgar Wallace was living there, a century later, but it was commodious enough and it was during his years there that Leigh Hunt's literary circle grew: and as he resumed his walks over the Heath and entertained his ever-widening circle of friends, his health improved and he was able to finish his narrative poem *The Story of Rimini*, which he had begun in prison.

He had met the aristocratic Shelley once or twice before his imprisonment, for Shelley was fired by radical principles while he was still at Eton, and had been sent down from Oxford for what was considered to be his atheism, when he published his immature pamphlet *The Necessity of Atheism*. With the fierce courage of extreme youth, he clung to his liberal beliefs and rejected a valuable estate in Surrey and a seat in Parliament, content to live on £1,000 a year. To many of his fellow writers this was affluence, and to millions of English people it was undreamed of wealth, but compared with the amount he had forfeited, it was little enough.

In 1811, when he was only nineteen, he married Harriet Westbrook, a schoolgirl of sixteen, and in June 1813 their daughter was born, but by the following April Harriet had left him, although she was pregnant again, their son being born in November 1814.

In the meantime, Shelley, a great advocate of Godwin's *Political Justice*, had met and fallen in love with Mary Wollstonecraft Godwin, the daughter born after Godwin's marriage to Mary Wollstonecraft. They eloped to France for a time and when they returned to England, Godwin, who had borrowed heavily from Shelley, to help him with the shaky finances of his *Juvenile Library*, refused to see them. Shelley pleaded that he and Mary had done no more than practice what Godwin himself had advocated in his *Political Justice*, but Godwin, exasperated, retorted that the book had been written many years previously and was a theoretical work, the principles of which would have been splendid in some Utopia, but not in London, where he and his daughter had been exposed to scorn, and his teaching had been perverted.

Shelley was now being dunned for money which he had lent to Godwin, but Godwin, saying that his conscience suffered greatly, asked for still more. Shelley, with a touching faith in humanity to abide by the rules of honour and goodness, was deeply grieved by his hypocrisy, but lived happily with Mary at Windsor, by now writing superb poetry, comparable with that of Coleridge and Wordsworth.

These poets of the end of the eighteenth century and the early years of the nineteenth, Scott, Coleridge, Wordsworth, Byron, Shelley and Keats, had broken away from the mannered and affected writing of the Augustan age, which had reflected a cynically material and prosaic acceptance of life, and had been inspired by a new romantic movement of questioning and wonder. As Hogarth in his drawing and painting, they strove to express in simple but imaginative language a realistic view of the world, unimpeded by sterile conventions.

In December 1816, Harriet Shelley's body was found in the Serpentine. Hardly anything is known of her life after she deserted Shelley, but little of any credit has come to light, although Shelley provided for her generously and allowed her to keep the children. A week or two after her suicide, Shelley and Mary were married, and he sought to recover the custody of his children, to whom he was devoted. Harriet's father, probably with an eye on the Shelley family's fortune, contested the case and eventually won it; and it was during these anxious months that Shelley visited Leigh Hunt in the Vale of Health, staying sometimes for several days.

Mary Shelley, in the preface to the first collected edition of Shelley's works, wrote of his 'gentle and cordial goodness that animated his intercourse with warm affection and helpful sympathy', and of the 'eagerness and ardour with which he was attached to the cause of human happiness and improvement'. His dream was to rid life of its misery and evil and he,

> dedicated to it every power of his mind, every pulsation of his heart. He looked on political freedom as the direct agent to effect the happiness of mankind; and thus any new-sprung hope of liberty inspired a joy and an exultation more intense and wild than he could have felt for any personal advantage.
>
> . . . He had been from youth the victim of the state of feeling inspired by the reaction of the French Revolution, and believing firmly in the justice and excellence of his views, it cannot be wondered that a nature so sensitive, as impetuous, and as generous as his, should put its whole force into the attempt to alleviate for others the evil of those systems from which he had himself suffered. Many advantages attended his birth; he spurned them all when balanced with what he considered his duties. He was generous to imprudence, devoted to heroism.

Leigh Hunt loved him dearly and Shelley, ever generous, helped him to pay his fine and settle his other debts.

At Hampstead, wrote Hunt, Shelley delighted,

> in the natural broken ground, and in the fresh air of the place, especially when the wind set in from the north-west, which used to give an intoxication of animal spirits. Here also he swam his paper-boats on the ponds, and delighted to play with my children, particularly with my eldest boy, the seriousness of whose imagination, and his susceptibility of a 'grim' impression (a favourite epithet of Shelley's), highly interested him. He would play at 'frightful creatures' with him, from which the other would snatch 'a fearful joy', only begging him occasionally 'not to do the horn', which was a way that Shelley had of screwing up his hair in front, to imitate a weapon of that sort.

In this year, 1816, John Keats was still working at St Thomas's for his

Licentiate examination and was also house surgeon, but at the same time his interest in poetry was growing and he was writing and experimenting. With Hunt's publication of *The Story of Rimini*, he also began to plan a long epic poem *Endymion*. *The Examiner* was now publishing poems of Wordsworth and Byron regularly. Keats, not yet known to Hunt, sent him his 'Solitude' sonnet, which Hunt accepted. Keats passed his Licentiate examination and settled down to the prospect of another year's study, for his membership of the Royal College of Surgeons. Still in lodgings at the Borough, his rather lonely life was cheered by his friendship with Joseph Severn, who at this time was apprenticed to an engraver, although he was already making experiments in water colour miniatures.

Cowden Clarke was always a welcome visitor at the Vale of Health and later that year he collected some of Keats' work and took it over to Hunt for his opinion. Hunt was enthusiastic and asked Clarke to bring Keats over to see him. So in October 1816, Keats had his first introduction to Hampstead, walking across the Heath with Cowden Clarke. The visit was a success. Hunt had shown Keats' poems to Godwin and Hazlitt, both of whom confirmed his high opinion of them, and Keats, diffident and shy, not yet twenty-one, was received into that distinguished literary circle.

Hunt's white painted cottage, despite its chronic disorder and the crowd of children, the invalid wife which Marianne Hunt had become, and Leigh's own dilettante fecklessness, opened a new world to the young Keats, for it was full of books and pictures. There were flowers and music, a zest for living, and above all conversation – sound criticism and discussion of life and poetry – to which he was eager to contribute.

Through Hunt he met Benjamin Haydon, the painter, who had been contributing art criticism to *The Examiner* since its founding, and Reynolds, a young poet of Keats' age, studying for the law, whose father was a master at Christ's Hospital. Haydon introduced him to William Hazlitt and Reynolds to many who were to be lasting friends, including Charles Dilke and Charles Brown.

John was now making the long walk from Southwark to Hampstead every week or two, and decided to move north of the river, to lodgings in Cheapside, which he shared with George and also Tom, who had now left school and, like George, was a City clerk.

For several months Keats had been having doubts about his future in medicine. Appalled by the hazards of surgical operation and the sufferings of the patients, as well as the dire results of his immediate master's incompetence and clumsiness, he began to wonder whether he could shoulder the enormous responsibility of undertaking such work himself.

'Lord, a man should have the fine point of his soul taken off to become fit for this world,' he exclaimed one day.

Finally, when he reached his twenty-first birthday, he broke the news to his trustee that he was giving up medicine and had decided to devote himself to poetry. Abbey, with astonished anger, pointed out to him that there was very little money left for him, but Keats, as impractical over money matters as Leigh Hunt, was undeterred. There was at least something left, and Hunt was now publishing his poems in *The Examiner*, along with those of Shelley, and hailing them both as members of the new school of poetry – a second wave of the revolution which had begun with Wordsworth and Coleridge. His mind was made up and he was gaining confidence in his own powers.

It was on 11 December 1816, very soon after making this decision, that at Hunt's cottage, he met Shelley for the first time. Shelley had come up from Bath, where he and Mary were living for a time, to pay Hunt a brief visit. Keats and Horace Smith were already there, having met for the first time. Keats had wanted to meet Horace Smith for a long time, but Smith was more interested in Shelley, and as they all set off for a long walk over the Heath, Keats was almost ignored. Smith said afterwards that Keats seemed very shy and unused to company. It was a cruelly class-conscious age still, despite the new spirit of liberalism, and Hunt recorded that Keats was 'sensitive on the score of his origins' and did not take to Shelley as warmly as Shelley took to Keats. There was no snobbishness in Shelley, and he was greatly impressed with Keats' work, as yet in its immaturity, and sincerely generous in his praise of it.

It was on this occasion, on first meeting Keats, that Shelley returned home to hear of the suicide of his wife Harriet, and the following January he married Mary. Her step-sister, Jane Clairmont, the daughter of Godwin's second wife, was one of the many young women who had fallen in love with Byron. She had pursued him relentlessly to Switzerland. Their daughter, Allegra, was born early in 1817, Jane coming back to stay with Shelley and Mary for the confinement. She took Allegra back to Italy, but Byron insisted on taking the child away from her and placing her in a convent. He then abandoned Jane and moved on to Venice, where he began his romance with the Countess Guiccioli. Jane, with no money, became a governess in Florence. Byron had been warned that conditions at the convent where he had placed

Allegra were bad but he left it too late. When she was four years old she died of typhus.

Keats' friendship with Hunt continued and Cowden Clarke often accompanied him during his walks over the Heath to Hampstead. Hunt introduced him to Ollier, the publisher, who was looking for new poems and encouraged Keats to make his first collection for a complete volume. Keats introduced his brother George to the Hunts' circle and Shelley was a frequent visitor, adding fire and sparkle to the friendly, brilliant talk, mainly fiercely radical, which they all enjoyed there.

Keats' first volume was nearly ready. Shelley, during a walk on the Heath, advised him to omit or revise one or two of the less successful poems, but Keats, still not quite at ease with him, did not take his advice.

On 3 March 1817, the day that his hospital appointment came to an end, the volume was published. Two days before, carrying an advance copy, he walked to Hampstead to show it to Leigh Hunt. They met in Millfield Lane and Hunt brought him back to Vale Lodge to celebrate. For Keats it was a magical day. He waited for the reviews. None appeared. Then one or two brief notices were published. He looked for Hunt's notice in *The Examiner.* Week after week he searched for it, but it was not to be written for another three months.

However, Reynolds and Haydon supported and encouraged him in his bitter disappointment and Reynolds' publishers, Taylor and Hessey, expressed an interest in the new young poet, particularly when he discussed with them his projected *Endymion.*

Both Tom and George disliked their City jobs, and the Cheapside lodgings that the three brothers were still sharing were damp and unpleasant. They decided in that spring of 1817 to move to Hampstead and took lodgings in the house of the local postman, Bentley and his family, at number 1, Well Walk, on the very edge of the Heath, next door to the old Green Man.

London was changing. Nash was building Regent Street. The Eyre family were developing their St John's Wood estate. In Hampstead, however, there was very little change as yet from the days of the eighteenth century. The main landowners, Eton College, the Dean and Chapter of Westminster and the Maryon Wilson family, were not free to sell land or grant building leases without legal action, and as they were all wealthy and in no great need of change, things remained much as they were. The fifth Earl of Chesterfield had obtained a private estate act to sell his Belsize land to four Hampstead men, but little development had yet taken place. The Eton College Chalcot estate was still essentially farmland. In 1811 there were six houses on it and by 1832 still only nine. In 1812 the Maryon Wilson family, after complicated negotiations, had granted William Coleman the right to develop fourteen acres of copyhold land on the eastern part of their estate, on which he built Downshire Hill, with its attractive, white stucco Regency houses and pleasant gardens. The beautiful little proprietary estate chapel of St John, with its portico and cupola, was built about the same time, designed probably by Cockerell, and the first houses in John Street were appearing.

Travelling to London was easier, for in these Regency years there were six coaches out of Hampstead and six in from London each day.

When John and his brothers moved to Well Walk the lime trees were just showing their pale green buds and all that summer the boys were out of doors, exploring the Heath and the surrounding countryside. It was not until the following winter that they realised how cramped their lodgings were and that the little house was crowded with the Bentleys' noisy small children. But the Bentleys were very kind to them, especially to Tom, the youngest.

Keats remained friendly with Hunt, but their relationship was never the same after the disappointment over the long delayed review in *The Examiner*. His two nearest friends now were the two who had been introduced to him by Reynolds – Charles Wentworth Dilke and Charles Brown. They had been among the first to take a plot of land from William Coleman in John Street and here they had built a pair of Regency villas, Wentworth Place, during the winter of 1815-16. Dilke and his wife Maria lived in one of them, Brown, a bachelor, in the other. Dilke, six years older than Keats, was a civil servant in the Navy Pay office with keen literary interests, who had already brought out a six volume edition of Old English Plays. Charles Brown had a small private income and a passion for the theatre and had already had one musical play produced at Drury Lane in 1814.

Leigh Hunt was running into money troubles again, for during the years following Waterloo the fear of Jacobinism died hard, the Tory strength grew and the circulation of *The Examiner*, too radical to be generally acceptable, declined.

In the end, Hunt had to leave the Vale in a hurry, to escape his creditors, for he owed more than £1,000. The generous and sympathetic Shelley offered him and his large family refuge for a time, and Keats was called in to help with the last minute packing and sort out what Hunt described as 'all the chaos of packed trunks, lumber, litter, dust, dirty fingers etc'. The following morning, Sunday, 6 April 1817 the family took a coach for Marlow, leaving Keats alone in the bare, dirty cottage which had once been the Mecca of his dreams. He walked back across the Heath, dreaming of the long epic poem *Endymion*, which was absorbing him increasingly and which Taylor had promised to publish. On Haydon's advice, he decided to leave his brothers in Hampstead and go away to the Isle of Wight, to begin it in solitude. He worked with nervous energy, self critical and often near despair, as he grappled with the technical difficulties of his work, and he was lonely. A few weeks later he moved to Margate, where Tom joined him, George being involved in a variety of jobs in the City once more.

He finished Book One of *Endymion* and began work on Book Two, but progress was slow, although in between times he was writing other poems. By June the boys were all together again at Hampstead, for money was running low. George had been involved in one or two unsatisfactory business ventures and Keats was worried about Tom, whom he feared was developing the tuberculosis which had killed their mother. To add to his worries, some adverse and even destructive notices of his first book of poems appeared and a few weeks later Hunt's long-delayed notice in *The Examiner*. Hunt was back in London by now, living first with his brother in Maida Vale and then at Lisson Grove North, and his review of Keats' work was not only far from encouraging but distinctly patronising.

Keats sought consolation and renewed confidence in long walks over the Heath with Severn, Reynolds and Cowden Clarke. He had great courage, in the face of a shattering disappointment, and studied anew the works of Wordsworth and Hazlitt, who at this time were his literary lions.

George and Tom went off on holiday to France, on money borrowed from Keats, while Keats was invited by Bailey, a friend of Reynolds, to share his rooms at Magdalen College, Oxford, for part of the long vacation. Bailey was reading for Holy Orders, and while he studied Keats worked steadily at Book Three of *Endymion*. This he was happy about as he wrote it, although disappointed when he re-read it.

By the beginning of October, Keats was back in Hampstead and at work on Book Four of *Endymion*, but now Blackwood's *Edinburgh Magazine*, which was fiercely against the Whigs and all radicalism, came out with a savage attack on Keats and the 'Cockney School of Poetry'. To the sensitive Keats it must have been torturing, and to add to his worries Tom was back from France and showing no improvement in his health.

Keats slipped quietly away to an inn at Box Hill to write the last part of *Endymion* and the poem was finished at Burford Bridge on 28 November 1817.

Back in Hampstead he heard that Wordsworth and his wife were paying one of their rare visits to London. Haydon, who had already met Wordsworth, when he had sat for him for one of the heads in his vast painting 'Christ's Entry Into Jerusalem', arranged for Keats to meet the great man for a few minutes, at the house of Wordsworth's brother-in-law in Queen Anne Street, and Wordsworth, who was becoming increasingly pompous, and impatient of any criticism of his own work, seems to have treated the young Keats kindly.

Keats set about the task of revising and copying *Endymion* for the printers, and became increasingly friendly with the Dilkes at Wentworth House, and also with Charles Brown, who had let his half of the house for the summer months, but was now back in residence. With Brown he often went to Drury Lane and Covent Garden and began to write theatrical reviews for the *Champion.*

At the end of December, Haydon gave his famous dinner party for Keats, Wordsworth, Monkhouse and Charles Lamb, which was a highly successful and convivial affair, Lamb, as usual, quickly becoming tipsy, and Keats reciting parts of *Endymion.* A few days later Keats met Wordsworth by chance, walking on Hampstead Heath, and Wordsworth invited him to dine at his lodgings in Mortimer Street, with his wife and sister-in-law, the Sara with whom Coleridge had been so deeply in love.

Mrs Wordsworth treated her husband with an awed deference, which fed his egotism and vanity, and when Keats disagreed with him on some point during a discussion, she placed her hand gently on his arm and said, softly but firmly, 'Mr Wordsworth is never interrupted.' Sara, though not very interested in Keats at this time, had more moral courage to argue with Wordsworth, but it must have been disconcerting and disillusioning for Keats; yet he always maintained that, despite the dogmatic manner he developed, Wordsworth was a great poet.

It was about this time that Keats met Coleridge, who had moved to Highgate the previous year. Keats was now dressing in the tradition of a radical poet, with open necked shirt and hair wild and dishevelled. 'A loose, slack, not well-dressed youth met Mr Green and myself in a lane near Highgate,' recorded Coleridge. 'Mr Green knew him and spoke.* It was Keats! He was introduced to me and stayed a minute or so. After

---

* They had met as medical students.

he had left us a little way, he came back and said 'Let me carry away the memory, Coleridge, of having pressed your hand!'

' "There is death in that hand," I said to Green, when Keats was gone; yet this was, I believe, before consumption shewed itself distinctly.'

Keats finished *Endymion* and sent it to his publisher. He was writing a great deal of poetry now and his mind was growing fast. George came of age in February 1818 and was to come into his inheritance. He wrote that Tom was better and they were returning to Hampstead, but John, fearing for Tom, hurried down to Teignmouth and saw at once that far from having improved in health, the boy was dying. George returned to London and made final arrangements to marry Georgina Wylie and emigrate to America. In April *Endymion* was published at last. Keats felt it to be inadequate and Taylor himself had been disappointed with it. Tom was anxious to return to Hampstead and he and John made the long coach journey back from Devon. On 28 May, George was married and a few weeks late he and Georgina set off by coach for Liverpool, on their way to seek their fortune in America. Keats and Brown went with them and then continued north for a walking tour in Scotland, while Tom was left in the care of the Bentleys at Well Walk.

Early in August, Keats returned to Hampstead, leaving Brown to continue his holiday alone, but he missed the letter Dilke had sent to him in Scotland, telling him that Tom had taken a sudden turn for the worse.

He left the coach at the Pond Street stop, and still not knowing of Tom's condition, dropped in at Wentworth Place before reaching Well Walk. The Dilkes broke the news to him and, distracted with grief, he hurried round to the cottage.

Brown had let his part of Wentworth Place to Mrs Brawne, a young widow with three children, Fanny, Samuel and Margaret, for the few summer months he was to be in Scotland, but Keats did not yet meet them. For the next few weeks he devoted himself to nursing the dying Tom; and to add to his pain the August number of *Blackwood's* published its most scathing review yet of Keat's work. It was even worse than the Cockney School jibe, still associating him with Hunt. 'Mr Hunt is a small poet, but he is a clever man. Mr Keats is a still smaller poet, and he is only a boy of pretty abilities, which he has done everything in his power to spoil,' said the notice, and ended: 'It is a better and wiser thing to be a starved apothecary than a starved poet; so back to the shop, Mr John, back to the plasters, pills and ointment boxes. . . .'

Keats was only twenty-two, worried about George who had failed to repay some desperately needed money, and had the additional sorrow of watching helplessly as Tom slowly declined. The wounding and unjustified attack on him in the *Edinburgh Review* seemed just another part of the nightmare through which he was living, yet he had sufficient trust in his increasing powers of thought and imagination not to lose confidence entirely. The *Quarterly Review* was nearly as derogatory, but other critics joined issue with the *Edinburgh Review*, some even conceding that Mr Keats had 'powers of language' and 'gleams of genius'.

Undeterred, he worked steadily on, developing his genius and a power of discriminating between the good and the indifferent in his writing. Severn was a good friend to him during these anxious days and he saw the Dilkes whenever he could spare time from Tom's sick bed, and also met the Brawnes. When Brown returned to Wentworth Place from Scotland, late in September, Mrs Brawne and her children moved to Elm Cottage in Downshire Hill, close by, and the families remained close friends.

Tom died in the early hours of 1 December, at the age of nineteen. Keats ran round to Wentworth House to tell Brown, who at once took charge of affairs. He begged Keats not to return to the lonely lodgings in Well Walk but to come and live with him at Wentworth Place. Keats, on the verge of a nervous collapse with grief and worry, gladly agreed. Brown looked after him well during those difficult weeks, taking him to see his friends, including Haydon, Hazlitt and Charles Lamb, and also the Brawnes, where Keats began to fall in love with the beautiful and stylish eighteen-year-old Fanny.

At Wentworth Place he settled down to serious work that winter. He spent Christmas Day with the Brawnes, which Fanny later was to recall as the happiest day of her life. His most serious poem at this time was *Hyperion*, but he was also pouring out a flood of lyrics and sonnets. During a visit with Brown to Dilke's parents at Chichester, he wrote *The Eve of St Agnes*, but early in February he was back at Wentworth Place, depressed by a shortage of money and the knowledge that Byron's work was selling extremely well and his own hardly at all.

The Dilkes decided to move to Westminster, where their son was going to school, and the Brawnes rented the Dilkes's part of Wentworth Place, moving in early in April 1819. On that day Keats drew his last hundred pounds from the bank, but their arrival stimulated him to write some of his loveliest poetry. With little prospect of ever being able to afford to marry, Keats turned away from the problems of the future and lived in the present. During the next few weeks he wrote his 'Ode on Melancholy', his 'Ode on a Grecian Urn' and, perhaps the best loved of all his poems, the 'Ode to a Nightingale', all under the plum tree in the garden of Wentworth Place, where a nightingale had built near the house during that exceptionally warm and sunny spring of 1819.

But the idyll was all too brief. He wanted desperately to marry Fanny. A letter came from George to say that their first child had been born and he needed more money for a new business venture in which he was involved. There seems to have been a good deal of muddle between the Keats' trustees and the solicitors, and money which should have been made over to John was never forthcoming. Brown was letting his part of the house for the summer, and John told Fanny he would go into the country for a spell, work hard, and try to make some money. He departed once more to the Isle of Wight, working principally on *Lamia*, but he was not well. The rapture of the earlier part of the year had departed and he wrote despairingly passionate love letters to Fanny. Brown joined him and they collaborated in the writing of a play *Otho the Great*, which they hoped Edmund Kean would accept, but then they heard that Kean intended to go on an American tour. They moved to Winchester. There was another letter from George, asking for money, and Keats went at once to London to try and raise some for him.

Early in September he wrote his poem 'To Autumn' – 'Where are the songs of Spring? Ay, where are they?' It was the year of the Peterloo massacres, and moved to pity and anger by the outrage, he decided to become a political journalist. He wrote to Brown saying that he loved Fanny too much to be able to return to Wentworth Place that winter. Dilke found him lodgings in Westminster, near his own home, but calling at Wentworth Place one day to collect some of his belongings, Keats found his love for Fanny so overwhelming that he could not face the thought of another separation. By the 21 October he was back with Brown and became formally engaged to Fanny.

The winter that followed was no repetition of the halcyon days of the previous spring. To add to the strain of his own emotions. Brown engaged Abigail a young Irish girl, as a housekeeper, with whom he was soon sleeping, and she became pregnant.

Keats, having laid his hands on some money for George and a little for himself, from his trustees, was busy preparing his new volume of poems for his publishers, but he was still far from well. It was a bitterly cold winter and with the new year came snow and freezing fog. Then George arrived at Wentworth Place with the news that Georgiana was expecting a second child and he must have money at once. Brown sent

Otho the Great to Covent Garden, for Macready to consider, but it was returned, apparently unread. George left after three weeks, having collected money that was due to him and an additional loan from Keats which, although neither of them realised it at the time, left Keats not only penniless but £10 in debt.

On the night of 3 February he returned from London, having taken an outside seat on the coach for cheapness, despite a bitterly cold wind. In a high fever, he staggered to Wentworth Place from the Pond Street coach stop. Brown saw that he was seriously ill and put him to bed, and as Keats sank between the sheets he had a small lung haemorrhage. He knew what it meant. 'That drop of blood is my death warrant,' he said to Brown. 'I must die.'

That night he had a far more serious haemorrhage, yet within a few days he was able to leave his bed and lie on the sofa in his peaceful little sitting room, with its french windows opening on to the garden. The doctor whom Brown had summoned to attend him was Mr G. R. Rodd, the surgeon of Hampstead High Street, whose wife was a friend of the Brawnes. Keats, having no illusions about the nature of his illness, offered to release Fanny from her engagement, but this, to his infinite joy and relief, she refused to do. Mr Rodd did not recommend too frequent visits, not only because it could upset them both, but because of the danger of infection to Fanny, but she sent him a short note every night.

Brown was jealous of Fanny. The hostility between Brown and Keats deepened as Abigail's pregnancy became obvious and Fanny began visiting Keats more often. Mr Rodd called in a specialist who recommended a more invigorating diet for Keats. It gave him more strength and confidence for a time and enabled him to complete his volume of poems for his publishers.

Fanny and Keats were now seeing a great deal of each other and were very happy. On 14 March he was well enough to make the journey to London, to dine with Taylor, and a week or two later was able to walk the four miles to Piccadilly, to the private view of Haydon's picture, at last finished, in which Keats' head and so many others appeared, and walk all the way back to Wentworth Place, declaring that he was getting better every day.

Brown was obliged to let his part of the house earlier than usual that year, in order to raise money for the baby he would soon have to support. He planned to spend the summer in Scotland, but Keats was not strong enough to go with him. Hunt was now living at 13 Mortimer Terrace, Kentish Town, a 'sort of compromise between

London and our beloved Hampstead', as he said, and considerably cheaper. He offered to find lodgings for Keats close by and sadly Keats left Wentworth Place. Hunt was now editing the *Indicator* as well as *The Examiner*, and he printed 'La Belle Dame Sans Merci' in the *Indicator*, but the improvement in Keats' health did not last and he missed Fanny sorely. He took long walks over the Heath with Severn, but he grew depressed in his loneliness and, without any justification, grew jealous and suspicious of Fanny's every move. It would have been improper for her to visit him at his lodgings without a chaperone and he did not go very often to Wentworth Place, as he found the partings almost unbearable, but she wrote to him constantly.

Towards the end of June he had another haemorrhage. His landlady told the Hunts and they moved him to Mortimer Terrace. His new book of poems was coming out any day, yet he knew he was dying. He began bitterly to brood on the *Blackwood* review of the previous year and the poisonous pen of Lockhart, which he said had brought about his end.

The only hope for him now, said the doctors, was to winter in Italy. The book came out in the last week of June and was generously reviewed. Even *Blackwood's* gave it an acknowledgement. His friends were good to him, but Keats was too ill to appreciate their kindness. Shelley wrote inviting him to stay with him at Pisa, but he declined the offer. He quarrelled with the Hunts over a letter from Fanny which, owing to the ineptitude of either Mrs Hunt or a servant-maid, had not been delivered to him for two days. He left the house and managed to reach as far as Well Walk. There, resting on a wayside seat, he was seen 'sobbing into a handkerchief'. That evening he arrived on the Brawnes' doorstep at Wentworth Place, so ill that Mrs Brawne took him in and nursed him for the next month. His publishers, on the strength of the success of the new volume, arranged for his journey to Rome, where there was a good English doctor, and Severn offered to accompany him. At the end of August he had another severe haemorrhage and again Mrs Brawne and Fanny nursed him lovingly.

On 13 September he said his farewells to the Brawnes and to Hampstead and set sail from Tower Dock for the three week long journey to Leghorn. During the voyage his health deteriorated and on one occasion he tried to commit suicide by taking an overdose of laudanum, but Severn was able to dissuade him.

They sailed from Leghorn to Naples and after a few days set out in a small hired coach for the week-long drive to Rome, where they arrived on 15 November, the kindly Severn doing all he could to encourage and cheer poor Keats. The English doctor had booked rooms for them close to the Spanish Steps in the Piazza di Spagna and for a week or two Keats seemed a little better, but on 10 December he had another severe haemorrhage, after which they occurred with increasing frequency and on the night of 23 February 1821, he died.

When the news reached Fanny she was heart-broken and mourned him for many years; and there were many others to grieve for Keats, who had shown such wonderful promise and who died so young, for he was a lovable character.

'I weep for Adonais – he is dead!' wrote Shelley at Pisa, a few months later, in his elegy on 'The Death of Keats'.

Leigh Hunt and his family, including the now tubercular Marianne, were still living in Kentish Town, but their fortunes were sinking. The political climate throughout the whole of Europe was becoming increasingly anti-Radical and the sales of *The Examiner* were falling disastrously. Lord Byron, still living with the Countess Guiccioli, had suggested to Shelley that Hunt might join them, to edit a new Liberal quarterly review. Shelley urged Hunt to come and offered to pay the fares for the family. John Hunt agreed to struggle on alone with the flagging fortunes of *The Examiner*, and in November 1821, Leigh Hunt and his family set sail for Leghorn. The weather was appalling and the six children and their parents were herded into one small cabin, with their servant in a closet leading from it.

By the time they reached Dartmouth, the ship had to be abandoned and it was not until the following May that they set off once more, this time from Plymouth, in a different ship.

When they eventually arrived at Pisa, Byron offered them rooms on the ground floor of his magnificent mansion, the Casa Lanfranchi. Here Shelley visited them, from his summer residence at Lerici. A day or two later Shelley, now twenty-nine years old, planned to return to Lerici, travelling post chaise to Leghorn and making the rest of the journey, with his friend Edward Williams, in a light sailing craft. It was a risky venture for the weather was uncertain. A sudden storm blew up, the frail boat collapsed and they were both drowned. When, a week later, Shelley's body was washed ashore, Keats' last volume of poems was found in his jacket pocket.

The bodies were ceremoniously burned on the shore, in the presence of Leigh Hunt and Byron, and Keats' poems were added to the funeral pyre.

The Hunts stayed on for a while with Byron, who at this time was writing *Don Juan*, working through the night into the small hours of the morning, with the help of gin and water. Marianne Hunt was too ill, for most of the time, to leave her room and Hunt found collaboration extremely difficult. The first number of the quarterly appeared, however, but the reviews were disastrous.

At the end of September, they all left Pisa to winter in Genoa, but already relations were strained to breaking point. Byron seemed to like Hunt well enough, but could not stand his wife, whom he described as dowdy and disagreeable and as impertinent as she was silly. As for the children, who romped unchecked up and down the magnificent marble staircase of the palazzo, he said they were like a 'kraal of Hottentots, dirtier and more mischievous than Yahoos,' and put his bull-dog on guard to prevent their using it.

In Genoa the two households lived separately, Mary Shelley joining the Hunts at the Casa Negrotto, a forty-roomed mansion for which they paid £20 a year, while Lord Byron, with the little Countess, now aged about twenty, took an even larger establishment. He was drinking heavily by now and becoming increasingly difficult. Three more numbers of the *Liberal* appeared, yet although they contained poems of Byron, Shelley, Hazlitt and Hunt, none of them was successful, and in July 1823, barely a year after the arrival of the Hunts, Byron departed for Greece, leaving them stranded.

Theodore Hook wrote in *John Bull* at this time: 'Byron is weary and sick to death of the Hunts; he repents that he ever went into partnership with him in the money-making speculation of the magazine. He writes word that 'Hunt is a bore'. 'He is,' says his lordship, 'a proser; Mrs Hunt is no great things; and the six children perfectly intractable.'

Eventually Colborn, the publisher, offered an advance on a collection of Hunt's writings and an autobiography, which enabled the family to return to England. By this time there were seven children, the youngest having been born at Genoa. They travelled across Europe by easy stages of thirty or forty miles a day, in a small travelling carriage, the box of which turned into a chaise with a hood. It was drawn by three horses, with the occasional help of one or two mules. For eighty-two guineas the ten of them were taken to Calais, being given breakfast and dinner each day and allowed four days rest on the way. At Calais they took the new steam-boat to London, where they arrived on 14 October, to receive the news that Byron, at the age of thirty-six, had died at Missolonghi.

The family did not return to Hampstead, but lived for a short time at Highgate, in a house at the lower end of Bromwich Walk, a footpath which once ran from the Grove down to the corner of Swain's Lane and the bottom of West Hill, through the grounds of Holly Lodge. Here, said Hunt, 'I took possession of my old English scenery and my favourite haunts. The country round was almost all pasture; and beloved Hampstead was near'.

He walked across the fields to the ponds in which Shelley had sailed his boats and saw again the 'very little brooks unknown to all but the eye of their lovers'; and here, on the Heath, he wrote his poem 'Gipsy June'. But his future looked bleak. He had a sick wife, a brood of young children and no money. His brother said that because of his long absence abroad, he had forfeited any stake in *The Examiner*.

For the next twenty years, Leight Hunt was engaged in a variety of journalistic ventures which, all too often, did not produce enough money to keep the bailiffs out of his long succession of homes. They included some short-lived weekly periodicals – *The Companion*, *The Chat of the Week*, *The Tatler* and *Leigh Hunt's London Journal*, as well as one or two novels, books of criticism and a volume of new poetry; and in his autobiography he says that it was not until Toryism declined with the rise of Louis Philippe that his small circle of readers began to expand.

From Highgate they were constantly on the move for the next few years – Epsom, St John's Wood, Somers Town, the Marylebone Road – and were never again to live in Hampstead. In 1833 they moved to a charming little house in Upper Cheyne Row, close to the home of Jane and Thomas Carlyle in Cheyne Row, and here they stayed for the next seven years. Hunt wrote of the Carlyles with far more affection and regard than the Carlyles of the Hunts. Carlyle could not but like Hunt, with his charming Georgian elegance and critical but generous mind, but he deplored the squalor and dirt of his home and could make little of his 'large, sickly wife' and the brood of 'well-conditioned, wild children', while Jane never forgave Marianne for borrowing and not returning, a fault which had caused such trouble with Haydon many years earlier.

In 1840 they moved to Edwardes Square in Kensington and after another eleven years to Hammersmith, where Hunt died in 1859, surviving Marianne by only two years, but the last ten years of his life were easier, for the Shelley family granted him a pension, and he was also awarded one from the Civil List.

Moreover, during these later years he had great pleasure from the success of one or two of his plays, which were presented at Covent Garden.

The first number of Charles Dickens' *Bleak House* appeared in 1852, seven years before the death of Leigh Hunt, and the lovable old man was deeply wounded by the popular assumption that Dickens had used him for the character of Harold Skimpole, that odious, irresponsible and selfish idiot of a man, a heartless snob, who bragged of having no common sense in regard to money and was for ever borrowing and cadging from his friends.

Dickens later denied this, although not very convincingly, and there are certain obvious resemblances – living in Somers Town in a state of squalor, yet with remnants of a shabby luxury, the invalid wife who showed signs of being a borrower, the large family of daughters. It is a bitter book – bitter in its description of the appalling slums of London, the unending delays in the Court of Chancery, the first attempts of women to achieve emancipation – but Harold Skimpole has no part in the construction of the plot. For all his admitted charm of manner and appearance, he comes and goes throughout the book like an evil spirit, always in debt, always borrowing, airing his false philosophies, including his heartless theory on how to treat poor Jo, and adopting an air of guileless, child-like candour to conceal an utter lack of principle. He adds nothing to the book and is a shameless travesty of the man who, for all his faults and weaknesses, discovered Keats and Shelley and helped them on their way to immortality.

After Hogarth's death in 1764, his Hampstead home at North End became the Bull and Bush, soon a favourite haunt of London's artists and writers – Gainsborough, Fuseli, Sterne and Garrick. The tradition continued into the early years of the nineteenth century, and to this part of Hampstead John Linnell, the landscape artist, came in 1822, taking first Hope Cottage and then, the following year, Collins' Farm, the farmhouse of the Eton College Wyldes estate. Here, with his young family, he lived for the next five or six years, painting many scenes of Hampstead and also doing a good deal of portraiture, including a painting of the daughter of the second Lord Mansfield, living close by at Ken House.

William Blake was a frequent and greatly loved visitor to the Linnells at Collins' Farm, an old man by this time and despite his brilliance both as an artist and poet, very poor.

He was born in London in 1757, the son of a hosier. It has been suggested that he may have been a descendant of the William Blake of Highgate, who published the *Silver Drops* and founded the orphan-age at Dorchester House, but there is no real proof of this. He was a dreaming, visionary child whom nobody properly understood and by the time he was ten years old he was already writing poetry and had become fascinated by the works of Raphael, Michelangelo and Dürer.

He was apprenticed to an engraver, studied for a short time at the Royal Academy schools and then began to earn his living as an engraver to booksellers. Flaxman became his friend and in 1783 helped with the cost of the publication of his first, privately-printed volume of poems, *Poetical Sketches*, which had been written between 1768 and 1777. They are lyrical poems utterly alien in spirit to the materialism of the eighteenth century, for they are fresh, and their language, with a delicate choice of simile, seems almost childish in its simplicity. They are the first poems of the English renaissance in poetry, which emerged from the Augustan formalism, and they may well have been the inspiration of the later poets, Southey, Wordsworth and Coleridge, yet the *Poetical Sketches* were never published. The whole issue was presented to Blake and no one knows what happened to it.

In 1789 Blake engraved the *Songs of Innocence* himself, his devoted, beautiful but quite illiterate wife, binding the copies for him by hand. He also produced the first of his prophetic books and in 1794 his *Songs of Experience*. Whether they inspired Wordsworth and Coleridge to write their *Lyrical Ballads* is not certain, but by this time his work was known to them and Charles Lamb was one of his deep admirers. His poems, said Wordsworth, were 'undoubtedly the production of insane genius, but there is something in the madness of this man that interests me more than the sanity of Lord Byron and Walter Scott'.

Blake found a kind patron in Thomas Butts, who for many years encouraged him in every way and bought a number of his paintings and drawings, but after Butts' death he fell into the unscrupulous hands of Cromek, who cheated him of the copyright of some of his designs and plagiarised others. Blake found his paintings were difficult to sell and his poetry brought him no money.

Gradually he sank into poverty and obscurity, respected only by a handful of discerning artists and poets who recognised the significance of his genius, and it was not until 1813 that he found a new patron in John Linnell, and through Linnell met John Varley.

Linnell set Blake to work on his illustrations for the Book of Job and commissioned him to engrave them. This, with other work for Linnell, brought him often to Collins' Farm, and Samuel Palmer, another friend of the Linnells, said that Blake was often to be found there, enjoying the summer air or playing with the children, who loved him dearly and delighted in the stories he told them of 'the lovely spiritual things and beings that seemed to him so real and so near'. Linnell's daughter, in later years, recalled with affection 'the cold winter nights, when Blake was wrapped up in an old winter shawl of Mrs Linnell's and sent on his homeward way, with the servant, lantern in hand, lighting him across the Heath to the main road'.

These were his last years, for he died in 1827, but his death was a happy one, 'radiant with ecstatic visions and spiritual rapture'.

While the Linnells were at Collins' Farm, William Collins, said to have been a distant relative of the Collins who owned the farm, was living in a cottage close by, having arrived in Hampstead with his young wife in 1823. He had known Hampstead since his boyhood, for one of his teachers had been George Morland, and his son, Wilkie Collins, named after Collins' close friend, Sir David Wilkie, said that it was here in Hampstead that his father 'found the footsore tramps; the patched or picturesquely ragged beggars; the brutish or audacious boys; the itinerant ratcatcher, with the dirt shine on his leather breeches, and his ferrets and cage of rats'.

Later the Collins, unable to obtain permission to build a larger house on the Heath, moved to Pond Street, and at both houses Sir David Wilkie was a frequent visitor.

Although Linnell was to paint many more scenes of Hampstead, his Hampstead pictures ranging over thirty years, from 1822 to 1856, in 1829 the family left Collins' Farm for their new house in Porchester Terrace, Bayswater. By this time an even greater artist was living in Hampstead, for John Constable had settled at number 2 Lower Terrace in 1821, the year that Shelley was drowned and that Leigh Hunt and his family were living at Pisa with Byron.

John Constable was born in East Bergholt, on the Suffolk-Essex border, in 1776, the son of a prosperous miller, who owned several windmills. Constable and William Turner, who was born the previous year, are today regarded as the two greatest English landscape painters, but while Turner became rich and famous during his lifetime and was given a splendid funeral at St Paul's Cathedral, John Constable could hardly earn a bare living. His work was never fully appreciated during his lifetime and it was not until 1814, when he was thirty-eight, that he sold a landscape to anyone but a personal friend.

His father wanted him to enter the Church, but John from childhood was interested in little else but drawing and painting and the lovely scenery surrounding his home. For about a year after leaving school he worked in his father's mills. To a wind-miller every change in the clouds and the sky must be studied with intense care, for the shape of the shadows and reflections are portents of the weather to come; and it was during these months that Constable learnt so much of the skies that he was to paint so magnificently. In later years his brother said: 'When I look at a mill painted by John, I see that it will *go round*, which is not always the case with those by other artists.'

Encouraged by the enthusiasm for the young artist's work of Sir George Beaumont, who had been a pupil of Richard Wilson, his father allowed John to go to London to see what prospects there were for him as a professional artist. Here he was befriended by Joseph Faringdon, another of Wilson's pupils, who recommended him as a student at the Royal Academy schools. He was a quiet, lovable soul, utterly dedicated to his art, and he worked steadily, dividing his time between London and his home, or the surrounding Suffolk countryside.

His 'Flatford Mill' was rejected by the Royal Academy, but the President, Benjamin West, Leigh Hunt's maternal uncle, consoled him by assuring him that the world would hear of him again, and added: 'You must have loved nature very much before you could have painted like this.'

During the next few years he exhibited several landscapes each season at the Academy, but they went unnoticed and unsold. It was from portraiture that he earned a subsistence, for at this time it was the only reasonably profitable branch of the art. Yet increasingly he concentrated on landscape painting. He aimed to be a 'natural' painter, giving a true impression of nature as he saw it, with its lights and shadows, the breeze rustling the leaves, the dew on the grass, the bloom and the freshness.

'The great vice of the present day is *bravura*', he said, 'an attempt to do something beyond the truth'.

In 1811 he and his childhood friend Maria Bicknell, daughter of Charles Bicknell, solicitor to the Admiralty, and granddaughter of Dr Rhudde, the Rector of Bergholt, fell in love and wished dearly to be married; but Maria's family opposed the idea, for Constable had not yet had any real success, and to the embarrassment of the Constable family it was Dr Rhudde who came out most strongly against the idea.

John and Maria's love letters during the next five years are sad and courageous and never hopeless, although John, hard as he worked, appeared to be making little material progress in his profession.

Early in 1815 Maria wrote that her father had at last given permission for John to visit her occasionally at their London home. A few weeks later John's mother, who had sympathised deeply with the thwarted love affair which was undermining his health, died suddenly of a stroke, and a few days later Maria's mother also died.

In June John was writing to Maria in deep concern over the fate of two of his cousins, who had been fighting at Waterloo, and of whom nothing had been heard. He was working at Bergholt for most of that year, spending much of his time with his ailing father, who died the following May.

He inherited a legacy of £4,000. He was forty and Maria twenty-nine. In October, refusing to wait any longer for Bicknell's permission, he and Maria were married. The old man soon forgave them and quickly became very fond of Constable. Dr Rhudde was not placated so easily, but when he died, three years later, he left Maria £4,000.

For a time John and Maria kept house modestly in Keppel Street and then in Charlotte Street, but in 1819, when John exhibited his 'View on the River Stour', later known as 'The White Horse', it was so much admired by some of his fellow artists that he was elected an Associate of the Academy; and in the following year he and Maria and their two children took their first, attractive little terraced house in Hampstead, number 2, Lower Terrace, where their third child was born.

It was an intensely happy marriage and Constable was doing some of his finest work. In 1821 he exhibited 'The Hay Wain' at the British Gallery, yet it attracted little attention. The following April he was writing to his friend Archdeacon Fisher that he had had 'some nibbles' and an offer of £70 for the picture, to form part of an exhibition in Paris, but was doubtful whether or not to accept it, although he wanted 'money dreadfully'.

He did no more about it at the time but went on working, and during the next year or two made several studies of Hampstead. By 1824 'The Hay Wain' was still unsold, but the discerning French collector who had earlier made an offer for it, wrote again to Constable saying he would like to send it to the Paris Salon. Fisher, who had the picture in his keeping, advised Constable to send it. 'I am too much pulled down by the agricultural distress to hope to possess it', he wrote. 'I would, I think, let it go at less than its price for the sake of the éclat it may give you. The stupid English public, which has no judgement of its own, will begin to think there is something in you if the French make your works national property. . . .'

So 'The Hay Wain' went to Paris, where it was received with unreserved admiration and won Constable a gold medal. His pure and brilliant colour, compared with the fashionable and dingy browns of most of the landscape artists of the day – even Beaumont had once told him that 'a good picture, like a good fiddle, should be brown' – set a new and lasting trend amongst French landscape painters.

Yet the Paris success seemed to have little effect on the appreciation of his work in England. Constable did not complain, nor did he become embittered, but on one occasion he wrote to Fisher: 'I do think I should have been broken-hearted before this time but for you.'

By 1826, with a family of five children now, he was writing: 'I am much worn, having worked hard, and have now the consolation of knowing I must work a great deal harder, or go to the workhouse.'

A sixth baby was born at the end of that year and Constable decided to take another house in Hampstead and let part of his London studio in Charlotte Street.

By August 1827 he was telling Fisher:

We are at length fixed in our comfortable little house in Well Walk, Hampstead. . . . I hope now that I am settled for life. The rent of this house is fifty-two pounds per annum, taxes, twenty-five, and what I have spent on it, ten or fifteen. . . . This house is to my wife's heart's content; it is situated on an eminence at the back of the spot where you saw us, and our little drawing room commands a view unsurpassed in Europe, from Westminster Abbey to Gravesend.

Here on 2 January 1828, their youngest son was born. About the same time Maria's father died and left them £20,000.

It gave them the financial security they so sorely needed but by this time Maria had become ill and in November of that year, 1828, she died of tuberculosis. It was a grief from which Constable never really recovered, although he went on working. He was devoted to his children, and although he retained the house in Well Walk, to which they came as often as possible, he took them to Charlotte Street for a time, in the care of a kindly housekeeper.

The following February he was at last elected an Academician but gratified as he was, he could not help remarking: 'It has been delayed until I am solitary, and cannot impart it.'

Yet there were still only a few people in England who realised his worth. William Blake, looking through one of Constable's sketch books and coming across the drawing of the avenue of fir trees on the Heath had exclaimed: 'Why, this is not drawing, but inspiration!'

Nevertheless, in 1829, at the time of his election to the Royal Academy, there were ill-natured comments in the newspapers and even Sir Thomas Lawrence, the President, on whom, by custom, Constable called when he received the news, made it clear in a wounding remark which was perhaps unintentional, that he considered Constable had been extremely fortunate in being chosen, at a time when there were so many other painters of great merit among the candidates.

In 1814, when a collection of pictures by Wilson, Hogarth and Gainsborough was exhibited at the British Gallery, there had been a note in the preface of the catalogue, acknowledging the long years of shameful neglect which Wilson had endured: 'The merit of Wilson's works is now justly appreciated; and we hope that since the period of his decease, the love and knowledge of art has been so much diffused through the country, that the exertion of such talents may never again remain unrewarded during the life time of him who may possess them,' it ran.

Wilson, born in 1714, had begun his career as a successful portrait painter, but in 1748 he went to Italy and concentrated on his real interest, which was landscape painting. In Rome his reputation as a landscape painter was soon established, but when he returned to London, in 1756, he found there was little or no interest in his work. George III, whose portrait Wilson had painted many years earlier, was interested in his 'Sion House From Kew Gardens' and sent Lord Bute to negotiate its purchase, but Lord Bute considered the sixty guineas which Wilson asked was excessive. When Wilson cheerfully suggested that the King could pay by instalments Lord Bute, bereft of any sense of humour, deemed the remark disrespectful and poor Wilson not only fell from royal favour but remained under a shadow for the rest of his life, until his death in 1782. Unable to sell his pictures, he sank into obscurity and poverty, living in a garret in the Tottenham Court Road and existing mainly on bread and porter, until some Welsh relatives rescued him and took him to Wales for the last year or two.

Yet John Constable was neglected as cruelly as Wilson had been, and as the years passed and his house and studio became increasingly crowded with unsold pictures, he ceased to expect the appreciation shown to so many of his lesser contemporaries.

His health was failing but in June 1833, he gave a lecture at the Hampstead Assembly Rooms on the 'History of Landscape Painting', which he later developed into a course of four lectures delivered in London, at the Royal Institution; and he lectured again at the Hampstead Assembly Rooms in 1835, on a beautiful June evening, when the skies over the Hampstead fields were at their loveliest.

He was painting until the last day of his life and he died quite suddenly, at the beginning of April 1837. He was buried beside his beloved Maria, in Hampstead churchyard, and was mourned not only by his family and friends but by many Hampstead residents who had come to love the kindly, sensitive John Constable.

IX

Highgate during the Nineteenth Century

At the beginning of the nineteenth century Highgate was still little more than a village, perched on the top of a steep hill, which had grown up round the Old Monk's Hermitage. It was not a parish and lay partly in the north-eastern corner of the long, narrow parish of St Pancras, which stretched four miles from north to south but was less than a mile wide, and partly in the parishes of Hornsey and Islington. In the population figures of 1801, of its 429 inhabited houses, 299 were in the parish of Hornsey.

There had been building down the High Street to Highgate Hill, northwards along Southwood Lane towards Muswell Hill, north-westwards along the North Road, westwards along Hampstead Lane and south-westwards down West Hill, but progress was very slow and the houses were scattered, for the most part set in tree-shaded gardens.

Behind the houses on the north side of the High Street and the Hill were fields and farmlands, woods and waste land. On the south side, stretching westwards to West Hill and cut by the ancient track of Swain's Lane, were the gardens and grounds of large houses, including that of Holly Lodge, the Georgian villa which Thomas Coutts bought in 1810 and the grounds of which spread over nearly the entire extent of the Highgate Rise, being bordered on the north and west by West Hill and on the east and south by Swain's Lane.

On West Hill itself there were a few charming white stucco villas backing on to the leafy Millfield Lane, Ken Wood, with its string of ponds and, to the south, Parliament Hill Fields.

William Paterson, who had founded the Bank of England at the end of the seventeenth century, had conceived the idea of collecting the springs of Ken Wood into reservoir ponds, as a water supply for Hampstead and Kentish Town, and they remained after the New River Company took over responsibility for the water supply of the district.

To the north of the heart of the village, with its green and its pond and the beautiful houses of the Groves, the Spaniards Lane and the North Road ran through woods and countryside.

As in Hampstead, there had been steady encroachments on the waste land, ever since the time that two acres had been enclosed for the schoolmaster's orchard and garden in the sixteenth century, and as late as 1806 permission was obtained from the trustees of the Waste Land Fund to enclose a strip of waste land lying on the south side of Southwood Lane. This was in order to build eight cottages for the poor, four to be for the benefit of Hornsey and the others for Highgate; but in 1818, with the Hornsey Enclosure Act, 198 acres of common land in Hornsey, Highgate, Fortis Green, Muswell Hill and Stroud Green were enclosed and all common rights ceased.

Wagons still struggled up the Highgate Hill and High Street to reach the North Road on their way to Finchley. It was hard on the horses as well as the carters, and it would sometimes take all day to haul a heavy load up from Holloway, although – or perhaps because – there were a number of inns on the way to offer them rest and long drinks.

In 1809 Rennie had the idea of cutting a tunnel, some two hundred yards long, through the hill on which Highgate stands, but a little to the east of the main road up Highgate Hill, where the slop is gentler. It was to run from where the Holloway Road joins Highgate Hill. A company was formed and the work began, burrowing through the heavy London clay. For several months things seemed to be going well and about a hundred and thirty yards of the tunnel had been bored. Then, one April morning in 1812, the whole thing collapsed with an enormous crash. Fortunately no lives were lost for it happened very early, before the men had begun their day's work, but all hope of building a new tunnel was abandoned and for a time Hornsey Lane was blocked. However, the work was not wasted. An open cutting remained and this was continued to form the Archway Road, which was opened the same year. Then, at the suggestion of John Nash, an archway was built across it to carry a continuation of Hornsey Lane, which was completed by 1813.

There was a heavy toll for using the new road – sixpence for every horse and a penny for each foot passenger – but after the initial problems of waterlogging were overcome it was successful in diverting traffic from the difficult climb up Highgate Hill. The original archway was thirty-six feet high and about eighteen feet wide, composed of three semi-circular brick and stone arches carrying a stone balustraded bridge, and when it was built it passed over pleasant countryside. The stone balustrade had to be replaced towards the end of the century by high iron railings, because of the suicidal tendencies which high bridges of this kind always seem to induce, but the archway held until 1900, when, with the increase of traffic both above and below, it was decided to pull it down and replace it with a single-span iron bridge.

The building of the Archway Road was bad for the business of the inn keepers on Highgate Hill but now it was the turn of the Woodman, at the corner of Southwood Lane and the Archway Road to prosper.

In Highgate village the little chapel was still standing, but, like the school, was fast falling into ruin. The school was rebuilt in 1819 but nevertheless was little more than a village school by now, where the boys were given only a rudimentary education. This was a situation that was to be found in many of the old-established grammar schools at the beginning of the nineteenth century. Their decline had begun after the Restoration. As prices rose, endowments became so inadequate that there were not enough funds for proper staffing. In 1795 Lord Chief Justice Kenyon was declaring that most of the ancient grammar schools had become 'empty walls, without scholars and everything neglected but the receipt of salaries'; and in some cases headmasters corruptly pocketed the bulk of the money that was available and employed a half-educated, inadequate master to do the teaching. This was the situation at Highgate where the Reader of the Chapel, who should have been teaching the boys, was a pluralist and handed over the work to the Chapel sexton.

Throughout the eighteenth century many boys of the upper classes were still taught at home by tutors, although increasing numbers were being sent to the fashionable schools such as Eton, Winchester, Harrow, Rugby and Westminster. Most of these schools had originally been grammar school foundations for the free education of the sons of local men, but as prices rose and headmasters discovered that their statutes allowed them to admit a certain number of fee-paying pupils, to augment their own small salaries, the practice of charging fees increased. The segregation between the fee-paying and free scholars grew increasingly rigid, and it was not long before the misnamed 'public schools' became entirely fee-paying.

At the same time, the Dissenting Academies provided a valuable education for a large number of the middle classes. They offered a curriculum more in tune with the changing times, which included science, mathematics, geography and living languages, as well as the Classics, and many of the public schools, freeing themselves from their ancient statutes which had prescribed rigid rules for the kind of teaching to be provided, copied the new academies. By the nineteenth century there was an increasing fashion for public schools and one by one the Dissenting Academies closed down. At the same time a Charity Commission was appointed to investigate the fate of many endowments which seemed to have gone astray or been put to purposes for which they were never intended, and it came to light that the boys at Highgate School were not receiving the benefits to which they were entitled, for since Sir Roger Cholmeley's endowment, which had now reached the value of £166 a year, several more bequests had been made.

In 1824 new rules were drawn up for the school. The master had to be a graduate in Holy Orders and instruction had to include Latin and Greek. Fee-paying boys were admitted, in addition to the forty free places, and with the additional money available the old grammar school quickly attained the status of a public school.

Shortly after this plans were made for the building of a new church at Highgate, for the old chapel was in a ruinous condition. St Michaels, designed by Lewis Vulliamy, was built in the Grove, on the site of the old Mansion House which William Ashurst had built in 1694 and which had stood empty, crumbling and haunted for years. It was a large church, designed for a congregation of fifteen hundred, five hundred of the seats being free and set aside for the poor. The question now arose as to which parish it was in – Hornsey or St Pancras – and the problem was solved by giving Highgate at last the status of a separate parish, with defined boundaries from just west of Ken House down to Swain's Lane, and as far east as the Holloway Road.

The church was consecrated in 1832, after which the old chapel was demolished and several of its monuments, including that of Coleridge, were moved to the new church.

A few years later, in 1839, the grounds of the old mansion, stretching down the hill behind the Church, were bought and laid out as a large cemetery by the London Cemetery Company. This had been founded by Stephen Geary, who had already achieved a reputation as an architect of gin palaces, at a time when the old cemeteries of central London had become grossly overcrowded. Many had to be closed and Highgate cemetery was the first of the new large cemeteries built on the outskirts of the city to replace them, being soon followed by Kensal Green and Brompton.

The first cemetery at Highgate covered twenty acres, but only seventeen years later an extension of another eighteen acres had to be laid out on the eastern side of Swain's Lane.

The ground was wooded and steeply hilly and Geary spent infinite pains in the designing of this enormous burial ground. The Gothic entrance has an abundance of turrets and buttresses, pinnacles and cupolas, with a bell tower over the Tudor gateway. He employed Ramsey, the landscape gardener, to create winding paths and flights of steps between the rises and dips of the hillside, with trees, shrubs and flower beds skilfully planted, so that it soon became a favourite Sunday afternoon walk for jaded Victorian Londoners, who came to enjoy the magnificent views and the vast masses of monumental marble which quickly accumulated.

The most spectacular sight was the Egyptian avenue, leading from half way up a flight of wide steps, made in the steepest part of the hill. The avenue, a hundred feet long, was approached by a large, dark entrance flanked by obelisks, and led past iron-bound stone sepulchres, each of which contained twelve coffins laid out on stone shelves. It rose on a gentle incline to a circular road, similarly flanked on both sides with sepulchres, the inner circle of the road being covered by a flat roof on which were planted trees and shrubs and a solitary, mournful cedar of Lebanon.

When the newer part of the cemetery was opened, an underground passage was built to convey the coffin from the chapel on the west side of Swain's Lane to the grave on the east side, the coffin being dropped through the floor of the chapel by means of an hydraulic lift.

Everything was new and discreet and very convenient and Highgate cemetery became a highly fashionable place in which to be buried. Among the illustrious Victorians whose graves can be found here are Michael Faraday, George Eliot, Henry Crabb Robinson, Christina Rossetti, William Rossetti and his wife, Elizabeth Rossetti, Lucy Maddox Brown, Friese Green, John Galsworthy, Charles Knight and Karl Marx, who wrote most of *Das Kapital* in the reading room of the British Museum and died in London in 1883.

It was in 1860 that Dante Gabriel Rossetti married the strangely beautiful, auburn-haired Elizabeth Siddal. At first they lived at his studio close to Blackfriars, but Elizabeth was too frail for the sharp, cold winds and fogs of the Thames waterside and after a month or two they moved to lodgings in Highgate, where they hoped her health would improve. But less than two years later Rossetti returned home one evening to find her lying dead, with an empty bottle of laudanum beside her.

She was buried in Highgate cemetery and Rossetti, distraught with grief, put into her coffin the poems he had written for her during the days of their courtship. Seven years later, by which time Rossetti was living in Chelsea, his friends persuaded him to retrieve the poems and arrange for their publication.

The Home Office gave permission for the exhumation and that dark night of 1869 saw one of the strangest scenes ever to take place in the cemetery. Rossetti was tortured with doubts and misgivings towards the last, feeling that he was robbing the beloved dead, and he was not present, but his friends, at dead of night, lit a huge bonfire close to the grave. The coffin was raised and opened and they found the poems intact, still wrapped in a tress of Elizabeth's red-gold hair. The coffin was replaced and the poems duly published the following year; but they brought Rossetti only bitterness and disappointment, for they were badly received by the critics for many years to come, *Blackwood's*, which had condemned Keats' first work, contributing to the general misunderstanding and denigration.

Today Highgate cemetery is full, terribly overgrown and neglected. Vandals have despoiled the monuments and desecrated the graves, so that the cemetery has had to be closed to the public. Now wild life is returning to the deserted gardens and at night time foxes have been heard, prowling round the broken catacombs and haunting the emptied graves.*

In 1816, the congregation of Roman Catholics to whom the Abbé Morel had ministered in Hampstead, were able to build for themselves the beautiful little Roman Catholic chapel of St Mary on Holly Hill. This was one of the first Roman Catholic churches to be built in England since the Reformation, and although the interior has been improved and embellished since then, the outside remains much as it was when it was built, with its white, stucco front, the large statue of the Virgin in a pedimented niche over the doorway and the bell tower surmounted by the Cross. In 1858 the community established the monastery known as St Joseph's Retreat on Highgate Hill. It was built on the site of the old Black Dog Inn and its surrounding six or seven acres of garden and orchard, which had served generations of drovers and carters toiling up the hill. The chapel of the Retreat ministered to

* Since writing this, the Highgate Society has begun the restoration of the cemetery. M. C. B.

the large number of Irish who during the mid-nineteenth century were living in Upper Holloway.

The first head of the monastery was the Hon George Spencer, who took the name of Father Ignatius, and his biographer wrote:

> In 1858 we procured the place in Highgate now known as St Joseph's Retreat. Providence guided us to a most suitable position. Our rule prescribes that our houses shall be outside the town, and yet near enough for us to be of service to it. Highgate is wonderfully adapted to all the requisitions of our rule and constitution. Situated at the brow of a hill, it is far enough from the din and noise of London to be comparatively free of turmoil, and yet sufficiently near for its citizens to come to our church. The grounds are enclosed by trees; a hospital at one end and two roads meeting at the other promise a freedom from intrusion and a continuance of the solitude which we now enjoy.

The new monastery was completed in 1876 and opened by Cardinal Manning, and since that time the Roman Catholic schools have been established next to it, lower down the hill. Above the Retreat, Lauderdale House had a succession of wealthy owners throughout the century and in 1868 it was bought by Sir Sydney Waterlow and known as Waterlow House. This was the year in which Andrew Marvell's cottage was demolished, and now all that marks the spot is a commemorative tablet low down on the wall adjoining the grounds of Waterlow House. In 1872 Sir Sydney bequeathed the house to Bart's Hospital as a convalescent home and took up residence in Fairseat, an old house close by. In 1891 the grounds were opened to the public, having been presented to the LCC as a 'garden for the gardenless'. Today Waterlow Park is a quiet and lovely place, most beautifully maintained, but the house, now a protected building, which Camden acquired with the park in 1971, is empty and shuttered, and no specific use has yet been found for it.

Late in the nineteenth century, Cromwell House, on the other side of the road, became a convalescent home for the sick children from the Great Ormond Street hospital, and farther up the hill, where the Bank ends, the Channing School for Girls was established in 1885, founded by the Misses Sharpe, great nieces of the poet Samuel Rogers, and still flourishing as an independent day school. There is also a junior school on the opposite side of the road, occupying Sir Sydney Waterlow's old house, Fairseat.

During these years Highgate School had been developing steadily and establishing the prestige which it enjoys today. In 1866 there were some two hundred boys at the school. The old building was taken down and the present attractive, red brick Gothic building, designed by Cockerell, rose in its place, still on the site of the original little sixteenth-century grammar school. The adjoining Crawley chapel was a gift of the widow of a former governor.

In 1876, under the Endowed Schools Act, the constitution of the school was remodelled by the Charity Commissioners. Today, with its twelve governors, it has seven hundred boys in the senior school, of whom a third are boarders, and two hundred and eighty in the junior school, their ages ranging from eight to ten years.

There are four boarding houses and eight day-boy houses, the boarding houses of the senior school being grouped, with the junior school, round the twenty-two acres of playing fields, which are only a few minutes walk away from the main school building, with its assembly hall and classrooms, library, gymnasium and laboratories.

The heart of Highgate changed very little throughout the century. As late as the 1860s the old hermit's pond stood in Pond Square and the Grove, South Grove, West Hill and Millfield Lane remained secluded and peaceful. In Millfield Lane was Ivy Cottage, where Charles Matthews, the comedian and one-time manager, with his wife Madame Vestris, of Covent Garden, spent the last years of his life, with his large collection of theatrical mementoes and pictures. At the charming little Millfield Cottage close by, John Ruskin spent some time of his childhood, with his parents. The Howitts lived at West Hill Lodge after they moved from the Hermitage.

In 1810 Thomas Coutts bought Holly Lodge as a country retreat from his mansion in Piccadilly on the corner of Stratton Street, which was joined to number 1, Stratton Street round the corner.

The Hoare family, whose banking business was eventually to be merged into that of Lloyd's, was already established in Hampstead, for the first Samuel Hoare had bought Heath House in 1790 and built The Hill close by for his son in 1807: but while the Hoares created their circle of literary friends and social reformers, particularly those concerned with the abolition of the slave trade, the Coutts entertained on a still wider scale, which included the reception of royalty, for Coutts was probably by now the richest man in England.

Thomas Coutts was born in Edinburgh in 1736 and when he was only sixteen came to London to join his brother James in his banking business. James died shortly afterwards and Thomas carried on the business by himself, quickly achieving a remarkable success. He married Susannah Starkie, who had been a maid servant of his brother's, and they had three daughters, all of whom married into the aristocracy. Fanny married the Marquis of Bute, Susan married Lord Guildford and Sophie married Sir Francis Burdett. In his later years, around 1804, Thomas, by now immensely rich and banker to George III, fell in love with Harriot* Mellon, the humbly-born actress who had made her first appearance at Drury Lane in 1795. His marriage to Susannah had been happy enough, but for the last four years of her life she had been insane; and a few days after her death, in 1815, by which time he was approaching eighty, he married Harriot, who was now nearly thirty-eight, and they spent their honeymoon at Holly Lodge.

Despite the humble origin of their own mother, Thomas Coutts' three daughters were highly indignant at the second marriage and treated Harriot abominably. The Burdetts were living in the Piccadilly House, where the youngest of their five daughters, Angela, had been born in 1814, and the Guildfords in the adjoining Stratton Street House, and when neither couple would condescend to receive Harriot, Tom Coutts asked them all to leave and installed Harriot as the sole mistress of the two mansions. The Burdetts eventually relented but for Harriot the wound had gone deep and the only member of the family for whom she had any real affection was the little Angela, too young at this time to understand what had happened.

Thomas Coutts died in 1822 and during the seven years of his second marriage he entertained in splendid style, both in Piccadilly and at Holly Lodge. Although Holly Lodge was not a particularly large house a very long room was built on at the side, for entertaining, and the wooded grounds on the wide sweep of the hill were magnificent.

Tom and Harriot gave splendid garden parties there during the summer, attended by royalty and members of the nobility. In 1815 *The Times* recorded that 'Yesterday the Prince Regent dined with Mr Coutts at his Highgate Cottage'. There is a note in the household records of the Duke of York dining there in 1820, after which he was taken upstairs 'to see the brilliancy of the atmosphere over London occasioned by a splendid Illumination on that evening in consequence of a Bill of Pains and Penalties which had been pending in the House of Peers against Caroline Queen of England having been given up on its third reading on Friday, the 10th November'.

Sir Walter Scott was a relative of Thomas Coutts and on his rare visits to London would visit Holly Lodge as well as Joanna Baillie in Hampstead, and he was always particularly kind to Harriot.

When Tom died he left his entire fortune, estimated at well over a

* Often spelt Harriet, but Harriot by the Burdett-Coutts.

million pounds, to Harriot. During the first year or two of her widowhood she travelled a great deal and her retinue was enormous, consisting usually of seven carriages, each drawn by four horses, carrying a companion, two doctors, which she felt necessary in case one fell ill on the way, and amongst other servants, two bedchamber women, one for her toilette and the other to keep watch at night, as she was afraid of ghosts.

Women though envious of her wealth often snubbed her but when she visited Abbotsford the kindly Sir Walter Scott warned her fellow guests to treat her properly and she enjoyed the visit enormously.

Five years after the death of Thomas, Harriot, by now fifty, married the twenty-six year old Duke of St Albans. There was inevitably a flurry of ill-natured gossip, but Sir Walter was one of the few who gave his blessing and in Harriot's reply to his letter of congratulation she sounds engagingly simple and sincere.

What a strange, eventful life has mine been, from a poor little player child, with just food and clothes to cover me, dependent on a very precarious profession, without talent or a friend in the world! [she wrote.] Is it not wonderful? Is it true? Can I believe it? – first the wife of the best, the most perfect being that ever breathed, his love and unbounded confidence in me, his immense fortune so honourably acquired by his own industry, all at my command . . . and now the wife of a Duke. . . .

Contrary to the expectations of most and the hopes of her enemies, Harriot's second marriage seems to have been as happy as the first. The Duke and the new Duchess were often at Holly Lodge, for Harriot loved it dearly. The Duke was Hereditary Grand Falconer of England and at Highgate he used to fly his hawks, his German falconers dressed in liveries of green and orange velvet, with steeply-crowned hats decorated with black plumes, and wearing long white gauntlets.

Harriot died in 1837 and to the dismay of the Burdetts left her entire fortune to their youngest daughter Angela, who by this time was a tall and rather plain young woman of twenty-three. She was living with her parents at 23 St James's Place, and the story goes that Sir Francis was so angry that Harriot had left the money to Angela and not to his wife, that Angela had to leave home within the hour, with her former governess, Miss Meredith, as her sole companion, and establish herself in the Coutts' Piccadilly mansion; and in accordance with the terms of the will she changed her name to Burdett-Coutts.

Sir Francis had changed greatly with the passing years from the radicalism of his younger days and had ended up as a staunch Tory. In 1810, shortly after pressing for the enquiry into the affair of Mary Anne Clarke and the Duke of York, he had been committed to the Tower for an alleged breach of privilege in the House of Commons, by publishing scandalous matter in Cobbett's *Weekly Register*, alleging intrigue and corruption in the House.

It was only a short imprisonment but Sir Francis had been hailed as a hero in the cause of common justice by the radical intellectuals, including Shelley, who had a great admiration for him and was a regular correspondent for a number of years.

The breach with Angela was soon healed, for it was, after all, none of her making, but from the time of her inheritance Angela, with Miss Meredith to help her, lived an independent life, dividing her time between Piccadilly and Holly Lodge. She mixed in the highest circles of society, entertaining lavishly and being entertained in return, enjoying her wealth and the power that it brought, and proud of her father's aristocratic blood.

In 1844 Sir Francis and her mother died, within a few weeks of each other, and she grieved for them sincerely, but when she had recovered from the shock she began once more to give her lavish entertainments.

After a ball at Buckingham Palace, when she was wearing her famous Marie Antoinette tiara, Tom Moore called, as she was preparing to send all her jewellery back to the bank. He asked her what the value of her dress had been the previous night. 'I think about a hundred thousand pounds', she replied calmly.

From the time that she inherited her vast wealth, in 1837, she became famous, and inevitably she received scores of begging letters. She was a sincere Church woman and despite her gay, full social life she took the responsibility of her wealth seriously and began to consider the ways of practical philanthropy.

1837 was also the year that the young Charles Dickens, less than two years older than Angela, who was to advise and help her so much in the years to come, was staying for a short time at Collins Farm. The thirteenth monthly part of *Pickwick* had just been published, but Dickens was grief-stricken by the death of his sister-in-law, Mary Hogarth, when she was only seventeen.

In May 1837, he was writing to Harrison Ainsworth from Collins' Farm, North End: 'I have been so much unnerved and hurt by the loss of that dear girl, whom I loved, after my wife, more deeply and fervently than any one on earth, that I have been compelled to once to give up all idea of my monthly work and to try a fortnight's rest and repose.'

He loved Hampstead and later that year was writing to Forster: 'You don't feel disposed, do you, to muffle yourself up, and start off with me for a good brisk walk over Hampstead Heath? I knows a good 'ouse where we can have a red-hot chop for dinner, and a glass of good wine' – and that became the first of many a good time they had at Jack Straw's Castle.

It was a year or two after this that Angela and Dickens met for the first time, for she and Miss Meredith had been greatly impressed and amused by Pickwick.

From some of the records it would seem that Angela was excessively class-conscious. Wordsworth, she said, was 'very similar to men of his class; a peasant; though I suppose he had genius'. She had a similar distaste for Coleridge. Yet this could have been mainly a distrust of radicalism and the fact that they had criticised her father for his change of political view. Bearing in mind the circumscribed rules of conduct which had been part of her upbringing and the rigid class-consciousness of her day, when with the rapid spread of industrialisation, the gulf between rich and poor was deepening, she was broadminded.

At first her philanthropy was mainly confined to the Church. By 1847 she had endowed the Bishoprics of Cape Town in South Africa and of Adelaide in South Australia, had built the Church of St Stephen's, Westminster and endowed the St Stephen's schools, but Dickens opened her eyes to the pressing needs of the industrial poor, whose numbers were increasing so rapidly during the middle years of the century.

Much of it was, in a sense, only piecemeal reform, but thousands lived to bless her name, and some of it has been of lasting benefit, such as the help she gave to the two small struggling societies which are now the NSPCC and the RSPCA.

She loved animals. At Holly Lodge she had as varied a collection as Lord Erskine had kept at Evergreen Hill, but her particular loves were dogs and horses, while for years her parrot travelled backwards and forwards with her, between Holly Lodge and Piccadilly.

In her younger days she had developed a warm, close friendship with the widowed Duke of Wellington and when they were seen riding together, in Hyde Park and the Green Park, many thought that, despite the disparity in their ages, they would marry.

The old Duke was devoted to her but in 1847, when she was thirty-three and he was in his late seventies, he wrote to her:

My dearest Angela!,
   I have passed every moment of the Evening and Night since I quitted you in reflecting upon our conversation of yesterday. . . .

You are Young! My dearest! You have before you the prospect of at least twenty years of enjoyment of Happiness in Life! I entreat you again in this way, not to throw yourself away upon a Man old enough to be your Grandfather! who however Strong, Hearty and Healthy at present! must and will certainly in time feel the consequences and infirmities of Age! . . . God bless you my dearest. . . . Ever yours Wn.

She was to live for another sixty years but he had only another five left, for he died in 1852.

By this time a devastating change had come over the approaches to Highgate from London. The first urban extension into the fields and farms to the north of the Marylebone and Euston Roads came after 1791. About the same time, Somers Town was built, occupying a triangular stretch of fields bounded by where the Hampstead Road, the Euston Road and the Pancras Road now lie. It had been intended as a middle-class development, but by the 1830s there had been many bankruptcies amongst the building contractors and the work was completed to lower standards by a fresh crop of speculative builders, who had bought up the land cheaply. Infinitely worse was Agar Town to the east, deliberately planned with nothing but the poorest tenements, which quickly became one of the worst slums of London.

Then the railways reached London. Euston Station was built in 1836, King's Cross in 1851 and St Pancras in 1868. Large areas of new building were destroyed to make way for them. Behind St Pancras Station alone seven streets of three thousand houses were swept away, but as this included Agar Town it was no great loss, except for the people who had been made homeless and could afford nothing better.

The value of the property in the immediate vicinity of the cleared area rapidly declined. The middle classes moved out and the poor moved in – mainly railway workers.

As the railway waste land spread the area became increasingly dirty and drab and the slums spread remorsely northwards. Kentish Town was still a village and as late as 1857 the traditional fair was still being kept near the Gospel Oak, where there was a hamlet of twelve or thirteen houses. Yet the district between Camden Town and Gospel Oak soon became railway land, with sidings, engine-sheds and workshops. The workers lived close at hand and Camden Town made a rapid descent in the social scale, while Gospel Oak was developed with working class houses, better than most but never approaching the standards of middle-class housing.

The slums spread into Holloway and to the foot of Highgate Hill, but here by virtue of the steepness of the hill, they stopped, while to the south-west of the village, north of the Prince of Wales Road, which cuts across the Kentish Town Road on its way up to Parliament Hill, there was hardly any development at all by the 1850s.

Highgate stood high and aloof from it all and as late as 1876 Edward Walford was writing that 'Highgate had about it that appearance of quietude and sleepiness that one is accustomed to meet in villages miles away from the busy metropolis'.

The old Duke of Wellington had disliked the railways intensely. In 1847 he was writing to Angela that he had arrived at Walmer Castle from Windsor Castle in ten hours, 'which was exactly the time which the journey took me in the good old days of post horses,' and the following year he was saying how foolish it was to allow 'the destruction of our excellent country in order to expend millions sterling on these Rail Roads! It appears to me to be the vulgarest, most indelicate, most injurious to health of any mode of conveyance that I have seen in any part of the world!' Yet in the early days the railways had arranged special facilities for carriage folk, so that they could drive on to the trains, on specially constructed wagons, make their journeys and drive off again, without leaving the comfort of their own carriages.

Life among the prosperous residents of Highgate was peaceful during these middle years of the century, undisturbed by the advancing but still distant urbanisation coming up from Kentish Town and Holloway. The cultural centre of the village was the Highgate Literary and Scientific Institution in South Grove, which had been founded in 1839, and here the Book Society met, as well as the Friendly Discussion Society, the Reading Society and the Bookworms. The choral society rehearsed here during the winter months and over the years a chess club, lawn tennis club, a skating club, a horticultural society and a chrysanthemum society were formed, while as early as 1850 the Yacht Club gathered round the ponds by Millfield Lane.

Yet they were not unmindful of the pressing social needs that were arising on their doorstep, for some of the old cottage property in the village and off the High Street was falling into a ruinous condition and, as elsewhere throughout the country, this was a time when, as the rich grew richer, the poor grew poorer. The idea of model dwellings was in the air, Prince Albert had inspired it with his design for a block of four flats for artisans, which was built near the Knightsbridge barracks for the Great Exhibition of 1851. Two years later Josiah Viney, the minister of the Congregational Church in South Grove, had promoted the building of similar flats for artisans and labourers in North Hill, called Verandah Cottages. This was a three-storeyed brick block of twelve flats, with verandahs to each of the four-roomed flats, which let at five shillings a week.

It was this same year, 1853, that Miss Barnett built St Anne's Church at the little hamlet of Brookfield, in memory of her brother who had died two years earlier. Brookfield is now part of Highgate but at the time it was described as a hamlet lying mainly in Kentish Town and partly in the chapelry of Highgate. The land was Miss Barnett's personal property, lying along the south west corner of the Burdett-Coutts estate, and she bequeathed her own house, next to the new church, for the Vicarage, Angela Burdett-Coutts donating the beautiful peal of bells.

The Vicar of St Michael's, in expressing his appreciation of Verandah Cottages, said that at least ten more of these blocks were needed throughout the parish, to rehouse some two hundred working-class families in Highgate.

The pond in Pond Square was sadly polluted by this time and had become a refuse dump. Over the years two ponds had developed in the marshy waste made by the hermit's digging and in 1845 they were made into one, but as a water supply they were no longer necessary, for by the 1850s the New River Company was supplying piped water to most Highgate households. Alexander Scrimgeour, living at Parkfield, where Witanhurst was later to be built, at the top of West Hill, suggested that the pond be filled in and similar model dwellings built on the site, but at a public meeting held at the Gatehouse in 1864, at which 350 local residents were present, the idea was rejected on many grounds, one of which was that Pond Square was common land; but it was agreed that something should be done about the pond and also about the provision of some new housing for the poor.

After a great deal of discussion, two committees were formed. Sydney Waterlow of Fairseat, whose Improved Industrial Dwellings Company had recently completed some flats in Finsbury, organised the Highgate Dwellings Improvement Company and W. J. R. Cotton of the Old Hall headed a committee to deal with the improvement of Pond Square. The pond was filled in with tons of earth and then planted with shrubs and flower beds, the Congregational Church and Angela Burdett-Coutts helping to finance the project. Under Waterlow's direction, Springfield Cottages were built in North Hill and in 1867 Coleridge Buildings in the Archway Road, by Shepherd's Hill.

At about the same time Angela Burdett-Coutts was busy with a somewhat different housing scheme of her own, in Swain's Lane, just below the cemetery. This was the model Holly Village, which in the first place she intended for servants on the Holly Lodge estate or for employees from Coutts' Bank. The village is composed of about a dozen small Gothic villas, some single, some double, with steeply sloping roofs and a profusion of gables and windows with pointed arches. They are grouped round a pleasant stretch of lawns and shrubs and enclosed by a low brick wall, the arched gateway building, which announces that they were built by Angela Burdett-Coutts in 1865, facing up the Rise to where Holly Lodge once stood. The village stands to this day, unaltered, although the yellow brick has darkened and the architecture is reminiscent of the cemetery on its flank, but the houses are roomy and pleasant to live in, and today they are freehold properties.

Pond Square did not stay tidy for long and as there were no funds for its maintenance, further plans were put forward for building on it, but again they were rejected, and early in the 1890s the centre of the square was planted with plane trees and covered with asphalt, making a pleasant, shady spot which remains to this day. This summer, as I sat in the sunshine at the foot of the steps leading up to the back entrance of the Prince of Wales and watched a group of young men quietly but with great skill and concentration, kicking a ball about under the trees, during their lunch time, I felt that the square was really being used and enjoyed in the way that was originally intended.

Not all the Burdett-Coutts enterprises were as successful and long-lasting as Holly Village. The Columbia Market in Bethnal Green was a failure and also the home for fallen women which Dickens had urged her to establish at Shepherd's Bush.

However, most of her donations proved to be of true benefit. She took an active and practical interest in the Ragged School Union and in the educational work of James Kay-Shuttleworth and she contributed to the foundation of many churches, reformatories, penitentiaries and model lodging-houses throughout the country.

At the same time she maintained her social life and entertained a wide circle of friends both in Piccadilly and at Holly Lodge. The Mansfields spent very little time at Ken House during these years, living mostly at Scone, so that Holly Lodge was by far the most important centre of entertainment in Highgate. A host of distinguished men and women were regular visitors, from the Duchess of Teck to Henry Irving and James Brooke, the Rajah of Sarawak. The house was conducted with all the splendour and formality of the two Piccadilly mansions and in the grounds there were vine houses, fig houses, mushroom beds, watercress beds, an apiary and a model farm.

Rajah Brooke declared that Angela Burdett-Coutts was the best friend he ever had and that he looked on Holly Lodge as home. He had been granted the complete overlordship of Sarawak by the Sultan of Brunei in 1846, and was devoted to this part of north-western Borneo and its people. He was a comparatively rich man but within a few years was needing money to defend Sarawak from the Dayak pirates who were harassing the coast. On a visit to England in 1847 Angela Burdett-Coutts lent him five thousand pounds and then bought a steamer which could serve as a gunboat and sent it out to him.

In 1871, in recognition of all her good works and beneficence, Queen Victoria raised Angela to the peerage, with the title of Baroness Burdett-Coutts of Highgate and Brookfield. Ten years later, when she was sixty-seven, she fell from grace in the Queen's eyes, by suddenly marrying her secretary, a young American of twenty-seven, William Ashmead Bartlett, who took the name of Burdett-Coutts at the time of the marriage.

Queen Victoria said Angela was a 'silly old woman' and thereafter treated her with coolness, but the marriage was happy and the new Mr Burdett-Coutts handled the somewhat difficult situation with great diplomacy. They spent more time at Holly Lodge now and Burdett-Coutts established a stable behind Swain's Lane and close to Holly Village, where he bred carriage horses.

During these later years of the century the buildings of Kentish Town spread up the Highgate Road and the open land between the Highgate Road and Highgate Hill and between Highgate Hill and the Archway was developed with houses of varying kinds, from the upper to the lower middle class, but Swain's Lane, West Hill, Millfield Lane and the heart of the village changed very little. Angela Burdett-Coutts lived on until 1906, the year of her silver wedding, and the only major development she could have seen from Holly Lodge, as she was taken through the grounds in her bath chair, pulled by a small pony, was the building of the blocks of large and very comfortable flats at Brookfield, which went up in 1902, at a time when similar blocks of mansion flats were being built in many other prosperous residential parts of London, including Hampstead.

During the 1880s there was a strong feeling that more open spaces should be provided for the public. The Hampstead Heath Extension Committee was formed, with the Duke of Westminster as Chairman and members who included Shaw Lefevre, Baroness Burdett-Coutts and Octavia Hill. Lord Mansfield was approached with a view to the purchasing of Parliament Hill Fields and Sir Spencer Maryon Wilson for the purchase of East Heath park. Lord Mansfield asked £1,000 an acre for his two hundred acres and Sir Spencer £1,800 for his fifty-six acres. It took five years to raise this sum of over £300,000. The Metropolitan Board of works contributed half the money, the City Parochial Charities £50,000, the Hampstead and St Pancras Vestries £50,000 and the rest came from private donations, so that in 1889 Parliament Hill Fields and the East Heath became a public open space. In the meantime, the Ecclesiastical Commissioners had presented Highgate Woods to the City of London, for an open space, in 1886, and gave the Queen's Wood to the borough of Hornsey in 1898.

The fifth Earl of Mansfield succeeded in 1898 and spent much more time than his father and grandfather had ever done at Ken House. Here he entertained on the grand scale for a few years, but in 1906 he died unmarried, and the estate passed to his brother, the sixth Earl. During the whole of the nineteenth century Ken House and its grounds changed hardly at all, remaining a large private estate which, with Parliament Hill Fields, protected the western approaches to Highgate. On the south side of Hampstead Lane, running westwards from the Gate House to the Ken Wood boundary, some spacious Victorian houses were built, the largest being Caen Wood Towers, which went up in 1871 and today is known as Athlone House, having become the geriatric department of the Middlesex Hospital. On the north side of the Lane, beyond some similar Victorian mansions, stretched the sports grounds and playing fields of Highgate School and then the Bishops Wood, where late in the century and during the early years of the twentieth century the Highgate golf course and the spacious houses and gardens of Courtney Avenue, Bishops Avenue and Winnington Road separated the old village from the spread of East Finchley.

X

Hampstead in the Nineteenth Century

At the end of the nineteenth century there were still only about twelve hundred houses in Highgate, an increase of some three hundred from the mid-century figure of nine hundred. Hampstead, a very much larger and more defined area, had a population of twelve thousand in 1851, which had increased from about four thousand five hundred at the beginning of the century, when there were an estimated six hundred and ninety-one inhabited houses, and it was to grow to a figure approaching eighty thousand by 1900, as the tide of urban development swept north-westwards from London and passed over it. Yet happily, the heart of the seventeenth and eighteenth century old town of Hampstead, perched on the hillsides, was already so closely built that there was no room here for further development and it has survived, its people cherishing its unique attractiveness. There are many places throughout the country where one may see cottages planted close together on hillsides, but in Hampstead, particularly on either side of Heath Street, there are substantial and elegant eighteenth-century houses, built at improbable angles and levels and creating intriguing surprises at every turn.

The building of nineteenth-century Hampstead is a complicated story. In the Kilburn area where there were a number of small landowners, some with villas on estates of less than ten acres, there was a succession of sales to speculative builders throughout the years, the quality of the houses and the market for which they were catering depending a great deal on the capital and credit of the undertakers, amongst whom there were many bankruptcies, especially during the economic depression of the years following the Napoleonic wars.

The ground of the Chesterfield estates belonged to Westminster and could not be sold until legal action was taken. The two hundred acres of Eton's Chalcots estates were similarly controlled. The four hundred and sixteen acres of the Maryon Wilson estate comprised nearly sixty acres on the east side of the Heath and three hundred and fifty-six acres of farmland in a wide, continuous stretch to the west and south-west of the old town, and by the terms of the will of the elder Maryon Wilson, who died in 1821, the main part of this estate also became legally controlled, for he made his heir, Thomas Maryon Wilson, merely a tenant for life, which meant that he could not make ninety-nine year leases to prospective developers, although the sixty acres of the East Heath became his personal property.

In 1752 Lord Chesterfield had sold his estates covering St John's Wood and part of southern Hampstead to Henry Samuel Eyre, and early in the nineteenth century the Eyre family began their building development here. In 1807 the Chesterfield family, in order to pay their debts, obtained a private estate bill which enabled them to sell off their Belsize estate as well, although the Dean and Chapter of Westminster do not appear to have done very well out of the deal and their legal position was never properly clarified.

The Belsize estate went to four Hampstead men who did very little in the way of development for several years. Some re-sold parts of their new properties, keeping only what they wanted for their own use or future sale, for they had been given the power to develop their estates as they wished. Belsize House, with forty-five acres of park and Sir Spencer Perceval in occupation, was part of this Chesterfield sale, but for the next fifty years it remained unaltered, with a succession of tenants.

However, a number of large villas were built in Belsize at this time, each standing in several acres of ground, and there was the beginning of development of smaller properties along Haverstock Hill.

On the Eton estate to the south there was no development at all for many years. It remained hay and grass farmland and was a profitable concern, supplying the fodder needed for the hundreds of horses engaged in London's transport. In 1796 there were five single dwellings on the estate and by 1832 only nine, including Steele's cottage and the farmhouses of Upper Chalcots and Lower Chalcots. It was a stretch of pleasant country which protected the seclusion of the new mansions of Belsize and the unique individuality of old Hampstead above it, but their security was shattered when Eyre announced a plan to build the Finchley Road as a toll road, in order to develop his estates to the south.

There was bitter opposition from Maryon Wilson and the people of Hampstead and Belsize. They saw a threat to their cherished privacy and foretold a day when they would be surrounded, but after much acrimonius argument, Eyre eventually won and in the early 1830s twenty years after the building of the Archway Road, the Finchley Road was built, from St John's Wood Chapel as far as the turnpike at the Swiss Cottage tavern, and here for the next forty years it ended.

On the Maryon Wilson estate, as we have seen, Downshire Hill and John Street, which later was re-named Keat's Grove, had been developed on copyhold land and the chapel of St John built.

In the heart of the old town, the little churchyard of St John's Church had filled up and early in the century the extension on the hill to the north was planned and consecrated. Above it, leading from Holly Walk, the little winding hill running along the west side of the new cemetery, Prospect Place, a cul-de-sac of two houses, looking straight down on to the cemetery, was built in 1814, and at the same time, just above it, Benham Place. This is a terrace of nine small houses which look over their neat little front gardens on to the weather-boarded backs of the Prospect Place houses.

Farther up the hill, where it bends to become roughly parallel with Heath Street down below, the Holly Place terrace of houses was built in 1816, at the same time as Abbé Morel's beautiful little St Mary's Church which stands in its midst.

However, when, in 1821, Sir Thomas Maryon Wilson, a rich bachelor and absentee landlord, found his hands tied by the terms of his father's will, he made no move for several years to make it legally possible for any further building on the fields and farmlands which still surrounded the old town. It was after the trustees of the Eton College estate of Chalcots obtained legal permission to develop their land that Sir Thomas Maryon Wilson became interested in the development of his manor estate. In 1829 he presented an estate bill to break the family settlement. It was no extraordinary measure, for many similar bills were presented to Parliament and passed during these early years of the nineteenth century. Sir Thomas argued that in making him a tenant for life, his father had not foreseen the development that was about to take place in north-west London. To his surprise and intense annoyance, he met with strong opposition and was reminded that during the argument against the building of the Finchley Road he had said that his father had wished to maintain the rural seclusion of Hampstead. Once more the copyholders joined together in vigorous protest against an infringement of their rights, as they had in the case of Mrs Lessingham half a century earlier: and it was now noised abroad that Maryon Wilson was planning to enclose the Heath, although he had never declared this to be his intention. Lord Mansfield joined in the outcry and *The Times* took a hand, by declaring, on 20 June 1829, that the rights of private property are always subordinate to the rights of the public.

His Bill was rejected. He tried again in 1830 and again he failed, and now, for the first time, there was a plea that the amenities of the Heath should be preserved for the benefit of London's poor, for as the slums of inner London grew ever more crowded and sordid, men and women with a social conscience began to preach the virtues of fresh air and the inestimable value of the few remaining open stretches of countryside near London, where the unfortunate slum dwellers could find brief respite from the squalor of their surroundings.

For the next thirteen years Maryon Wilson did no more about the development of his Hampstead property, but in 1843 he planned an estate on his freehold sixty acres which he called East Heath Park. As a preliminary he built an approach road and the viaduct over the most easterly of the Upper Hampstead ponds, which by this time had been leased to the New River Company. Yet people had become so suspicious of his ultimate intentions and the forces against him were so strong, the he was refused permission to build and had to abandon the idea.

By this time there was more building on the Eyre estate in South Hampstead and on the Belsize lands. Kilburn was developing and houses were also going up on parts of the manor estate, on the fringes of the Heath and to the west of Frognal, on land which had been acquired from the Maryon Wilson family before the restrictions imposed by Sir Thomas's father.

One of the oldest houses to be built during the 1830s was John Thompson's Frognal Priory. Thompson was an eccentric who had made his money as a pub auctioneer and he had a passion for antiques. The Priory stood where Frognal Close has since been built, and commanded a wonderful view over the Finchley meadows. It was a large, red brick house in imitation Gothic, with a wealth of turrets and towers, twisted chimneys and mullioned windows set with coloured glass, imitation carving in stucco and a welter of coats of arms belonging to every family but his own. It also had an overpoweringly ornate entrance porch, which was, in fact, genuine, having been taken from a medieval Shropshire manor house. In this extraordinary house he displayed all the furniture and pictures – both genuinely antique and faked – which he had collected in the course of his life, and for which he had a genuine affection. He was inordinately proud of his possessions and loved to display them not only to guests but to casual visitors, and when he died he left it all to his niece, who was married to a crook named Gregory. Gregory owned a publication called *The Satirist*, and made money by stirring up scandals and then blackmailing the people concerned by threatening to publish all the details. He was at last prosecuted and imprisoned for attempted extortion, and when he was released he moved into the Priory with his wife and proceeded to enjoy the fortune which Thompson had left her. She died and he went on spending the inheritance with such abandon that it soon dwindled away. Piece by piece he sold all the contents of the Priory and when everything had gone he disappeared and was never heard of again.

The lease expired and the strange place fell into a state of ruin, for despite its appearance of solid antiquity it was by no means strongly built. The Maryon Wilson bailiffs installed a caretaker and his wife for a time and after the caretaker died the old woman lived alone in the crumbling, empty folly, soon becoming as odd as the house itself and convinced that she was the owner, but eventually she had to be moved and the place was demolished.

There were a number of large mansions in West Hampstead during these middle years of the century, which have all now vanished. In 1844 Mr Cannon, a retired India merchant, built Kidderpore Hall, the grounds of which are covered today by Kidderpore Avenue and Kidderpore Gardens, although part of the house was incorporated in Westfield College, when it was founded in 1882. The beautiful Mrs Thistlethwayte, who in her day had been Laura Bell, the famous courtesan, moved from Grosvenor Square after her husband's suicide in 1887 to Woodbine Cottage, which stood in several acres of ground opposite West End Green: and here she lived in comfortable seclusion, with her flower gardens and kitchen gardens, greenhouses, stables and paddocks, horses and dogs, until she died, when the place was pulled down and the site covered with houses and flats.

On the Eton College land building began in 1830 but then came the news of the building of the London and Birmingham railway. Building plans were suspended, for it was feared that the railway would cut right through the estate, but the railway company agreed to build a tunnel instead, so as not to disfigure the landscape. At the same time, the Commissioner of Woods and Forests approached Eton with a plan to buy Primrose Hill as a permanent open space. At first they could not agree over the price, but eventually Eton found some Crown land in

Eton and in 1842 exchanged thirty-two acres of this for the fifty-three acres of Primrose Hill and its surrounding grassland.

Building continued on the Eton College estate and also on Belsize, but Maryon Wilson, though he presented Bills years after year, was refused permission to build even along his Finchley Road frontage.

A new factor had now to be considered. With the arrival of the railways, Hampstead Heath became much more easily accessible to London's East Enders. By 1860 the Hampstead Junction Railway had opened and on Bank holidays people flocked to the Heath. After the closing of the fair at West End, fairs had been held at South End Green and White Bear Green but had never been particularly popular. Now, however, a new and larger fair was established in the Vale of Health and about 1863 Donald Nicoll built the Vale of Health tavern.

There was a good deal of building in the Vale during these mid-Victorian years of small, unattractive houses and Maryon Wilson deplored its vulgarisation and the establishment of the fairground, with the hawkers and costermongers who lined the East Heath Road on Bank holidays, the steam hurdy-gurdies, the swings and roundabouts, coconut shies and Aunt Sallies, hooplas and peep shows, waxworks and shooting galleries, but this was all on copyhold land and had the consent of the copyholders.

He had done a good deal to improve the appearance of the Heath. In 1845, when he built the Viaduct bridge, people had appealed to him to plant more trees on the Lower and Middle Heath, and within the next year or so he had planted tree belts near the Vale of Health, as a screen to the grounds of a laundry, as well as several new plantations of willows, firs and Turkey oaks, the willows in Platts Lane and East Heath Road being still particularly beautiful. He was prepared to do more. 'I had a very large collection of cedar trees and curious oak trees raised at Charlton, in order to place on Hampstead Heath,' he said, 'but they have all died, or become too old to transplant'.

In exasperation, he threatened to build a new Agar Town on the Heath, with short leases, and establish brick fields, laundries and sand pits. This he never did, but in 1866 he sold a quarter of an acre of sand and ballast to the Midland Railway for the building of the Belsize tunnel. This sand was taken from either side of the Spaniards Road, so that to this day the road stands above the level of the Heath, like a causeway, instead of being in a slight depression, as it once was.

At the same time he ordered the building of a house near the flagstaff, which he had put up in 1845 to mark the site of the old Hampstead beacon. This had been the most northerly of the long line of beacons reaching down to Dover, all of which had been lit in times of national danger or rejoicing, and it was close to the Whitestone Pond, the highest pond on the Heath, which is named after the white milestone nearby, marking the spot as 'IV miles from St Giles' Pound'.

As the builders put up Maryon Wilson's first house on this strategic point of the Heath the inhabitants of Hampstead pulled it down. Gurney Hoare took him to Chancery, and while the question of the extent of his manorial rights was still being debated, the Metropolitan Board of Works approached him, asking whether he would be willing to sell the Heath. He said he was not prepared to negotiate and in any case it was still not clear whether he was in a position to sell it.

The problem of the intractable but much tried Sir Thomas Maryon Wilson was solved by his death, in 1869. The property went to his brother, Sir John Maryon Wilson, and although the manorial rights were still undetermined, the Board of Works offered to buy them from him. Sir John accepted their offer of £45,000 and by 1871 negotiations were completed and the Heath became public property, although by this time the original five hundred acres of heathland had dwindled to two hundred, because of the small but steady encroachments of the copy holders or straightforward grants over the centuries.

While the struggle for the Heath was being waged, building continued on the Chalcots estate. All through the 1840s and 1850s it went on, the countryside of rolling meadows disappearing before the advance up the hill of the numerous contractors. By 1867 Steele's cottage had been demolished but then there was a pause, with a hundred and twenty acres to the north-west still under grass. Swiss Cottage was developed. On the Belsize estates the mansions which had been built earlier in the century disappeared, as a new generation sold them for development of smaller properties. Building took place with no particular planning, each of the individual small estates being divided into building lots by its owner.

One of the failures was St John's Park which, during the 1850s, was developed between Haverstock Hill and the low-lying fields to the north, through which the Fleet brook ran. This estate, like the Fleet Road, built at the same time, was too near the river, which had become an open sewer. In 1860 the Metropolitan Board of Works converted the noisome Fleet stream into a culvert, but by then it was too late to redeem St John's Park, which had become seedy and shabby, and Fleet Road, which was soon a place of tenements and lodging houses and became even more depressed when the extension of the railway from St Pancras was built.

On Hampstead Green, facing Pond Street, were several large Georgian houses, built when Pond Street was one of the most fashionable parts of Hampstead. Here, to the consternation of the residents, the Metropolitan Asylums Board established a temporary smallpox hospital, with huts and fever sheds, during the smallpox outbreak in London of 1870. Protests were in vain and it put a stop to any further building. The smallpox patients were not moved until 1872 and then only to be replaced by imbeciles, and by 1876, when there was a further outbreak of smallpox in London, the smallpox patients were back there again. Within a few years it had become the permanent North Western Fever Hospital and the mansions, some of the finest in Hampstead, were deserted and eventually demolished. In Pond Street itself, while the eastern side is now occupied by the new building of the Royal Free Hospital, and Hampstead Green has practically disappeared, on the western side some of the eighteenth-century smaller houses have survived. Numbers 33 to 35, with their carved door canopies, are early eighteenth century, numbers 17 to 21 a little later: and several of these houses are now used as offices in connection with the hospital.

It was not until 1875 that Spencer Maryon Wilson, son of Sir John, planned the wide, tree-lined Fitzjohn's Avenue. It was, in effect, a southward extension of Heath Street, running due south to Swiss Cottage, although it was not until several years later that the heart of the old town was cleared and the intersection simplified. The new Fitzjohn's Avenue, cutting across the old Conduit fields, was opened in 1876, and then the building of the houses began. A few were architect built, some by Norman Shaw, who lived in one of them for a time, others by T. K. Green, but most were put up by speculative builders: and they were all enormous, T. K. Green's houses being built in what Sir Nikolaus Pevsner aptly described as 'crude elephantine Gothic'. Yet to the mid-Victorians, with plenty of servants available to maintain these huge houses, they were enormously impressive and desirable. Within such easy reach of London, they became fashionable, and for the first few years many prosperous Victorian artists made their homes here.

The land between Fitzjohn's Avenue and the Finchley Road soon filled up with similarly imposing houses, intended for the wealthy Londoners of the 1880s, and so they remained for a time, although the artists soon found their mammoth dimensions overwhelming and moved out, making room for equally rich business men.

Gradually, year by year, more streets were laid out and more houses built, but it was not until 1887, after the passing of the 1883

Metropolitan Streets Improvement Act, that work began on the clearing away of the centre of the old town.★ It was demolished as far as Perrin's Court, which has happily survived, making the High Street very much wider on the west side, and giving a clear run from Heath Street to Fitzjohn's Avenue.

By 1900, when nearly all the old mansions of central and west Hampstead had disappeared and the dreary waste of railway land had developed between the Finchley Road and the Kilburn High Road, many of the owners of the Victorian houses in the still exclusive parts of Hampstead were finding them too unwieldy to manage and were moving out to the suburbs. In Belsize Avenue and Rosslyn Park houses were being turned into girls' schools, boarding houses and private hotels. The ponderous, uniform houses of the 1880s were falling out of fashion and people now preferred the Norman Shaw type of house, with its steeper pitched roof and gables and its warm, red brick, which was used a good deal in the development of the north and western parts of the Maryon Wilson estate, as for example the house which Norman Shaw built for Kate Greenaway at number 39 Frognal Lane in 1885, but much of the building of this part of Hampstead did not take place until the turn of the century and the early years of the twentieth century.

During these years of expansion the affairs of Hampstead were conducted by the Hampstead Vestry, which acted as a parish council and attended to such matters as the installation of gaslight and then electric light, the cleaning and lighting of the streets, poor relief, the provision of schools, the building of roads and the maintenance of boundaries and footpaths. The members were mostly public-spirited tradesmen and the local gentry took little part except when matters of important local interest were involved. In 1876 the Town Hall on Haverstock Hill was opened and served as a Vestry Hall until 1900, when Hampstead became a part of London and the first Hampstead Borough Council was formed, under the control of the London County Council.

The population of the new borough had now risen to over eighty-two thousand and nothing like the old social intimacy could be maintained, but Hampstead retained its tradition as a place where artists, writers and members of the learned profession liked to live. There were a number of thriving societies where they could meet and for many years throughout the century the churches, more than twenty of which were built as the borough developed, did invaluable work in creating social ties amongst the new inhabitants.

★ See Chapter Five, pp. 90, 91.

There had been a subscription library in Hampstead since 1833, first in Flask Walk and then in the High Street, moving finally, in 1885, to Stansfield House, at the corner of Prince Arthur Road, the early Georgian House where Clarkson Stansfield, the artist friend of Charles Dickens, had come to live in 1847. Then the Vestry took a hand, with the provision of public libraries, and the Central Library in the Finchley Road was opened in 1897, the year that the Heath Protection Society was formed. It was at this time that Sir Spencer Wells, the owner of Golders Hill House, died. The house and estate came on to the market and were bought in with funds raised by the Hampstead Heath Extension scheme, being handed over to the London County Council as a public park in 1899.

Building in Hampstead went on. In Frognal Gardens Sir Walter Besant, the novelist and historian of London, who was also the first president of the Hampstead Antiquarian and Historical Society, built his house in 1892, and in the following years the area to the west was developed, many of the houses being designed by Philip Webb or C. H. B. Quennell.

At Mount Vernon, the North London Hospital for Consumption was built in 1880 and has since become the National Institute for Medical Research. The old workhouse at New End was enlarged several times throughout the century. It became a military hospital in 1915 and has been a hospital ever since, known as the New End Hospital.

Part of the old Vane House became the Royal Soldiers' Daughters' Home, which had first been established in Rosslyn House after the Crimean War, and remained until only a few years ago, when the house was demolished and new buildings put up on the site, the Home having been moved to a new building behind.

The number of famous people – writers, artists, architects and actors – who were living in Hampstead during the later years of the nineteenth century is legion. At Oak Hill Lodge George Smith, the publisher, of Smith, Elder and Company, lived from 1863 to 1872 and here gave his weekly receptions, attended by Thackeray and Anthony Trollope, George Henry Lewes and George Eliot, Wilkie Collins, Mrs Gaskell, Millais and Lord Leighton. In the Grove, George du Maurier lived at New Grove House, where he wrote Trilby and Peter Ibbotson, and his close friend Canon Ainger, chaplain to Queen Victoria, who gave du Maurier many an idea for his Punch drawings, was nearby in Upper Terrace.

Bell-Moor at the top of East Heath Road was converted by Thomas

Barratt, the historian of Hampstead, from four old houses, in one of which Canon Barnett and his wife had formerly lived, and here for more than thirty years Thomas Barratt made his valuable Bell-Moor collection of prints and manuscripts and wrote his history, which was first published in 1912.

In Gangmoor close by the Duveen family were living about this time and at Pitt House Sir Harold Harmsworth. In the Vale of Health Alfred Harmsworth, father of Lord Northcliffe, lived at Rose Cottage and other residents of the Vale included Charles Knight, Rowland Hill, Douglas Jerrold, Lady Dufferin and George Jealous, the proprietor and editor of the first Hampstead newspaper, the *Hampstead and Highgate Express.*

At the Admiral's House in Admiral's Walk Sir George Gilbert Scott was living, from 1856 to 1864.

Hampstead on the hill and in its central parts was fashionable and prosperous, and even with the decline of church-going, after the 1880s, a strong community spirit survived and it preserved its identity, but on the fringes, in Fleet Road and on the Kilburn side, it was rapidly becoming overcrowded and sordid, the houses let out in flats and tenements and growing dingier and more depressing every year.

XI

The Twentieth Century

By 1905 the Heath Extension Committee had raised £42,000 to buy eighty acres of the Heath on the north side of the Spaniards Road, which had belonged to the Eton College estate of Wyldes, and this land was handed over to the London County Council as a permanent open space. There remained two hundred and forty acres of the estate which were still fields and open countryside, and Dame Henrietta Barnett saw this land as a site for a garden suburb. In 1906 the Hampstead Garden Suburb Trust was formed and the land bought from the Eton College trustees. Barry Parker and Raymond Unwin, who had just planned Letchworth Garden City, were called in to develop, in co-operation with Sir Edwin Lutyens, the new Hampstead Garden Suburb, which geographically is not in Hampstead but Hendon, and Raymond Unwin came to live at Wyldes Farm. It had been in the Collins family from 1785 to 1834, during which time it was known as Collins Farm, but it was called Wyldes Farm again when Raymond Unwin bought it in 1906, and he lived here until 1940.

North End still keeps its rural atmosphere and the lane leading to the farm could be anywhere in the deep countryside.

The Bull and Bush was considerably altered and enlarged in 1924 and the garden is now a car park, but some of the old brick work is there and can be easily traced. The old place clings to its three hundred years of history and happy memories and is full of mementoes and relics.

The Hare and Hounds close by was destroyed by a bomb in the

Second World War and has been rebuilt. Just over the borough boundary, on the North End Road, is the Manor House Hospital, opposite Golders Hill Park; and beyond the park, Ivy House, where Anna Pavlova lived from 1912 until 1931, is now a drama school.

Pitt House, where Lord Rothermère was living from 1905 to 1908, was demolished in 1952 and two houses built in the grounds, but Byron Cottage still stands.

Jack Straw's Castle was severely damaged during the war and not rebuilt until 1962. Many deplore the new building. Weather boarding, oriel windows and toy turrets don't bed together happily, but it is a salute to the past and very comfortable inside, with its Wat Tyler and Dick Turpin bars on the ground floor and Dickens room on the first floor, while the Turret bar and dining room on the second floor have magnificent views over the Heath.

The houses which stood in Heath Brow just to the north of Jack Straw's Castle – Heath Brow, Fern Lodge, Heath Brow Cottage and Heathlands – were all destroyed during the war and the land on which they stood has now been merged into the Heath, but the Old Court House survived and is now a home for old people.

Heath House still stands and The Hill, which Samuel Hoare built in 1807 as a wedding present for his son, was bought by Lord Inverforth in 1925. On his death, he bequeathed it to the Manor House Hospital, and as Inverforth House it is now the women's section of the Hospital.

At the Elms, on the eastern side of the Spaniards Road, where Mother Huff once had her tea gardens, Sir Joseph Duveen was living early in the century, but since 1957 it has been the St Columba's Hospital.

Lord Erskine's Evergreen Hill stood until 1923, when most of the old house was demolished and a smaller one built on the site. Heath End House next to it has survived, but is now turned into three houses, Heath End House, Heath End Cottage and Evergreen Hill. Alongside them is the entrance to Spaniard's End, a development of the 1950s of a private road and large houses on the grounds of John Turner's house, The Firs. The Firs is still there, although much altered now and converted into three houses, while the stables and outbuildings have been rebuilt as very attractive cottages.

The Spaniards has happily survived and the block of luxury flats opposite Lord Erskine's old house was built on the site of the vast Mount Tyndal, a house which had been built not many years earlier, in the present century.

The Vale of Health is still a small, isolated community, with no room left now to extend. If you approach it from the East Heath Road the signpost leads you on to a narrow, woodland path, with a road for vehicles alongside it. As you walk down to the Vale, the large pond shines through the trees on your right, but the first houses – some of the last to be built in the Vale – are disappointing and dull. Then comes a small, dour-looking block of modern flats painted battle-ship grey and called Athenaeum Court, in tribute to the Athenaeum Club which once stood here, but originally there was a small hotel on this site, built soon after the Vale of Health Hotel went up in 1863. This second hotel was intended as a holiday resort for wealthy London invalids but the idea never caught on and it became successively a factory, a lecture hall and a club. The Salvation Army had it for a few years and in 1910 it became the headquarters of the Anglo–German Club, which did not survive the outbreak of the First World War, but it was not demolished until 1958 when Athenaeum Court was built.

Round the corner are Byron Villas, which are no improvement on the first houses, and even the LCC plaque on number 1, proclaiming that D. H. Lawrence lodged here for a while in 1915, does not redeem them, but beyond, running down to the Heath and the lake, the houses are older and interesting and end in the sumptuous new block of flats, Spencer House, built on the site of the Vale of Health tavern. During its last years, the tavern let off its top floors as artists' studios, and it was in one of these that Stanley Spencer completed his famous picture 'The Resurrection in Cookham'.

From the terrace of Spencer House there is a superb view over the lake and the Heath and alongside it is the fair ground, quiet enough during the week but bursting into vigorous, cheerful, if noisy, life during summer weekends and on Bank holidays.

Turning back to Byron Cottages again and the roadway leading from East Heath Road, there is a small triangular green ahead, with some early Victorian houses facing it, one of which bears a plaque commemorating the fact that Rabindranath Tagore once lived here. The narrow, steep passage running up by the side of this house leads to the old part of the Vale, an enchanting place where the houses and cottages are built all at sixes and sevens and the paths and roads make their way as best they can, twisting and turning between the garden walls, with no numbers or street names to help anyone to find them. Perhaps, in this delightful seclusion, nobody particularly wants to be found again.

Edgar Wallace lived in Leigh Hunt's old house, Vale Lodge, for several years, and Compton Mackenzie at Woodbine Cottage.

After Keats' death, Mrs Brawne and Fanny stayed on at Wentworth Place until Mrs Brawne's tragic accidental death in November 1829. With a candle in her hand, she stood by the front door, saying goodbye to some friends, when a gust of wind set her dress alight and she died of her burns. Keats' sister Fanny, who married a Spaniard, Senor Llanos, lived there with her husband from 1828 until they left for Spain in 1831, where they remained for the rest of their lives. In 1833, twelve years after Keats' death, and her brother now dead as well as her mother, Fanny Brawne married a Portuguese Jew, Louis Lindo, twelve years younger than herself. A few months later her sister Margaret married a Portuguese diplomat and both women spent most of the rest of their lives abroad.

In 1838 Wentworth Place was bought by Miss Eliza Chester, an actress who in her younger days had attracted the attentions of the Prince Regent. On his succession to the throne she had been given the equivocal appointment of Court Reader at Windsor Castle, a service which William IV and most certainly Queen Victoria found superfluous. When Eliza bought Wentworth Place she was in her forties. She converted the place into one large house and added the drawing room on the east side, now known as the Chester Room, as well as the conservatory. She did not stay for long, moving to Kensington, where she died in 1860, but while she was at Wentworth Place she did a good deal of entertaining and gave what were termed 'literary teas', diversions at which, it is said, Charles Dickens was sometimes present.

From the 1840s until the end of the century there were many occupiers of the house, including a doctor, who had a practice there, and a clergyman. For a short time it was a school, but the last occupier, who was there for twenty-five years, was a lover and keen student of Keats' work, and he strove to restore the atmosphere and furnishings of the house as it has been in Keats' day.

In 1895 the Hampstead Literary and Antiquarian Society asked the Society of Arts to place the memorial plaque on the house and the following year a group of Hampstead residents formed the Keats Memorial Committee, the librarian of the newly-formed Hampstead Libraries acting as honorary secretary.

Sir Charles Dilke, grandson of Charles Brown, presented a valuable collection of Keats' books, letters, first editions and manuscripts, which were displayed in the New Central Library in the Finchley Road for several years, but in 1920 Wentworth Place came on the market. The Mayor of Hampstead launched a National Committee to raise £10,000 to buy it. The money did not come in very quickly but eventually

£4,650 was raised, more than £2,500 coming from the United States, and the balance was contributed by individual members of the committee.

The house was bought and handed over to the Hampstead Borough Council, who agreed to maintain it. As the Keats Memorial House it was opened in 1925 by Sir Arthur Quiller-Couch, and the first curator, the scholarly Frederick Edgcumbe, was installed. It was he who began to form the museum, using the Central Library collection as the nucleus. Over the years, until his death in 1941, it grew – and is still growing.

The Keats Museum and Branch Library were built next door by the Hampstead Corporation in 1931, an invaluable source of information to everyone interested in this period of English literature and its poets and writers. The house itself suffered a certain amount of bomb damage during the last war, but it was put right, and none of the relics was lost. Today Keats' sitting room, with the french windows leading on to the garden, is as much as possible as it was when he lived and wrote there, as well as Brown's room at the front of the house, where Keats was moved during his fatal illness, and watched the gypsies from the Heath pass by.

The beautiful Fenton House has also been opened to the public in recent years. The Fenton family remained there until the middle years of the nineteenth century and joined with the Hoares in the controversy with Maryon Wilson over the building on the Heath. It then became the home of Mrs David Murray, a great-aunt of Lord Mansfield, and in 1956 it was bought by Lady Binning, who bequeathed it to the National Trust, together with her outstanding collection of European porcelain and some beautiful eighteenth-century furniture, as well as her picture collection which includes Constable's 'View of Hampstead Heath Under a Stormy Sky'. In 1952 the Benton-Fletcher collection of keyboard musical instruments – harpsichords, virginals, spinets, clavichords and early pianos, all of them in perfect working order – which he had presented to the National Trust, was moved to Fenton House, and adds to the delight and interest of the place, which still has the feel of a private home, the oldest of the large houses in Hampstead to have survived.

During the early years of the century there was more building in Hampstead. In 1907 the red brick, Neo-Georgian University College School, with its willow-fringed frontage, was built in Frognal Lane, when the school moved from Gower Street, and in Ellerdale Road, leading off the west side of Lower Heath Street, the King Alfred's

School, which is now in North End Way, opened at number 24, in 1910.

Gardnor Mansions at the corner of Church Row, had gone up as early as 1898, but with the new century similar blocks went up, in other parts of the old town, large and comfortable, with provision for servants' quarters.

1907 also saw the opening of the Hampstead Tube Station on the corner of Heath Street and the High Street, opposite Holly Hill, and the same year the extension to Golders Green was opened, serving the new Hampstead Garden Suburb.

The Hampstead Tube Station is the deepest in London, 192 feet below street level, and it seems hardly to have changed since the day it was built. Its crimson and white tiles and small lift, with the disembodied voice telling you to stand clear of the gates, seem to have been overlooked, but have an air of not minding in the least and preferring it that way.

There were scores of famous people living around Frognal during the first half of the century, Anton Walbrook, Anne Ziegler and Webster Booth and E. V. Knox. Upper Frognal Lodge, number 103, was the home of Ramsay Macdonald from 1925 to 1937. Hugh Gaitskell lived in Frognal End, Sir Walter Besant's old house at 18, Frognal Gardens. Kubelik and Frank Salisbury lived in West Heath Road, Henry Arthur Jones in Arkwright Road.

Moving eastwards, Mary Webb lived in number 12 of the old cottages in Hampstead Grove, John Galsworthy at Grove Lodge, next to the Admiral's house in Admiral's Walk, from 1918 until his death in 1933, John Masefield at Weatherall House, which had once been the second Long Room of the Spa days, Gerald du Maurier at Cannon Hall from 1916 until 1934, Katharine Mansfield and Middleton Murray at number 17 East Heath Road for a short time after their marriage in 1918. In Church Row, where John James Park, the first historian of Hampstead lived and died, early in the nineteenth century, Wilkie Collins lived at number 25 for a time, Lord Alfred Douglas at number 26, and later George Gilbert Scott Junior, and then Sir William Rothenstein. George du Maurier was here before moving to Hampstead Grove and other famous names, in later years, were Compton Mackenzie and H. G. Wells.

After the First World War more of the large Victorian houses of Hampstead declined in fashion. There were no servants to run them and with the advent of the motor car people were moving into flats and buying country weekend cottages. The large houses in such roads as

Fitzjohn's Avenue and West End Lane were divided into flats and there was a time when Belsize seemed to be developing into a rather forlorn bed-sitter land, but after the Second World War these districts revived and have become fashionable again, while the more modern and manageable houses in the roads surrounding the West Heath never lost their exclusiveness and value.

Several of the largest of the old houses have been lost, however. The Longmans' beautiful Mount Grove, at one time called The Rookery, came down and the modern block of flats, Greenhill, was built on the site. Thomas Barratt's Bell-Moor was replaced by the Bellmoor flats. Weatherall House gave way to the Wells Council flats in 1948. The Jacobean Holly Hill House was demolished in 1926 and University College Junior School established there. The house which George Steevens had adapted from the Upper Flask came down in 1921, when the Queen Mary's Maternity Home was built on the site.

The Lower Flask had been rebuilt as the Flask in 1874 and in the High Street the old King of Bohemia was rebuilt in 1935, but Norway House, one of Hampstead's oldest houses, with gardens stretching back to where Gayton Road and Gayton Gardens were built, came down in 1931. It had been a school in the early nineteenth century, described by F. E. Baines, in his *Records of Hampstead*, as 'the best school for young gentlemen in the parish'.

Yet a great deal of old Hampstead has survived and in the High Street, particularly on the west side, many of the buildings above the modern shop fronts have changed very little.

The Embassy cinema at the bottom of Holly Bush Vale was originally a drill hall but in 1919, by which time it was run-down and no longer used for its original purpose, Norman MacDermott converted it into the Everyman Theatre. It quickly became one of London's most distinguished Little Theatres, presenting carefully selected plays of distinction. He staged a good deal of Bernard Shaw but also tried out new plays, the most famous at the time being Noël Coward's *The Vortex*. Norman MacDermott gave up the theatre in 1926 and Raymond Massey took over for the next five years but then had to close down. For a short time the theatre was used as a Drama School, but then it re-opened as the Everyman Cinema, maintaining the tradition of the theatre, which still continues, of showing films of real merit.

For several years the Embassy theatre at Swiss Cottage was Hampstead's only theatre. This had been the Hampstead Conservatoire of Music, the principal of which, for many years, was Cecil Sharp, the founder of the English Folk Dance society. The policy of play selection at the Embassy was similar to that of the Everyman, and since it ceased to be a commercial theatre it has become the Central School of Speech and Drama.

Since the end of the Second World War, Hampstead has been well supplied with theatres. In 1967 the Round House in Chalk Farm Road was opened, the theatre having been converted from a hundred-year-old railway engine shed. There is the little 'Theatre at New End' and also the Hampstead Theatre Club at the Swiss Cottage Centre which, designed by Sir Basil Spence, was built, along with the new library and swimming baths, as a replacement of the original social centre and library in the Finchley Road, just before the borough became part of Camden.

Down beside the Hampstead tube station, at the bottom of Upper Heath Street, is the new Kingswell shopping precinct, modern and attractive, but the little Back Lane of early nineteenth-century cottages which encircles it, curving round from Heath Street to Flask Walk, seems to challenge it to extend no further. Some of the shops in this part of Heath street have caught the Carnaby Street and King's Road fever of the 1950s and bear strange names, but are none the worse for that.

During the twenties and thirties there were as many artists living in Hampstead as in Chelsea. At 47 Downshire Hill lived the Carline family, nearly all of whom were artists, and at the Slade School, Sydney Carline met Stanley Spencer, who ultimately married Sydney's sister Hilda. The Carlines were a friendly, hospitable family and their circle included Gilbert Spencer as well as Stanley, Henry Lamb, John Nash, James Wood, Richard Hartley, John Duguid and a host of others who were often to be found at the delightful if draughty old house, with its wisteria-hung wrought iron balcony overlooking the garden, particularly at weekends, playing not very serious croquet or having tea in the first-floor drawing room.

Although Stanley Spencer spent most of his life in Cookham, where he was born, he had many connections with Hampstead. In 1924 this strange, mystical genius moved into one of the Vale of Health tavern's studios with Henry Lamb, and the following year he married the equally mystically inclined Hilda Carline. Here they spent the first few years of their turbulent marriage and Spencer completed the picture which brought him fame, 'The Resurrection in Cookham'. Few people understood it when it was exhibited at the Goupil Galleries in 1927, but the Contemporary Art Society bought it and presented it to the Tate Gallery, where it now hangs.

By 1933, when they had two daughters, the marriage had almost broken up and Hilda was back in Downshire Hill, but Spencer continued to visit her, even after the divorce and his marriage at Cookham to Patricia Preece. Despite the long liaison which had preceded it, this second marriage was a failure from the outset, for a week or two after the wedding Spencer made it clear to Patricia that he wanted both women for his wives.

The Carlines moved to number 17 Pond Street, and Spencer, in love again with Hilda, moved first to a top room in 188 Adelaide Road and then to number 179, writing often to Hilda and occasionally seeing her; but for most of this six months living in retreat, working hard to pay off an accumulation of debts and meet his heavy commitments and at the same time enjoying the solitariness of his existence.

Early in 1939 he met Daphne Charlton, living at 40 New End Square with her husband, in the eighteenth-century house where Tennyson's mother had lived for the last years of her life. A few months later Spencer and the Charltons were staying together in a village in the Cotswolds but by the end of the year he was visiting Hampstead again. 'I was up to Hampstead in December 1939,' he wrote. 'It was getting dark and misty when I went for a stroll in the late afternoon to the place where early this summer I painted the Vale of Health.' He could not forget Hilda and gazed up at the Studio where they had known much happiness, in between the quarrels, but as she was no longer there, the place seemed unreal. 'I find it hard to believe that it is marked on the map. There is no connecting it with any place outside it. It seems only to have a ghostly existence. It is a place that has been formed by lovers,' he said.

He even contemplated re-marrying Hilda, although he was still legally married to Patricia, but although they wrote long letters to each other and were, in many ways, reconciled, Hilda would not consider it, while he regarded the new relationship as a spiritual marriage and would probably never have gone through another ceremony, even if it had been possible.

In 1942 Hilda suffered a mental breakdown and for a time was insane. She recovered, but in 1947 she developed cancer, and she died in the New End hospital in 1950. Spencer spent his last years in Cookham where he died, also of cancer, in 1959.

In Highgate the building over Dartmouth Park at the beginning of the century, with Dartmouth Park Hill running form the point where Highgate Hill meets the High Street and then due south to the junction of Fortess Road and the Junction Road opposite Tufnell Park station, made a continuously built up area from Kentish Town to the southern approaches of Highgate – and it is difficult to tell where one ends and the other begins, but the old part of the village on the top of the hill has changed hardly at all. Highgate is still a rather vaguely defined area. On the east, beginning from the foot of Highgate Hill, it is bounded by the Archway Road and some of its eastern tributaries, such as Shepherd's Hill and Wood Lane, beyond which it merges into Crouch End and Hornsey. It also includes, to the north-east, the Highgate Woods, which reach almost to Muswell Hill. Its northern boundary is Aylmer Road, which is the beginning of the Great North Road, this boundary running from the Archway Road and North Hill as far west as about Bishop's Avenue. And its western boundaries are formed by Ken Wood and Parliament Hill Fields.

At the foot of Highgate Hill, on the left hand side, in the middle of the pavement, the Whittington stone still stands – a memorial restored by W. Hillier in 1935, surmounted by a reclining, slumbrous looking cat and enclosed by an iron railing. The memorial inscription does not perpetuate the legend. It states merely that Richard Whittington was three times Lord Mayor of London – in 1397, 1406 and 1420 – and Sheriff in 1393. Nevertheless, there is abundant evidence of Whittington's beneficence, for on the opposite side of the hill is the large Whittington Hospital and beyond it the Whittington School, while on the left side, beyond the stone, the extension to the hospital is taking shape. Beyond it stretches the wall of St Joseph's Retreat and then Lauderdale House. On the opposite side, all the old houses are there, Cromwell House which in 1924 became a Mothercraft Training Centre and today belongs to the Church Missionary Society, Ireton House, Lyndale House, the houses on the Bank and the Channing School. In the High Street many more old houses have survived than in Hampstead's High Street and, as in Hampstead, above the shop fronts there are many traces of the eighteenth-century houses from which they have been adapted.

Just as the High Street looks much as it did a century ago, with the school on the corner of Southwood Lane, so do Southwood Lane and the North Road, with their eighteenth-century houses. There have been a few additions of modern blocks of flats, those in North Hill, the extension of the North Road, Highpoint One and Two, which were built during the 1930s, being among the earliest and most successful of this type to be seen in this part of London.

The Gatehouse is now rebuilt in reproduction Tudor but Pond Square, South Grove and the Grove are unchanged as well as West Hill,

Millfield Lane and Brookfield, apart from a little building up after bomb damage, yet they have maintained an air of vitality and there is no hint of decay. This is still a fashionable place in which to live and there have been as many distinguished residents here in recent years as in the past, including John Drinkwater and J. B. Priestley, while the president of the Highgate Literary and Scientific Institution today is Yehudi Menuhin.

The greatest change during the century came soon after the First World War, when the Burdett-Coutts Holly Lodge estate was sold and the whole of Highgate Rise developed with roads, houses and flats, the flats being built in an unfortunate imitation Tudor fashion best described as Tudor-Georgette. However they are pleasant enough to live in and have magnificent views. The estate is well planned, with a few of the trees from the old garden still standing, at the top of the Rise, around Robin Grove, where the largest and most expensive houses are built, and the whole place is beautifully maintained.

Kenwood remained in the Mansfield family until 1918, although they were not living there, the place having been let from 1910 until 1917 to the Grand Duke Michael of Russia, who dwelt there in a state of magnificence. As early as 1914 there had been talk of selling it for building land. Plans were shelved during the war but in 1918 talks began again. The Kenwood Preservation Council was formed and Lord Mansfield gave a year's option for a selling price of £340,000. This amount was not forthcoming and the option lapsed, but by 1922 with the help of private donors, one hundred acres were bought, which included the meadows between the Parliament Hill Fields and Kenwood.

Then in 1925 Lord Iveagh bought from Lord Mansfield both the house and the 74 acres of land surrounding it, with the provision that it should pass to the nation. He was only just in time, for the house had already been emptied and the sale of the park in building lots had already been arranged.

Lord Iveagh refurnished the house with some beautiful eighteenth-century furniture and his own picture collection, which included the work of Reynolds, Romney and Gainsborough, as well as Rembrandt's 'Portrait of the Artist' and Vermeer's 'The Guitar Player'. Two years later Lord Iveagh died and in 1928 the house and the estate were opened to the public, the house as a museum and picture gallery, administered by the London County Council, now the Greater London Council.

This has become one of the most delightful resorts of north-west London. The house is beautiful and a splendid example of eighteenth-century living at its best, and the estate is a wonderful stretch of woods and hills and grassland, with the chain of ponds running up close to Millfield Lane. There are eight ponds altogether, including two bathing ponds and the boating pond. On the stock pond coots and moorhens, dragon flies and water rats live amongst the willowherb and on summer evenings there are concerts round the large pond near the house, while on Sundays there are celebrity concerts in the Orangery – beautiful music in idyllic surroundings.

Highgate has its Gatehouse Theatre at the Community Centre in Jackson's Lane. The Literary and Scientific Institution has a lending library, a reference library, reading room and lecture hall, where lectures are given and social events held all through the winter months. The newer Highgate Society established next door, at 10a South Grove, keeps a watchful eye on conservation and environmental affairs as well as running a number of community services and an information centre.

There is a Gatehouse Theatre Club at the Old Gate House and a Holly Lodge Theatre Group which presents plays and also organises theatre visits and drama lectures.

And now, since 1965, Hampstead and Highgate are part of the large borough of Camden. They have not lost their identity and are benefiting from the added facilities which the new arrangement affords them, schools, libraries, hospitals, council flats, many of which are replacing some of the worst congested areas behind the Kilburn High Road, and homes for old people, among which Highgate already had the excellent Goldsmith Court in the Archway Road, built in 1950 to replace the bomb-damaged Coleridge Buildings.

There are clubs to cater for all tastes and all ages, from sports clubs to civic societies, antiquarian societies to study groups, and the Camden Historical Society keeps alive a constant research into the histories not only of Hampstead and Highgate but the whole of the borough, from Bloomsbury and St Giles to its most northerly point at North End.

BIBLIOGRAPHY

Barratt, Thomas J., *The Annals of Hampstead*, A. and C. Black, 1912.

Berry, Paul, *By Royal Appointment*, Femina Books, 1972.

Clarke, W., *Life of Mrs Mary Anne Clarke*, T. Kelly, 1809.

Collis, Maurice, *Stanley Spencer*, Harvill Press, 1962.

Gittings, Robert, *John Keats*, Heinemann, 1968.

Hampstead Scientific Society, *Hampstead Heath – Its Geology and Natural History*, T. Fisher Unwin, 1913.

Howkins, F., *The Story of Golders Green*, Ernest Owers, N. D., ca.1923.

Howitt, William, *The Northern Heights of London*, Longmans Green, 1869.

Hunt, Leigh, *Autobiography*, Cresset Press, 1948.

Le Breton, A. L. *Memoirs of Mrs Barbauld*, Bell and Sons, 1874.

Leslie, C. R., *Memoirs of the Life of John Constable*, Longmans, 1845.

Lindsey, John, *The Lovely Quaker*, Rich and Cowan, 1939.

Lysons, Daniel, *Environs of London*, London, 1811.

Maurois, André, *Ariel*, Bodley Head, 1924.

Maxwell, Anna, *Hampstead*, James Clarke, 1912.

Norman, Philip, *Cromwell House, Highgate*, London Survey Committee Monograph.

Orpen, Sir William, *Outline of Art*, George Newnes, N.D.

Palmer, Samuel, *History of St Pancras*, Samuel Palmer, 1870.

Park, John James, *The Topography and Natural History of Hampstead*, London, 1818.

Patterson, Clara Burdett, *Angela Burdett-Coutts and the Victorians*, John Murray, 1953.

Pepys, Samuel, *Diary*.

Pevsner, Nikolaus, *The Buildings of England – Vol. 2 London*, Penguin, 1952.

Pike, E. Royston, *British Prime Ministers*, Odhams, 1968.

Preston, J. H., *The Story of Hampstead*, Staples Press, 1948.

Prickett, Frederick, *The History and Antiquities of Highgate*, F. Prickett, 1842.

Spencer, Gilbert, *Stanley Spencer*, Gollancz, 1961.

Summerson, John, *Georgian London*, Barrie and Jenkins, 1970.

Thompson, F. M. L., *Hampstead – Building a Borough – 1650-1964*, Routledge and Kegan Paul, 1974.

Wade, Christopher, *The Streets of Hampstead*, High Hill Press, 1972.

Walford, Edward, *Old and New London*, Cassell, 1890.

Watson, L. E., *Coleridge at Highgate*, Longmans Green, 1925.

White, C. A., *Sweet Hampstead*, Elliot Stock, 1903.

Wroth, Warwick and A. E., *London Pleasure Gardens of the Eighteenth Century*, Macmillan, 1896.

Camden History Review – Numbers 1 and 3.

Chambers Encyclopaedia of English Literature.

Dictionary of National Biography.

Index